LD

A WARRIOR'S HEART

A WARRIOR'S HEART

The True Story of Life Before and Beyond *The Fighter*

MICKY WARD
with **JOE LAYDEN**

FOREWORD BY MARK WAHLBERG

B

BERKLEY BOOKS, NEW YORK

THE BERKLEY PUBLISHING GROUP
Published by the Penguin Group
Penguin Group (USA) Inc.
375 Hudson Street, New York, New York 10014, USA
Penguin Group (Canada), 90 Eglinton Avenue East, Suite 700, Toronto, Ontario M4P 2Y3, Canada
(a division of Pearson Penguin Canada Inc.) • Penguin Books Ltd., 80 Strand, London WC2R 0RL,
England • Penguin Group Ireland, 25 St. Stephen's Green, Dublin 2, Ireland (a division of Penguin
Books Ltd.) • Penguin Group (Australia), 250 Camberwell Road, Camberwell, Victoria 3124, Australia
(a division of Pearson Australia Group Pty. Ltd.) • Penguin Books India Pvt. Ltd., 11 Community
Centre, Panchsheel Park, New Delhi—110 017, India • Penguin Group (NZ), 67 Apollo Drive,
Rosedale, Auckland 0632, New Zealand (a division of Pearson New Zealand Ltd.) • Penguin Books
(South Africa) (Pty.) Ltd., 24 Sturdee Avenue, Rosebank, Johannesburg 2196, South Africa

Penguin Books Ltd., Registered Offices: 80 Strand, London WC2R 0RL, England

This is an original publication of The Berkley Publishing Group.

The events described in this book are the real experiences of real people. However,
the authors have altered their identities in a few instances.

FIRST EDITION: June 2012

Library of Congress Cataloging-in-Publication Data

Ward, Micky.
A warrior's heart : the true story of life before and beyond the fighter / Micky Ward with
Joe Layden ; foreword by Mark Wahlberg.
p.   cm.
ISBN 978-0-425-24755-6 (hardback)
1. Ward, Micky.   2. Boxers (Sports)—United States—Biography.   3. Irish American
boxers—Biography.   I. Layden, Joseph, 1959–   II. Title.
GV1132.W24W37 2012
796.83092—dc23
[B]
2011053313

PRINTED IN THE UNITED STATES OF AMERICA

10   9   8   7   6   5   4   3   2   1

*Penguin is committed to publishing works of quality and integrity.
In that spirit, we are proud to offer this book to our readers;
however, the story, the experiences, and the words are the authors' alone.*

To my mother and father,
who passed away in the last year.
And to my wife, Charlene, and my daughter, Kasie,
whom I love dearly.

ACKNOWLEDGMENTS

So many people have influenced my life and career. I'd like to take this opportunity to recognize some of them now. If I've forgotten anyone, I apologize.

My brother, Dicky Eklund; all my sisters; Arthur Ramalho; Mickey O'Keefe and his sons, Brian and Timmy; Richie Bryan; Jimmy Poulin; all my cousins in the Lutkus family, the Ward family, the Libera family and the Greenhalge family.

And a special thanks to my uncle Gerry, who was like a second father to me, and to Ray-Ray Greenhalge, my biggest fan.

Johnny Dunn; Ouchie McManus; my little league coaches, senior league coaches, wrestling coaches and football coaches.

Kenny Fleming; all my wife's friends; Ricky "Smiley" Russell; Mike LaPoint and Kevin LaPoint; Stevie and Paul McGuire; Tony Ducharme; Tucker Hartigan; Craig Noonan; Mike Ryan; Jorge Vasquez; all my friends from The Acre; the Kozombolis family; Scott Silver.

Pat Lynch; Lou Dibella; Bob Arum; Kathy Duva; Al Valenti; everyone at Team Micky Ward Charities; Mark DeVincentis; all my friends at Caesars Palace and Bally's Atlantic City; everyone at Everlast; my nephew Sean Eklund; Eric Wayne; Big Daddy; Norman Stone; John McGonigle; Kippy

Acknowledgments

Diggs; Ricky DeFelice and everyone at Newport Construction; Teamsters Local 25.

Chris Nowinski and everyone at the Center for the Study of Traumatic Encephalopathy (CSTE) at Boston University School of Medicine.

Chuck Zito; Tony Underwood; Dave Mendoza; Freddy Roach; Teddy Atlas; Bob Papa; Max Kellerman; Jim Lampley; Larry Merchant.

Thanks to everyone who helped bring my story to Hollywood, especially Mark Wahlberg, a great actor and friend. Thanks to Christian Bale, Melissa Leo, Amy Adams, David O. Russell and everyone else associated with *The Fighter*.

My legal and management team, especially Nick Cordasco, Darren Prince, Paul Litwin and Kevin Broderick.

Thanks to Berkley Books for giving me a chance to tell my story in even greater detail, and to everyone else who made this book possible: my coauthor, Joe Layden; my editor, Denise Silvestro; and my agent, Frank Weimann.

And, finally, thanks to my good friend Arturo Gatti, one of the toughest fighters ever to set foot in a boxing ring. I miss you, my brother.

Boxing is the magic of men in combat, the magic of will, and skill, and pain, and the risking of everything so you can respect yourself for the rest of your life. —F. X. TOOLE, *ROPE BURNS*

Boxing is the only sport you can get your brain shook, your money took and your name in the undertaker book. —JOE FRAZIER

While early childhood experiences may impel, they do not compel. In the end, evil is a matter of choice. —ANDREW VACHSS

FOREWORD

by Mark Wahlberg

I was eighteen years old when I first met Micky Ward. At the time, I was just a kid from Dorchester, trying to figure out exactly what I was going to do with my life. Like most young guys who had grown up in blue-collar towns across Massachusetts and the rest of New England, I was a big fan of Micky's. We were inspired and captivated by him, not just because of his prowess in the boxing ring (which was substantial) but because he was one of us. Nothing was ever handed to Micky; he fought for everything he got. And he didn't know the meaning of the word "quit."

Micky and I hit it off right away. We spoke the same language, had a lot of the same interests and mannerisms. I was a boxing fan, and that's what drew me to Micky, of course. But as we got to know each other, I came to realize just how much we had in common. Like me, Micky came from a sprawling Irish-Catholic family, at the head of which was a strong-willed mother. (How can you not be tough when you're raising nine kids?) Like me, Micky was the second-youngest, almost the baby of the family, which meant he learned at an early age how to find his own way in the world, and how to create elbow room at the dinner table. Both of us had been in scrapes with the law and were determined to turn things around and do something meaningful with our lives. And, like me, Micky knew what it was like to grow up in the shadow of a talented older brother who was the apple of his mom's eye. The parallels were almost too eerie to ignore.

Life and business took us in different directions after that initial encounter. Micky stayed in Lowell, and I headed out West to build a movie career. But I continued to follow his efforts as a professional fighter. We remained friends and kept in regular contact. Hollywood can be a frustrating and challenging place, and sometimes I'd think about Micky and the obstacles he'd overcome on the path to becoming a world-class fighter, and I'd find inspiration in his story. Micky is a few years older than me, but really we were climbing and struggling at the same time, throughout the 1990s. I always felt a kinship with him. And I always thought his life would make a fantastic movie.

Around 2005 we began talking seriously about producing that movie. I had no idea then what a long and remarkable journey it would be. The story of Micky Ward and his older brother, Dicky Eklund, was both unique and challenging, and the more deeply I became involved, the more I wanted to do right by them and to make a movie that would truthfully and accurately depict their relationship and their family and Micky's hardships and triumphs. It's never easy to get a movie made in Hollywood, but *The Fighter*, as Micky's story came to be known, was one of the most daunting projects I've ever been involved in. Actors came and went, as did directors. There were significant legal, financial and scheduling issues to overcome. Months became years.

"Don't worry, Micky," I said on more than one occasion. "We're going to get this movie made."

He never questioned me, never doubted my sincerity. That's just the kind of guy Micky is: He takes you at your word, because he knows there's nothing more important than a man's integrity. You make a promise, you follow through. Simple as that. There was no way I could let him down. So I built a boxing ring in my house and trained like crazy so that when we eventually got around to filming, I'd look like a real boxer as opposed to an actor pretending to be a boxer. That was crucial, I thought, to the success of the movie. And, again, I felt an obligation to Micky. If I was going to play this guy, who was such a tremendous athlete and such a courageous, humble man, then I owed him a full investment. I couldn't imagine having Micky watch this movie and be disappointed in the way it turned out.

So I put in the time (often with Micky right by my side, helping me train, offering advice and encouragement). As did Christian Bale, who played Dicky. And Melissa Leo, who played Micky's mom, Alice Ward. And Amy Adams, who portrayed Micky's wife, Charlene. And, of course, David O. Russell, who directed *The Fighter*. It took years to get to the starting line, but once we arrived, everyone was fully committed. And in the end we produced a movie that was released in 2010 and won a bunch of awards but, more important, was faithful to Micky and his family and to the city of Lowell; a movie that inspired people in much the same way that Micky Ward inspired a generation of kids growing up in New England.

Including me.

Today I am proud to count Micky among my closest friends and to note that he remains the same levelheaded straight shooter he's been all his life. Fame hasn't gone to Micky's head. At his core, he's still a humble, working-class kid from Lowell. He's a devoted husband and father, a guy who probably took more punches than he should have, because he knew of no other way to fight, but who has no regrets about any of it.

Now he's written a book, and I couldn't be prouder of him. *The*

Fighter was Micky's story, but it's virtually impossible to condense someone's entire life into a two-hour movie; there are limitations to the form. If anyone has earned the right to expand upon that, it's Micky. So here it is, the whole story, from his childhood in Lowell all the way to his epic three-fight series with the equally courageous Arturo Gatti. It's great stuff. In fact, there's enough here to make another movie.

And maybe someday we will. I know this: I'd be honored to have the chance to play Micky Ward again.

A WARRIOR'S HEART

PROLOGUE

JUNE 7, 2003
Atlantic City, New Jersey

Eventually, for every fighter, it comes down to moments like this.

A flurry of hands trying to work magic on your battered face and body as you slump on a stool in your corner between rounds. Adrenaline-soaked cotton swabs protrude from your nostrils; an endswell struggles to flush the blood pooling along the harsh ridges of your cheekbones and eyebrows. Your heart is racing, your head is throbbing. It's natural at a time like this to wonder what you've gotten yourself into, and how you're going to get out. Fatigue makes cowards of all men. You get tired, you get hurt, you want to quit—it's as simple as that. I figured that one out real early. It's a normal response; it's human nature.

Of course, there's nothing normal, nothing natural, about boxing. It's as brutal and primitive a game as there is, and the truth is, you don't really have a choice about the exit—but merely the way you'll pass through the door. With courage and dignity . . . or something else.

The crowd at Boardwalk Hall has come here tonight with a certain set of expectations, based on prior performance and reputation. I don't want to let them down, and neither does my opponent—that much I know for sure. Because I know him. I know his heart and I know his personality. He is my equal, in every sense of the word. We've already fought twice, Arturo Gatti and me, and each time we put on a show for the ages, the kind of fight that brings people back to boxing, the kind you don't see too often. That's what I heard, anyway, and I suppose it's true. Each fight went the distance—twelve brutal and bloody rounds—and here we are now, six rounds into another epic. Across the ring I can barely make out Arturo's face, but I know he's tired, I know he's hurting.

I also know he won't quit.

And neither will I.

I got this far in my life and career not because I was the most gifted athlete, but primarily through stubbornness and tenacity. That's what separated me (and Arturo) from other fighters—that refusal to give up. This may sound barbaric, but I would rather die in that ring than quit. I will give every ounce of energy I have in there, fighting until there is absolutely nothing left. Your body can do so much more than you think it can; people are just afraid to go to that dark, scary place where you don't know what will happen, or how much it will hurt. I've been there a few times, so I know. And I've never given up, never surrendered. For me, the physical anguish is nothing compared to what I would feel the next day, looking at myself in the mirror, knowing I had given less than a complete effort.

That, to me, would be unbearable.

Maybe that's a gift, too, like quickness or speed or agility or strength. You can hone and develop it, just as you can with any other skill. But if it's not there, it's not there. People have told me I have the heart of a lion. Come on . . . Everybody's heart is the same. What they're really talking about is something intangible, something I don't really even understand myself. It's the will to go on, to keep fighting under the harshest of circumstances, no matter how much shit gets piled on top of you. And this is true inside the ring or outside the ring.

Quit on my stool?

No fuckin' way.

Like anybody else I have my own narrative—history and circumstance that go a long way toward shaping the person I am and the man I still hope to be. You can't escape your past, after all—can't run or hide from any corner of it, though God knows I've spent a lot of years trying. It taps you on the shoulder when you least expect it, and sucks the breath right out of you.

There was a time when I was known primarily within the insular world of professional boxing. I had a reputation—not undeserved—for giving as good as I got, and for leaving it all in the ring. To a fighter, that's not a small thing; in fact, it's what separates the good ones from the great ones. I wasn't necessarily the most gifted boxer on the planet, but no one tried harder; no one dug deeper. Eight years removed from my last fight, I still feel pretty good about that. Even when I have trouble remembering things; or when I'm lying in bed, watching television, and I look up too quickly and my vision doubles. When you've had numerous concussions, there are bound to be a few scars. What the hell? It ain't the worst one, that's for sure.

I'm pretty fortunate. Got to spend most of my adult life making a living doing what I love best: boxing. And while I may not have acquired the degree of celebrity (or the bankroll!) of some of my contemporaries, like Sugar Ray Leonard, Mike Tyson or Oscar De La Hoya, I came away financially stable and with a story interesting enough to have attracted the attention of Hollywood. How many working-class Irish Catholics from Lowell, Massachusetts, get to see their life transformed into a hit movie? I still find it hard to believe. The last two years have been a minor miracle to me, a second go-around for a guy who would have been happy running a gym and hanging out with his family.

You know the family, right? If you've seen *The Fighter*, you know a little about the extended Ward clan, depicted in all its crazy, brilliant dysfunction by the director David O. Russell and a trio of clever screenwriters. They did right by me, as did my friend Mark Wahlberg, who trained his ass off and came away with not just the physique of a fighter, but enough skill and heart to have given a few guys more than they bargained for if he ever wanted to lace up the gloves for real. Mark's a little better-looking than me, of course, but I couldn't have picked a better celluloid version of myself. Same is true of Christian Bale, who played my big brother Dicky Eklund, in all his twitchy, loose-limbed, crack-addled glory. Watching those guys together, sparring and fighting and loving each other the way only brothers can . . . Well, it felt like I was watching my life, which I guess I was.

I'm no critic, but I think *The Fighter* is a great film. And it basically gets the story right. Or part of the story, anyway. There were a few times when we were making the movie that I got a little queasy about the way they were taking liberties with some facts or condensing so many elements into one. Like that part about my mother and sisters all coming down to the gym for a big family intervention? Nah, never happened. The gym is a fighter's sanctuary. Always has been, always will be. The core of the story, though? The part about my relationship with Dicky, and how I had to do my own thing for a while in order to realize my potential as a fighter?

Yeah, they got that part right, even if some of the details were left out.

"Mick, you gotta understand," Mark Wahlberg explained to me one day. "We're taking your whole life and squeezing it into a two-hour movie. We don't have room for everything."

So here I am, writing a book about my life, one that will include all the drama and characters from the movie . . . and a whole lot more. Like my transformation from boxer to brawler, from a fighter who danced his way to mediocrity before discovering that he could take a punch about as well as anyone out there. See, the funny thing is, if you look at tapes of me when I was younger, I was more of a dancer. I didn't become the fighter people recognize today until I was in my late twenties, early thirties. I think I just grew into my body. For the longest time I didn't have the confidence that I could take a punch, and when I realized I could, everything changed. That cuts to the core of being a fighter: when you stand in there and get hit, and you don't go down, and you don't get your brain scrambled. It's an amazing feeling. Even better, something so primal that it's almost incomprehensible, is when you do get dazed—when you're practically out on your feet—and yet somehow you have the will to go on. I was lucky; I was blessed with a good chin. Sure, I went down in a few fights, but I always got up and fought back. Every fighter is scared, every fighter gets hurt. It's how you deal with adversity that counts. You either quit or you keep going.

The Fighter ended on a wonderfully upbeat note: my 2000 victory over Shea Neary in London, for the World Boxing Union light welterweight championship. Some people have told me that I never really won a major title. Well, in boxing these days, with so many different governing bodies, one title is pretty much as meaningful as another, and if they want to call this one a world championship, I'll take it. Neary was unbeaten when I fought him, and one of the top-ranked fighters in the division. And I beat him. No one can take that away from me.

So it made sense to let the credits roll after that fight; let the audience walk out of the theater feeling good about what they'd seen. The bloody postscript, though, was pretty damn good, too. I fought five more times after beating Neary, with three of the fights coming against Arturo Gatti, the greatest warrior I've ever known.

Arturo brought out the best in me, and I'd like to think I brought out the best in him. Through thirty rounds of boxing we beat each other bloody, neither one of us willing to quit. I won the first fight, in May of 2002, by a majority decision. That one was named Fight of the Year by *Ring Magazine*. Six months later, in Atlantic City, we faced each other again. That one was the biggest payday of my career: one million dollars. Unfortunately, this time Arturo emerged with the decision. Afterward he said, "I used to wonder what would happen if I fought my twin. Now I know."

I couldn't have put it better myself. I never felt any animosity toward Arturo, never worked up any of the venom boxers often need before stepping into a ring and trying to beat another man into unconsciousness. I had nothing but respect for him—respect that grew with each encounter, reaching a peak on that particular night, June 7, 2003, when we fight for the third and final time. There is no title at stake. In fact, for me, there's very little on the line. Arturo has been guaranteed a million dollars; I have been guaranteed $750,000. Regardless of the outcome, I know this is going to be my last fight, and more than a few people have suggested I act accordingly. You know, take the money and run—or at least walk—away with my brain intact. Go off into the sunset and relax. But I said, No fuckin' way; I don't want to be remembered that way. Like I said—I'd die in that ring before I quit.

And I very nearly do.

For a while I was doing really well, even dropped Arturo late in the sixth round. Too late, as it turned out. He's saved by the bell and recovers sufficiently between rounds. Me? I'm shot. That was my chance and it wasn't enough. As I rise from my stool to start the seventh round, my legs turn to jelly. They talk about "hitting the wall" in boxing and endurance sports. I'd always thought it was just a cliché. But you know what? It's real. I got nothing left to give. Still, there's no way I'm throwing in the towel. I try to stay away from Arturo, try to move and jab, buy some time, but he catches me with a thunderous left hook that lands flush on my temple. I know right away I'm in trouble. The punch shakes me to the core, causing a loss of equilibrium and something that I can only describe as a sort of temporary paralysis. That's what happens when you get hit in the head so hard that your brain sloshes about in its own soup and then crashes into the side of your skull. It's just like being in a car crash. The effect is immediate and profound.

I don't go down, but while trying to regain my composure I realize that I'm no longer fighting just one opponent, but two. My vision has doubled. I throw a woozy left at Arturo's head and catch only his ghost. To protect myself, I lean into him, trying to narrow the distance between us as much as possible. It's my only chance for survival. When the round ends I stagger back to my corner, exhausted, disoriented.

"I can't fuckin' see!" I tell Dicky, who helped train me for the fight. "I mean . . . I can see, but I see a lot of him."

"What are you talking about?" he says.

"There's something wrong with my eyes!"

The only conceivable strategy, aside from quitting on my stool, is to slug it out with Arturo for the final three rounds, never let him get far enough away to jab and counterpunch. If I can feel him, maybe I can hit him. So that's what I do, to limited effect. I conclude the fight on my feet, but absorb a tremendous amount of punishment along the way and wind up losing by a decision for the second straight time.

After the fight one of the docs comes to my dressing room and does the usual post-fight examination. Since my vision has not returned to normal, he suggests I be taken to a nearby hospital for an MRI and CAT scan. So they bring me to the emergency room and stick me in one of those little triage bays. And guess who's right next door? Arturo Gatti! Turns out the guy has suffered almost as much damage as I have, including a broken hand. He smiles broadly through the welts and bruises.

"Hey, Mick," he says. "You okay, brother?"

"Yeah, man. I'm fine. How 'bout you?"

Arturo nods, gives a little thumbs-up.

"Hell of a fight, huh?"

CHAPTER 1

Fighters are mostly born, not made. You're either blessed with courage and an ability to harness fear, or you're not. I really believe that. But a boxer? Well, that's something else. A boxer is a tactician, a strategist . . . an athlete. A boxer is made, not born, his technique honed through endless hours in the gym, skipping rope, working the speed bag and heavy bag, pounding his trainer's mitts until his knuckles bleed and sparring so often that headaches become his best friend.

I followed Dicky into boxing, the way little brothers so often trail their older siblings. He took me to the gym for the first time when I was seven years old. Dicky was in his mid-teens by then, and already something of a boxing prodigy, on his way to winning three Golden Gloves titles, an Amateur Athletic Union (AAU) title and a New England championship. They called him "The Pride of Lowell" and that's exactly what he was. A quick puncher with the angular build of Thomas Hearns and the lightning jab of Willie Pep. Dicky could have been just like

"The Hit Man." The sky was the limit. He had as much talent as anyone I've ever seen—more talent than me, that's for sure. But Dicky was his own worst enemy. Crack got the best of him and he pissed away some of his most productive years. *The Fighter* begins at the tail end of that downward spiral, with Dicky already an addict hanging on to lost glory.

In the beginning, though, he was my hero.

I boxed because Dicky boxed. Simple as that. Not that I was a reluctant student. I liked boxing right away. In fact, I loved everything about it, from the musty smell of the gym to the never-ending soundtrack—the machine-gun smack of leather on leather. Even before then, really, I was attracted to the *idea* of boxing. Two of my sisters were married to fighters, and I was raised in a town where boxing was like the unofficial sport. Some of my earliest memories revolve around impromptu sparring sessions in the basement of our house, with Dicky or one of his buddies on their knees encouraging me to bang on them with everything I had. And they didn't treat me with kid gloves (so to speak). They'd hang out, and when they got bored they'd set up a little ring and start whacking me around a little.

"Come on, Mick," Dicky would yell. "Don't be a quitter."

I'd fight with everything I had. Once in a while, if got lucky, I'd catch one of them hard enough to get a reaction.

"Jesus Christ!" they'd say. "Little guy's got a wicked shot!"

By the time I started tagging along with Dicky he was already established as a fighter, and everybody in town knew who he was. There was a bit of folklore surrounding Dicky, the stories about how Ouchie McManus, a well-known local trainer, would throw a dozen boys into the ring and let them wale on one another until one remained standing. Dicky, nine or tens years of age and nothing more than a bag of bones, always seemed to be the last to leave the ring. Or he would sneak off to

Rockingham Park, a thoroughbred racetrack located just over the border in Salem, New Hampshire, so that he could take part in amateur
fight cards. They did this every so often at the Rock, and usually the
shows, which were barely above the level of underground brawls, with
the crowd betting feverishly on the outcome, included jockeys from the
local colony. By twelve years of age, Dicky was a semi-regular participant
in these events, always fighting under a pseudonym, and routinely giving these pint-sized grown men everything they could handle. I still
laugh when I picture it—scrawny little Dicky bobbing and weaving, his
fists fluttering, baffling some twenty-five-year-old jock who couldn't
believe the balls on this little kid.

You pull shit like that and you're bound to become something of a
folk hero around town, and that was definitely the case with Dicky.
Wired and wiry, he was a kid with boundless energy and limitless potential, and a self-destructive streak, to boot. It wasn't like my mom approved
of him running off to Rockingham Park to fight jockeys; he just did it.
See, there was no harnessing Dicky. The very traits that made him a great
boxer—a motor that never quit, a compulsion to train, and a generally
addictive, hyperactive personality—eventually got him into trouble,
as well. And while it's true that my mother was one of the first successful female boxing managers, and thus something of a pioneer in the
sport, she wasn't crazy about either of her little boys fighting at such a
young age.

Mom had nothing against boxing in general. Hell, it was part of
the culture in Lowell, and part of the fabric of our family. But we were
her babies—me especially as the second-youngest of nine children (spread
out over two marriages and fifteen years). I suppose my parents just
wanted to protect us as long as they could.

Especially Mom.

My mother got a bad rap over the years for being a little too emotional and involved in her kids' lives. But criticism comes with the territory when you're a woman clawing your way through a world dominated by men. I'm not saying it was easy growing up in a house full of females (it wasn't); nor do I completely excuse some of the business mistakes Mom made when she was working on my behalf. But ultimately I take responsibility for all of that, and I never doubted for a moment my mother's loyalty or love.

But let's be honest: The Ward clan wasn't exactly the Brady Bunch. Sure, we were both blended families, but that's pretty much where the similarities end. Here's a quick glance at the family tree:

My mother was married first to a man named Dick Eklund. Together they had four children before the relationship broke apart. But even after they separated and my father, George Ward, entered the picture, and three more children were born, my mother and Dick Eklund remained legally married. So those kids all got the Eklund surname. Only the last two, me and my little sister, Sherrie, were born after George and my mother married, and thus were given the Ward name.

Anyway, just for the record, here's the whole family, in descending order, from oldest to youngest, with nicknames (everybody had one in my family) in parentheses: Donna ("Stemp"), Gail ("Red Dog"), Dicky ("Bird"), Phyllis ("Beaver"), Cindy ("Tar"), Kathy ("Pork"), Alice ("Bagels"), Micky ("Bear Head"), Sherrie ("Dirty Sally"). Don't ask for an explanation—in most cases I can't even remember, although I think they all had something to do with physical characteristics.

It's probably one of the great understatements in the history of understatements to suggest that Mom was busy; she was overwhelmed. And, yeah, she was protective and tough as nails. Becoming a boxing manager hardened my mother; I don't think there's any question about that. She worried incessantly about Dicky, fought valiantly on his behalf. But she definitely loved all of her children to the same degree. I laugh and joke with Dicky all the time:

"Ah, you were always Mom's favorite."

"That's right," Dicky will respond with a smile. "I was."

But it wasn't really like that. He was older, and in some ways, once he turned pro, Dicky was the breadwinner of the family. He was also the first boy, and a kid who lived in a manner that would make any parent lose sleep. It was probably hard for Dicky, between being a boy surrounded by so many women and the expectations placed upon him by family and the sport of boxing. I don't make excuses for his drug abuse or his drinking, or for the opportunities he missed. But let's be honest: That was all the kid saw when he was growing up. That was all any of us saw. Okay, maybe not the drug abuse, but the drinking?

Oh, yeah. Most definitely.

It may be a cliché, of course, considering the Wards are an Irish-American family from Massachusetts, but drinking was simply part of the culture. We'd have extended family gatherings at a nearby lake on the weekends, and they'd start out as harmless little barbecues, like something out of a Norman Rockwell painting. But as the day progressed and the drinking escalated, things would take a darker turn. Everyone would be playing horseshoes or softball or whatever, and all of a sudden someone would say the wrong thing, and someone else would start snarling.

"Who you callin' an asshole?"

"You! Asshole!"

Boom!

Before you knew it, fists were flying and blood was flowing. You'd see better fights on a typical Sunday at the lake with our family than you'd see in most boxing clubs. And I'm talking about the adults, not the kids. My cousins and I would watch these epic encounters from the safety of the sidelines, with a mix of horror and amusement.

But the next day? When everyone was lying around, nursing hangovers? Nothing but warmth and affection. We all loved one another. I can say that with absolute certainty. But when my family drank, fighting was inevitable. It's the strangest thing—you grow up seeing that sort of behavior, and you actually get used to it. I know it's not normal, of course, but it sure seemed normal to me at the time; it was all I knew.

So you can see how fighting was in my blood. Boxing, too. My parents eventually warmed to the idea of Dicky taking me to the gym. It was a rite of passage for a lot of kids in Lowell. You reached a certain age and you learned how to throw a proper punch. No different from learning how to throw a baseball or a football. I was seven when I started regularly hanging out at the gym, which probably sounds a little young, but it wasn't. Not for my neighborhood. I spent part of my youth in The Acre, maybe the toughest part of Lowell, which is saying something. The Acre had already produced a bunch of terrific fighters, including Beau Jaynes, who at one time held New England titles in five different weight classes. Beau fought more than 250 amateur and professional fights before hanging up the gloves. Along the way he also married my sister Donna. She was one of two members of the family who married boxers; the other was Red Dog, whose husband was a man named Larry Carney, another former New England champ. Larry was a big, strong guy, fought at middleweight and light heavyweight. Those guys were a lot older than me so I never really got to see them in the ring, not as active fighters, anyway. But they both had a profound impact on Dicky. He admired them and wanted to be like them, and they happily took him under their wing.

Dicky was a natural athlete: lean, thin, fast, always in tremendous shape. He was an effortless runner, loose-limbed and tireless. He played baseball as a kid and was pretty good at it, but the pace of the sport didn't fit Dicky's temperament. Boxing, with its constant motion, was more his speed. And he couldn't get enough of it. He was always shadowboxing around the house, flicking off jabs and practicing his footwork in front of the mirror. Whether any of this would have happened if my sisters hadn't married boxers, I can't say for sure. Boxing seeped into the pores of kids in The Acre (we had several friends and cousins who boxed), and maybe Dicky would have become one of those kids anyway. But this much is clear: Larry Carney and Beau Jaynes got him hooked.

And Dicky got me hooked.

Although Dicky was always a handful, he was a fundamentally good kid who looked out for his little brother. He didn't have much of a choice, since I was practically attached to his hip. See, Dicky used to take me everywhere with him. I can remember walking down to the train station with Dicky and sitting next to him while we rode into Boston; then we'd switch lines and ride the T down to Randolph to hang out with some of Dicky's pals. The whole trip I'd be looking up at Dicky, listening to him talk a hundred miles an hour—*rat-a-tat-tat*—about whatever popped into his head. He was twelve years old, maybe thirteen, and I couldn't have felt safer.

Crazy, right? I mean, what family sends two little kids out on their own like that? Sure, the world was a less hostile place back then than it is today, but come on. I'm five and Dicky's twelve, and we're going to friggin' Randolph? Alone?! Today, as a parent, that boggles my mind. But that was the way we lived. We used to do that kind of thing all the time, partly because there was no stopping Dicky, but also because it comes with the territory when you grow up in a family that big: You take care of yourself or you get help from other kids. Dicky watched over me, and I admired him for it. Even as he got a little older and started fighting farther from home, and as our time together naturally diminished, he made sure that I understood I was in his heart and his head. He'd bring home stuff whenever he went on the road: T-shirts, posters, memorabilia . . . even equipment. I was the only kid in the gym wearing boxing shoes from England, I can tell you that much.

We were a passionate, emotional family. The volume around our house was always cranked to the limit. Everybody yelled, everybody fought, everybody hugged it out afterward. Weird things stick out in my mind, like the way my sister Phyllis used to try to get me to eat onions. I don't even remember why it was so important to her, but it was. My sisters took turns cooking, and Phyllis's specialty was spaghetti sauce. For some reason she'd put a pile of onions in the sauce and I'd always pick them out and stack them up on the edge of my plate. Phyllis would sit there and watch me combing through the pasta, growing increasingly agitated, until finally she'd explode.

"Just eat your friggin' spaghetti! What's wrong with you?"

"I don't like onions."

Then she'd smack me on the back of the head. I got knocked around with some regularity by my sisters, although I never felt like I was in any danger or that they didn't love me. But there wasn't a lot of impulse control around my house. You said whatever popped into your head; if someone got on your nerves, you let them know it. And if your little brother was being a pain in the ass, then maybe you slapped him to keep him in line. I didn't take it personally. And anyway, once I got a little older and stronger, and learned my way around a boxing ring, that all naturally went away.

Interestingly enough, my father wasn't a fighter. George Ward had been a pretty good swimmer in his youth, so obviously he had some athleticism, but it wasn't like some families, where boxing is passed down through the generations. Still, they accepted it, mainly because of Larry and Beau. And because we weren't like the typical suburban American family (that's putting it mildly), where the mother frets obsessively about her son, or the parents are really on top of their kids for doing the right thing. It just wasn't like that around our house. There was a lot of fighting and drinking; a lot of crazy stuff. I never had to worry about Mom or Dad meeting me at the front door and asking me whether my homework was done. There wasn't a lot of talk about education or going on to college or whatever. In recent years I've spent a lot of time talking to my daughter about the value of education. But when I was a kid? I didn't even know what college meant. Some of my sisters finished high school; some didn't. Dicky dropped out in eighth grade. I stopped going to school midway through eleventh grade. Eventually I went back and got my GED. Not exactly the way I wanted to get a diploma, but I got it. And I'm proud of that.

Hey, I'm not saying my parents were bad people because they didn't care about higher education. It just wasn't on the to-do list. Like a lot of people their age from working-class neighborhoods, school wasn't a priority in their lives. Having grown up the way I did, and having seen what poverty and drugs and crime can do to a person when he doesn't have the tools to change his life—and having spent my career in one of the toughest businesses around, fighting and absorbing more concussions than anyone should have to endure—I have developed a slightly different take on the matter. I think education is the most important thing in a kid's life.

For me, though, as a little guy growing up in Lowell? It just wasn't a big part of the equation.

——————————

I learned the fundamentals of boxing at the West End Gym on Middlesex Street, in a neighborhood known as the Grove, under the guidance of Arthur Ramalho, a former cook who opened the club in 1968, in one of the many old and empty textile mills that cluttered the Lowell landscape. They were reminders of a more prosperous time, when Lowell was a manufacturing hub. When I was a kid, I'd hear stories about the old days, about how Lowell was considered the birthplace of the American Industrial Revolution. That, however, was just a history lesson to me and most other kids, and the image of Lowell as a rich and vibrant town, with an abundance of thriving plants (offering jobs and opportunity) along the banks of the Merrimack River was no more real or relevant to our lives than a brittle old black-and-white photograph.

Boxing offered hope to kids, or at least a way to pass the time and stay out of trouble, which could be found on just about any street corner in the city. Don't get me wrong. I love Lowell. Always have, always will. I live today in a house I bought with money I made as a fighter, less than a mile from where I grew up. I have friends I've known for forty years. I have family and a lengthy network of support. Lowell is a huge part of who and what I am. I'm proud to call it home. But let's be honest: It's seen better days. And that was true even when I was a kid growing up in the 1970s and early '80s.

Every day I'd walk or ride my bike past derelicts and drug addicts. The West End Gym was a sanctuary. When you walked through the doors, you belonged to Arthur Ramalho. Left behind were disputes with other kids, simmering feuds or racial biases, and any form of laziness or arrogance. There was nothing pretentious about the West End Gym. It was dark and rickety, with paint peeling off the walls and an assortment of plumbing and other structural issues. Hot as hell in the summer (no air-conditioning) and cold enough in the winter that you had to train in full sweats. Not that anyone seemed to mind. If you found your way to the West End Gym, and you had the guts to stay there awhile, eventually you fell in love with the place and its crusty old trainer, and you came to believe in the trite sayings that hung from the walls and served as inspiration:

No Pain, No Gain.
The More You Sweat, The Less You Bleed.

Probably no surprise that a man who decorated his gym in this manner—a man who had also worked at a reform school, and therefore spent a lot of time around troubled kids—would be fond of saying things like, "Building boys is better than mending men."

Maybe you laughed at those words when you first walked into the gym. Before long, though, you understood what they meant, and you believed in them with all your heart. West End Gym was a haven for kids of all ages, and it remains as such today. Forty-some years after throwing open the doors, Mr. Ramalho still runs the place, which has barely changed at all. A couple dozen other gyms have come and gone in that time, but the West End Gym is still standing. In fact, training scenes for *The Fighter* were filmed at the West End Gym, and Arthur even had a cameo as a cornerman. (Hey, even in Hollywood you can't re-create that kind of authenticity; nothing beats the real deal.) A lot of people say that Micky Ward represents boxing in Lowell. It's a nice compliment, but I don't really see it myself. If not for Arthur Ramalho, none of us would have learned how to box. He's a legend in town, and deservedly so. There's probably no one who has done more for the youth of the city over the last half century. As far as I'm concerned, Mr. Ramalho *is* boxing in Lowell.

I can still remember my very first trip to the gym—Dicky made me carry his duffel bag. Everything about the place appealed to me—the noise, the smell . . . the orderliness of it all. The gym was busy as hell, kids sparring in two rings, others working various stations: speed bag, heavy bag, skipping rope, shadowboxing. Every few minutes a bell would sound and the kids would trudge from one station to another, sweat-soaked and exhausted. There wasn't a lot of talking, aside from the instructive chirping of Mr. Ramalho and his various assistants, including a guy named Mickey Carney, who was the brother of Larry Carney.

Dicky was good about showing me around when we first arrived, introducing me to some people and making sure I was comfortable before he went off to work out. Mickey Carney then stepped in and volunteered to "train" me for a little while. He showed me how to properly wrap my hands (one of the most fundamental parts of the boxer's daily routine; a lot of people today use gloves or gel wraps for convenience, but I'm a traditionalist—I still do it the old-fashioned way), then we did some shadowboxing, working mostly on technique and timing. I'd done some of this stuff at home, by myself, so I had an idea of what to expect. But this was different. It was very cool to put on the wraps for real, and to be throwing punches at the air at a real boxing club.

I don't know why it hooked me so quickly and completely, but it did. I absolutely loved being in that space, among the fighters and trainers at the West End Gym. I started going a few times a week, learning to do more with each visit. Before you knew it, I was sparring. There were tons of kids, and although most of them were quite a bit older than me, it always seemed like there would be a couple boys my age. I'll admit to a little anxiety. First thing I'd do when I got to the gym each afternoon was take a good, long look around the place, try to figure out which boys were roughly my size or age.

Wonder who they're going to put me in with today. That kid? He's my age, but taller. Maybe that one? Nah . . . he's my size, but two years older. What about that kid over there? Jeez, I hope not. He looks tough!

It took a while to realize that appearances mean nothing in the gym. Well, almost nothing. Obviously you don't want to spar with someone twice your size. But the truth is, size is less important than experience when trying to set up an equitable sparring session. A smaller guy can sometimes move a bigger guy around the ring, simply by knowing what to do. Similarly, a younger kid who has been training for a few months can outbox an older kid who might have been recently introduced to the sport. And of course there's that thing I mentioned earlier: fatigue. You get tired and you want to quit; you get smacked in the nose and taste your own blood for the first time, you want to jump over the ropes, run through the door and never come back. No need to be ashamed of those feelings—they're perfectly normal. The trick is figuring out how to channel the fear. The kids who could do that? They were fighters, and I figured out pretty quickly that I could be one of them.

Sparring became part of my regular routine. Today, most gyms are pretty careful about letting kids get hit. They worry a lot more about concussions than they did back when I first started, which is a good thing, obviously. I wasn't really concerned about doing any long-term damage, and I don't think anybody felt like they were putting kids at risk by letting them spar after only a few sessions on the heavy bag. That was just the way things worked.

"Hey, Mick—Jimmy wants to go a couple rounds. You up for it?"

"Sure am."

The West End Gym provided everything a kid needed to learn the sport of boxing: headgear, gloves, wraps . . . even mouthpieces. They used to keep a pickle jar filled with used mouthpieces soaking in disinfectant. If you needed one, you just reached into the jar, rinsed it off, and popped it between your teeth. Disgusting, huh? I have no idea how often they changed the liquid. Never asked, mainly because I was always prepared. At the very least, after seeing that jar, I made sure that I brought my own mouthpiece to the gym.

I had my first fight when I was still only seven years old, maybe a month after I was introduced to the West End Gym.

"Hey, there's a fight card next week," Dicky said to me one afternoon. "Want to give it a try?"

"I don't know. Think I'm ready?"

He was standing next to Mr. Ramalho at the time. They looked at each other, smiled. Dicky shrugged.

"Sure, Mick. You'll be fine."

My opponent was a kid named Joey Roach, the younger brother of Freddy Roach, who would go on to become one of the greatest trainers in the fight game. Joey was a few years older than me, maybe ten or eleven, but since matches were arranged by size and weight, I guess the "promoters" figured we represented a fair fight. Maybe lineage had something to do with it—each of us had an older brother who was already well-known in the amateur ranks.

Anyway, it wasn't exactly the most memorable debut. We were part of an outdoor card at this place called the Harbor House in Lynn, Massachusetts. If I was scared or nervous, it wasn't because I was worried about getting my lights turned out by Joey Roach; it was because I didn't know what to make of the weathered old guy assigned the task of tying my gloves before the fight. His name was Charles Scioli, although everyone called him "Skeets." I didn't know it then but Skeets was a legend in New England boxing circles. He'd fought only a few times when he was younger, but he'd fallen in love with the sport and had devoted much of his life to it, volunteering as a ring announcer, amateur promoter, glove man, and all-round facilitator. Skeets was a little guy, barely over five feet tall and maybe a hundred pounds, but with his leathery skin and a voice like sandpaper, he cut a formidable figure in the ring, especially to a little boy fighting for the very first time.

"Get over here, kid!" Skeets coughed. "Let's get you ready."

I remember him grabbing my hands and shoving them into the gloves—only twelve-ouncers, but they must have looked like pillows on my tiny seven-year-old fists. The bell sounded and I shuffled to the center of the ring, where Joey Roach was waiting. He hit me square in the face within the first ten seconds. I hit him back. Neither of us did any real damage. We circled and poked and jabbed for about a round and a half, until the skies opened and the canvas became slippery as ice. Then they stopped the fight, brought us both to the center of the ring and raised our hands in unison.

Each of us went home with a trophy.

It was the perfect outcome for a kid new to the sport: no blood, no injuries, no shame. Boys are highly sensitive at that age. You lose, you want to quit. You get hurt, you want to quit. Better to have it be an exhibition and just leave it at that. Let them go in and fight their hearts out, and then congratulate both combatants. See, it's very personal, boxing. It's the most intimate of confrontations. When you lose a boxing match, it's not just about coming up on the short end of an athletic competition, like losing a tennis match or something. It's about getting *beat*—physically and mentally—by another person. It's about punishment. I think any kid who gets in the ring deserves a big pat on the back. Like they say: Those three steps from the floor to the ring apron are the longest three steps of your life.

And for a fighter, it's a journey that must be repeated . . . over and over and over.

CHAPTER 2

No more than a few days passed before I was back in the gym, training and sparring and preparing for my next fight. I was seven years old and bitten by the boxing bug. Back in those days the rules were pretty lax. In the amateur ranks, especially, you could fight all the time if you were so inclined. And you didn't have to look long or hard to find an opponent. There were a half dozen gyms in Lowell alone, countless others when you stretched out to Boston and the South Shore. Every weekend boxing fans would congregate at clubs or small venues up and down the New England seaboard. There were fight shows all the time, and an ambitious, hard-nosed kid could compete two or three times a week without anyone questioning his sanity.

I wasn't quite that zealous in the beginning, but I did like going to the gym as often as possible. If you'd asked me at the time, I doubt I could have put into words what was so appealing about the sport. Looking back, though, I think it had less to do with sport or competition, or even putting on gloves and trying to hit another kid, than it did with the atmosphere of the gym.

See, Lowell is an incredibly diverse place, as much of a melting pot as any small city in the Northeast. I was born in a Portuguese section of Lowell, then moved at a very early age to The Acre, which was a mix of Irish, Greek, Puerto Rican and African-American. I'm not saying there wasn't any racial tension in the neighborhood, because that just wouldn't be true. Generally speaking, though, everyone learned to get along. You had no choice. I heard my share of racial epithets when I was growing up, and it always bothered me, probably because I spent so much time in the gym, where race was rarely an issue.

First time I walked into the West End Gym I noticed that white kids were in the minority. Irish and Italians once dominated boxing, but those days had long since passed by the time I put on a pair of gloves. The fight game by then was primarily the province of black and Hispanic kids, and they far outnumbered the white kids on most days at the West End Gym. That was fine with me, because there was no color in the gym, anyway. We were all chasing the same thing, even if we couldn't quite define exactly what that thing might have been. I supposed some of us had vague aspirations to become *champions*. But we didn't really know what that meant, and we didn't talk much about it. We talked about working hard and getting better. To that end, we offered support and encouragement to one another. I noticed right from the beginning the generosity of my fellow fighters. If some kid was having trouble catching on—if he just couldn't figure out the rhythm of the speed bag or how to throw a particular combination—other kids would offer to help out.

Funny thing about boxing: It's an individual sport. One guy gets in the ring and squares off against another. But in some ways it actually offers a more collegial atmosphere than any of the traditional "team" sports, and I know, because I've played most of them. I can honestly say that the camaraderie of the gym is unique; it runs much deeper than it does in other sports. The friendships that are forged in the gym can work small miracles in the outside world, transcending boundaries of race and class. Think about it. Let's say you're a little white kid (like me) going to a tough, urban school district populated by black and Hispanic kids. Maybe you're a little timid about being a minority, about being physically unimpressive. Maybe you're shy and quiet . . . lacking confidence. Then you go to the gym and start training, and you're surrounded by all these other kids, a rainbow coalition of boys in boxing trunks and T-shirts. You start to make friends and earn their respect. Those things follow you to school. All of a sudden you're walking down the hallway and you run into one of your buddies from the gym, and he introduces you to one of his friends.

Just like that, everything changes. You talk with one another, the black kids and white kids and Hispanic kids. You learn to understand one another, and to appreciate your cultural differences. There isn't just tolerance; there's acceptance.

And friendship.

Okay, I know all sports do that to some degree, but boxing is unique. It's so demanding and painful that few people are really built for it. And the few who stick with it share a lifetime bond. This may sound strange, given that boxing is such a potentially dangerous pursuit, but in many ways I think it's one of the healthiest sports around.

Don't get me wrong—I don't advocate boxing as a singular pursuit, especially for young kids. Variety is crucial to developing not only conditioning, but a healthy, lifelong enthusiasm for sports and physical fitness. I tried just about everything when I was growing up. For a while, up until about thirteen or fourteen years of age, I preferred baseball and football to boxing. They were less rigorous, more fun (in the traditional sense of the word), and most of my buddies from school were playing, as well. I was an infielder in baseball (second and third base), a free safety and quarterback in football. By junior high school, though, it was apparent that a lack of size would be more than a minor obstacle to my football aspirations, so I began to concentrate on other sports in which diminutive kids could excel. My cousin Brian McMahon got me into wrestling when I was in seventh grade. Eventually I won a city title and finished second at the New England Boys Club Championships. In eighth grade I won the New England Junior Olympic title at one hundred pounds.

By high school I'd given up most of the other sports, although I did run cross-country. At first I just thought it would provide an opportunity to do some complementary training. No big deal. Nothing too strenuous. Boy, was I wrong. I'd done a fair amount of roadwork for boxing, but nothing that long or hard. Runners, I quickly learned, share a mindset with boxers: Both learn to cope with extraordinary discomfort on a daily basis. So do wrestlers. In fact, that's why you'll see a lot of high school wrestlers running cross-country in the fall—to get ready for the winter season.

Running is hard. Running is painful. I've suffered dozens of broken bones, lacerations and concussions in the boxing ring. But here's the God's honest truth: I've never been in more pain than I was a few years ago, when I hit the wall while trying to run the Boston Marathon for the first time. Didn't drink enough water on a very hot day, went out too hard and totally underestimated the challenge. By twenty miles it was all I could do to put one foot in front of the other. I staggered home in four and a half hours, about an hour slower than I had hoped. For the next three days I could barely get out of bed.

So I understand runners. I admire them. The rewards they seek are mostly quiet and personal.

Just as they are in boxing.

Dicky was a terrific all-around athlete, infinitely more gifted than I was. A lot of people have told me that if Dicky had possessed my drive and desire—my focus—he would have been a world champion many times over. I don't doubt that for a second. He was amazing to watch when he trained, so quick and versatile. In the gym, everybody is different. Some guys can go easy, some can't. Dicky could spar with anybody, regardless of age, size or ability. Anyone. Me? I could only train or fight one way: all out. Dicky could work with little kids or grown men. Lightweights or heavyweights. Didn't matter. He'd instantly adjust to the pace and the requirements of the sparring session. And he could do this even if he'd just come off a weeklong bender. Physically speaking, the guy was a marvel.

Even though I didn't do a lot of fighting until I was in my early to mid-teens, I was around the sport all the time, in part because I was training, but also because of Dicky. His career was reaching a peak around that time. Although he'd started drinking and was occasionally getting into trouble with the local cops, Dicky hadn't yet developed a taste for crack. He'd gotten his girlfriend pregnant at sixteen, married at seventeen, and, in the hope of supporting his young family, turned pro shortly thereafter. And why not? It wasn't like he lacked the resume. Dicky had won a New England Golden Gloves title at 126 pounds when he was only fifteen years old. Most kids at that age are still fighting in the Silver Mittens competition (for younger fighters), but Dicky stepped right up in class and beat a bunch of older guys. He won ten of his first eleven professional fights, and eventually, in 1978, earned the biggest opportunity of his career: a fight against Sugar Ray Leonard.

At the time Ray was one of the hottest young fighters in the game, just two years removed from his dazzling gold medal performance at the Summer Olympics in Montreal. Athletically gifted and lightning quick, and carefully handled by his backers, Leonard had won his first ten professional fights heading into his match with Dicky. As I've learned over the course of my career, there are few things more important in boxing than having a powerful and knowledgeable management and promotional team in your corner. There's no union in boxing, no organized league to oversee competition and guarantee the equitable treatment of its athletes. The cream does not necessarily rise to the top in boxing. Sometimes the cream sits and waits for the right opportunity. And spoils in the process.

Dicky wasn't supposed to beat Ray Leonard. He represented another step in Ray's journey to a world title. I don't mean he was merely an opponent. Dicky had talent. He could stick and move, and everyone knew it. Physically, stylistically, he was similar to Leonard, and the two of them would put on a good show. But there was a definite trajectory to Ray's career: straight up, like a rocket. Dicky, meanwhile, had lost his previous fight. And he lacked the network of support that surrounded an Olympic champion (my mom was his manager).

He also lacked the discipline.

Dicky got all fucked-up drinking one night just a few weeks before the Leonard fight, and got in a motorcycle accident. Nothing too serious, thank God (and I mean that literally—Dicky sometimes seems to have a guardian angel watching over him; I don't know how else to explain the fact that he's still alive), but he was pretty sore for a few days afterward and even appeared at one of the prefight press conferences leaning on crutches.

Having waited most of my career for an opportunity like this, I can only shake my head in disbelief at some of Dicky's antics. He was only twenty-one years old and facing a media darling and future champion—a future Hall of Famer, for Christ's sake! How could he not have taken it more seriously?

I didn't see it that way, at the time, of course. I was only twelve years old when Dicky and Ray climbed into the ring at Boston's Hynes Auditorium on July 18, 1978, and I was appropriately starstruck. That fight was a huge deal in Lowell and there was such a buildup to it. Everyone knew all about Ray and his Olympic accomplishments, and how he seemed destined to be one of the great welterweights of his era. And of course, everyone knew Dicky, the Pride of Lowell. Several busloads of fans made the trip down from Lowell to Boylston Street that night. They drank on the bus and then practically sold out the beer concession at the auditorium. It was a running gag in Lowell (and especially in my family) for years afterward that there were better fights on the buses and in the stands that night than there were in the ring.

Obviously it was a partisan crowd, with virtually all of the five thousand spectators cheering for Dicky. Even the black guys were pulling for him! Imagine that: a white Irish boxer getting cheered by black fans in Boston; a black fighter hearing racial slurs from white and black fans alike. It was unbelievable. And I had a front row seat to the mayhem, close enough to see not only Dicky fighting Ray Leonard, but my sister Gail nearly coming to blows with Ray's brother, Roger.

"Dicky's gonna kill him!" Red Dog yelled. "And then he's gonna kill you!"

"Shut up, lady!"

They jawed at each other the whole night. Never let up. A couple times Red Dog had to be restrained. Meanwhile, I took it all in, with wide-eyed disbelief.

What the heck is going on here?!

I thought Dicky fought well that night, and really held his own with Leonard. He got knocked down twice and ultimately lost a unanimous ten-round decision. But he fought gamely and went the distance with a man who would come to be regarded as one of the greatest boxers in history. No one can ever take that away from him.

And, of course, there was that awesome moment in the ninth round, when they were fighting in close quarters and their feet became entangled, and Ray fell to the canvas. As Dicky retreated to a neutral corner, the ring official quickly ruled that Leonard had merely slipped. Much has been made about that moment in the years since, about how Dicky always clung to the notion, fictitious or not, that he once knocked Ray Leonard down. With me and most people who know him well, Dicky will admit that it wasn't a knockdown. But if someone approaches him on the street, a boxing fan, for example, and asks him about that moment—"Did you really knock Sugar Ray Leonard down?"—Dicky will just sort of smile and wink.

"Hey, I can't say I did or I didn't. I don't know whether it was a punch or a slip. All I know is, he went down."

That entire night was a spectacle unlike anything I'd ever experienced. In all honesty, I can't say that it made me crave the spotlight, that I came away from Boston possessed with a desire to become a world champion. Mainly I just found the whole thing bewildering. I didn't even care if Dicky won the fight—I just wanted to see him get home in one piece. I remember stopping by the dressing room before the fight to wish Dicky good luck. He seemed completely at ease with what he was about to do, which is pretty cool when you consider the magnitude of it all. I knew he was fighting a superstar, a great boxer, and I was legitimately worried about him emerging from the ring safely.

And when I went into the dressing room after the fight? No tears, no anger. Dicky had gotten a little roughed up—a few welts here and there, some swelling on the cheek and above the eye—but nothing substantial. He sure as hell didn't look like he'd gone ten rounds with Sugar Ray Leonard. Seriously, now. Think of some of the people who can make that claim—Roberto Duran, Marvin Hagler, Thomas Hearns—and the damage they sustained in the effort. Dicky looked pretty damn good, by comparison. Practically unblemished.

That fight was a big moment for our family, and for the city of Lowell. Ray was top five in the world at the time, and clearly headed toward a world championship. Losing a ten-round decision to a guy like that wasn't a bad thing for Dicky. He was young enough to bounce right back. No one in the sport would have suggested that his performance was anything less than incredible. But here's the thing: Dicky didn't bounce right back.

He went away.

If he had fought again a month later, maybe two months later, he might have found himself right back in the hunt for a title shot. He'd proven his value as a fighter and performer; people wanted him to fight again. The sport loves a guy like Dicky. It would have welcomed him with open arms. But for some reason that I've never quite figured out—because of his addictive personality, I guess—Dicky never capitalized on the Leonard fight. Instead, shortly afterward, he went out and started partying pretty hard, got all banged up drinking and lost his focus. More than a year went by before Dicky returned to the ring, to face a kid named Fernando Fernandez, who had beaten my brother-in-law Beau Jaynes on the undercard of the Leonard–Eklund fight. I can only imagine how Dicky must have felt about that one. Beau was one of Dicky's first trainers, his idol. It was strange enough that Beau had fought on the undercard of one of Dicky's fights, but now here was Dicky trying to settle a score against the guy who had beaten Beau.

A New England champ, Fernandez was no walkover. Dicky won a unanimous decision despite the lengthy layoff, but he fought only twice in the next eighteen months, and lost both bouts, including a rematch with Fernandez. By that time, in early 1981, Dicky had discovered coke. Before long his boxing career was in the shitter. He'd stay in the game for four more years, losing about as many fights as he won, before finally calling it quits. Cocaine is an insidious thing: You use it once, and it's down the rabbit hole you go. Dicky got sucked in.

Over the years, our mom has taken some heat for what happened to both Dicky's career and my career. It's been suggested that perhaps Dicky shouldn't have fought Leonard at that time, that he wasn't quite ready for a fight of that magnitude. And that Mom should have done a better job of protecting him and guiding his career, carefully nurturing him through the right lineup of opponents. Same thing with my career (although my mother had less to do with managing me than she did with Dicky). But here's what I think: Mom did the very best she could. She was not just Dicky's manager, but his confidante and friend. She was his mother as well as his manager, and while that relationship may have complicated things, it also provided Dicky with the strongest of allies.

In ways too numerous to catalog, Mom took care of Dicky. While she may not have had the smarts of a seasoned manager, she was someone he could trust, and she did what she thought was right; she forced her way through doors that weren't even open a crack. Given her limited connections, I think it's remarkable that Dicky even got the Leonard fight. Thirty, thirty-five years ago, no one wanted to work with a female manager. There weren't many of them around, and even fewer who were taken seriously. In the same way that Barbara Roach (mother of Freddie and Joey) blazed a trail for female judges in boxing, our mother was influential in creating opportunities for women who wanted to be part of the managerial or promotional end of the business. Jesus . . . talk about an old boys' network! I can't imagine what it must have been like for my mother. Now, was Melissa Leo's portrayal of Mom in *The Fighter* over-the-top? Yes and no. The hair wasn't quite that big, the clothes not quite that tight (most of the time, anyway). But she was every inch the passionate, devoted mother depicted on-screen, and if you tried to push her around, you could expect to be pushed back.

Hard.

Bottom line: Better and more powerful management is always beneficial to a fighter. But it's not essential. Not if you're good enough. I just think that if Dicky had stayed busy and sharp, if he'd kept fighting instead of laying off for the better part of two years, more opportunities would have come his way, regardless of who was managing him. He was a talented fighter and he could have been competitive with any welterweight in the game at that time. A more well-connected manager might have provided a straighter path to the top, with a little more money along the way, but that's just an excuse. Ultimately, it's Dicky's responsibility. He wasn't in the gym. And when a boxer isn't in the gym, he's not serious about fighting. The dirty work—the hard, sweaty preparation—is done quietly, when no one is watching. You either embrace that life, or you don't. If Dicky had stayed in the gym, Mom could have gotten him more fights. But he didn't.

And that's on Dicky. No one else.

I don't recall specific business conversations between Mom and Dicky in the wake of the Leonard fight; I was too young to be anything but an observer. I just remember him going out all the time with his friends. For many years afterward my mother was haunted by Dicky's downfall—it killed her that she couldn't turn it around for him.

Sometimes they'd argue. "What are you doing, Dicky?" Mom would yell. "You gotta stay sharp. You gotta get back in the gym!"

But he was his own worst enemy, a kid blessed with talent and cursed with the alcoholic gene. Dicky could never sit still. The gym was his sanctuary, just as it was mine. It gave him focus . . . a reason for living. He was fine as long as he was off the streets. Unfortunately, Dicky also craved excitement and immediate gratification. He's never been a patient man. When he got a little bit of fame and money (in Lowell, it didn't take much), suddenly everyone wanted to hang around him. Dicky was the biggest thing since sliced cheese around here, and his success attracted a wide circle of enablers and sycophants. People knew who he was. He had some money in his pocket. Pretty soon he had girls hanging on his shoulder (his first marriage didn't last long) and guys buying him drinks and offering him drugs.

I don't think Dicky was crushed by the loss to Leonard, and that's something I've never really understood. An armchair psychologist might suggest that Dicky went into a downward spiral of despair and self-pity after losing to Sugar Ray. Uh-uh. Just the opposite. I mean, obviously he wanted to win the fight. But the fact that he lost? I honestly don't believe it bothered him as much as it should have. Instead, Dicky realized pretty quickly that simply by having fought Ray, and by lasting the full ten rounds, he was . . . *special.*

Maybe, at the time, that was all he wanted. All he needed.

His biggest mistake was coming back to Lowell and hanging out around here. Not necessarily around family, but "friends" who would take him out drinking and treat him like a king.

"Come on, Dicky," they'd say. "Let's go have a beer. Maybe two or three. My treat."

I'll give these people the benefit of the doubt: Maybe they thought they were helping Dicky through a hard time. In reality, though, they were making him worse, feeding his addictive personality. I'm not letting my brother off the hook. I mean, it's him, too. I know a thing or two about addiction, and while I do believe that it's a powerful disease, and not just a weakness, I also believe in personal accountability. At some point you have to look in the mirror and take stock of yourself. You have to accept responsibility for your actions.

See, even though he's often too fucked-up and self-absorbed to realize it, the addict creates a ripple effect, his deeds and misdeeds impacting an ever-widening circle of friends and relatives and acquaintances. I never stopped loving Dicky, and today we're as close as we've ever been. But there were a lot of years when I harbored anger and resentment for what he did to himself and to our family, for the way he squandered his own talent and opportunity, and how he wasn't always there for me when I needed him.

And how sometimes, even when he was there, I almost wished he wasn't.

CHAPTER 3

I was an average student in school. Not great, not terrible. I wasn't a dumbass, although sometimes I sure felt that way. I definitely lacked interest and motivation when it came to classwork. If you could fast-forward thirty years and put the ten-year-old version of Micky Ward in a modern-day classroom, I'm sure they'd slap the little guy with a diagnosis of ADD. Same with Dicky, though our symptoms manifested themselves in different ways. Now that I know people who have it, and I hear their stories and see the way they behave . . . God, it sounds just like me. But no one ever talked about ADD back then. Boys were boys, and most of them were a handful in one way or another. The prevailing wisdom was that they all needed a good kick in the ass once in a while.

I was basically just an underachiever. I wasn't disruptive or disrespectful. It was more a case of being unable to focus on the simplest of tasks. If a subject didn't hold my interest, I'd check out. I'd be sitting there in the classroom, daydreaming, staring out the window. Suddenly the teacher would ask me a question, and I'd have no idea what she was talking about. For a while, sports helped; they kept me engaged and motivated to at least remain eligible to play. But, man, almost every year I scraped by with grades that barely allowed advancement. I don't ever recall passing with flying colors or anything like that.

Neither was I a troublemaker in the traditional sense of the word. Didn't make life hard for teachers, didn't pick on other kids. Generally speaking, I was quiet and respectful. My parents taught me to be polite with my elders and patient with children. I always kept that in mind, and still do to this day. Nor was I the class clown, telling jokes and stuffing shit up various orifices just to get a laugh. And I definitely wasn't a punk. Jesus, there were enough of those to go around—guys who thought they were tough, talked a good game and usually targeted the weakest students in school. I hated those kids. You never saw them in the gym; or, if you did, you saw them only briefly, because their weakness was revealed almost instantly. They were all talk, incapable of doing the work required to become a real fighter, unwilling to take guidance and, ultimately, afraid of getting hit.

In short, they were bullies, and I had no need for them, no patience with them.

I never went looking for a fight, but I recognized pretty early on the value of standing up for yourself. For better or worse, a reputation is quickly earned and not so easily altered. By junior high a lot of kids knew I was a boxer, and that alone provided some relief from the torment routinely heaped upon the apparently weaker kids in school. I was small, too. Like, tiny. But most of the time size didn't matter. If other kids knew you were training seriously, and winning legitimate boxing matches, they naturally were less inclined to give you any shit.

Occasionally there were skirmishes in the school yard, or on the way home from school; silly little confrontations sparked by nothing more than making eye contact with the wrong person. Most of these, however, ended without a single punch being thrown, simply because the other kid backed down. And the honest truth is this: Most of them could have kicked the shit out of me. They were almost always bigger, older, stronger. My budding reputation as a boxer, though, provided just enough ammunition to save my ass on countless occasions. We'd be standing there, toe to toe, snarling, me looking up at the other kid (who was often a head taller), waiting to see which of us would blink first.

"Come on, you motherfucker," I'd say, trying to sound as cocksure and tough as possible. "You want to fight?"

I'd hold my ground, heart racing, pulse pounding in my temples.

Oh, God, please let him say no. Please let him say no.

The great majority of the time, the other kid would eventually take a step back, mutter, "Fuck you," under his breath and walk away.

And then I'd breathe a sigh of relief. Funny thing is, I'm sure I was just as scared as they were. But I was a scrapper, and I pushed through the fear. They were frightened not only because I was a boxer, but also because I was Dicky Eklund's little brother, and they figured I must be able to fight, too. Who knows? Maybe they were worried about Dicky coming after them.

Look, I'm not trying to suggest that I was the toughest little shit in town. I got poked around here and there. It's not like I never lost a fight—in the street or in the ring. I wasn't that kind of guy. I'm not ashamed to say I got my head kicked in or whatever. It is what it is. The point I'm trying to get across is that I learned a valuable lesson at a very young age: Respect is earned. If you stand up for yourself, people will generally leave you alone.

Most of them, anyway.

I was about twelve years old the first time this strategy failed to produce a victory by forfeit. It happened in July, while my little sister, Sherrie, was going to summer school. There was a kid who had been picking on her every day in class, and while she was generally capable of taking care of herself, his taunting had started to wear thin. Sherrie would come home in tears almost every day, and eventually I offered to meet her after school and walk her home. While I was waiting for Sherrie, this kid walked out of school, and immediately I confronted him. He didn't back down an inch, and within a few seconds we were flailing away at each other. He was significantly bigger than me, but he didn't know how to defend himself, and I basically beat the crap out of him. Unfortunately, I also broke one of the knuckles in my right hand in the process—the first in what would prove to be a long history of hand injuries.

Another time, when I was about fourteen years old, I was walking home one night from my girlfriend's house on Westford Street, when I passed a bunch of kids hanging out on the front porch of a house. They were a little older, and obviously had been partying a little bit, a fact that no doubt contributed to the exchange of insults that followed.

Rather than crossing the street, or just walking on by, I stopped in my tracks, and basically told them to kiss my ass.

The next thing I knew, five kids jumped off the porch and began chasing me. For a moment I was frozen. I was used to one-on-one confrontations. Five-on-one? No, thanks. Even I wasn't that stupid. I turned and began running as fast as I could, until I got to a house I recognized. It belonged to my friend Jay Simon. Jay was a good athlete, played baseball and boxed. He was a small kid, but strong and tough, and I figured he'd help me out. But he never had a chance.

By the time the front door opened, the gang had already descended on me. They kicked and punched and beat on me for a good two or three minutes, raining blows down on my head and back as I tried to simply cover up and shield myself, until finally the light came on and Jay threw open the door, with his parents standing behind him.

"Let's get the hell out of here!"

The assault ended as quickly as it had begun, with the group scattering in all directions, laughing and hooting as they ran off.

I wasn't badly hurt, really, just bruised and shaken up a little. More than anything else, I was angry and embarrassed, a response echoed by Dicky when I saw him the next day and told him what had happened.

"I got jumped," I said.

Dicky paused, let the words sink in for a moment. There was something about that term—*jumped*—that struck a chord in anyone with a properly functioning moral compass. Say what you want about Dicky—he was an addict and a convicted felon—but he was never a punk, never a bully.

"How many were there?" he asked, his tone deadly serious.

I shrugged.

"How many?!"

"Four or five."

"Which?"

"Which what?"

"Which was it—four or five?"

"Uhhh . . . five, I think."

"You know who they were?" Dicky asked.

I knew where this was going, although I wasn't sure exactly how it would play out.

"No. I mean . . . some of them. Not all."

Dicky smiled. "Okay. Don't worry about it. I'll get their names."

Over the next couple days, armed with a list of names and addresses, Dicky drove me and our friend Ricky Underwood (who was about eighteen years old at the time; Dicky was about twenty-two) to each of their homes (well, four out of five, anyway; the last one we never found) and arranged a series of grudge matches. Each boy was given an ultimatum by Dicky: Get in the car, drive with us to a nearby park and give my little brother, Micky, a shot at a fair fight.

Understandably, each one of them was at first reluctant to accept the offer.

"Uh . . . I don't think so," they'd sheepishly respond.

And then Dicky would smile.

"All right, then you can fight me instead."

Well, in that case . . .

The prospect of getting their asses seriously kicked by a professional boxer was enough to convince each of the boys that they'd be better off fighting with me. They all seemed like they were scared shitless, although that probably had more to do with Dicky and Ricky hovering nearby than it did with my less-than-imposing physical presence. I didn't care. I was furious at these guys for having ganged up on me, and for making me feel so humiliated. I wanted to get back at them. I detested bullies; I didn't understand anyone who preyed on people who were smaller or weaker. And I didn't want to be perceived as either of those things.

So I fought each one of them. The battles lasted no more than a few minutes apiece. Three or four punches, followed by some whining and crying, and finally a submission. If not for Dicky stepping in and putting an end to the proceedings, I would have killed them; or tried to, anyway. I couldn't believe the rage and anger that I felt. To be honest, the payback I sought was not equivalent to the offense committed.

I wanted to hurt them. I wanted them to understand that what they did was wrong, and that they deserved to be punished.

"Easy there, Mick," Dicky said, wrapping his arms around me, holding me close. Then he turned to my opponent. "Get the fuck outta here. And consider yourself lucky."

You want to know the strangest part? I got to know some of those kids; to this day, I'm actually friends with a few of them. I have respect for them as grown men, as responsible adults. But when you're a kid, and you're drinking, sometimes you do stupid things. I know—I did some stupid things myself. That doesn't mean they deserved a free pass for their behavior. There's right . . . and there's wrong. What they did was wrong. I'm no angel, but I think I've always had a reasonably sensitive and accurate moral compass. Where it comes from, I can't really say. I was raised in a loving family, but it was certainly a crazy family, and one that didn't always adhere to the rules and regulations of civil society. Everyone drank and fought. Dicky did some serious jail time.

And so did my father.

I was twelve or thirteen years old the first time it happened, although I'm pretty sure Dad had been in trouble with the law prior to that. This was a culmination of complaints and investigations that ended with Mom and Dicky supporting the family, and Dad behind bars.

My father was never violent, never stole a penny in the traditional sense of the phrase. He was, and is, a terrific guy, warm and friendly and fun to be around. I never saw him raise a hand in anger to any of his kids—he just didn't have it in him. But I don't think he was the greatest businessman, or even the most ethical businessman. Part of this, I suppose, stemmed from the fact that Dad was overwhelmed by the family situation he had at least partially inherited. A decade younger than my mother, George Ward came to a chaotic, stressed household. He was in his early twenties and suddenly taking care of a wife and four children, none of whom were his. Within a decade there were five more children, a mountain of debt and no way to accommodate the needs of everyone who called him "Dad."

If that sounds like I'm making excuses for him, well, maybe I am. I love my father and I think he did his best under the circumstances, so I choose to believe that he was guilty of nothing more than taking shortcuts and getting buried beneath more work than he could possibly handle. The authorities, however, had a different take on it. My father held a lot of different jobs, but primarily he was a roofing contractor, and eventually he was convicted of fraud for failing to complete work for which he had been contracted and paid. This happened a few times, both while I was a kid and while I was an adult. I always get in trouble trying to defend my father about this stuff. Obviously he should have been more careful. But it wasn't like he was a thief. In my opinion it's bullshit to say he stole from anyone, or even to suggest that he didn't intend to complete the work he had been paid to do. Sometimes he would overbid and get the job anyway. Three days later, after handing over a down payment for the job, the client would discover that another roofer was willing to do the job for half what my father's crew was going to charge, and the client would try to cancel the deal and seek reimbursement of the down payment. By that time, though, my father typically had cashed the check and spent the money. The cops tend to frown on that type of business practice, and my father more than once paid a price for it. The fact that some of his customers were elderly, and claimed to have lost a large chunk of their life savings, made the misdeeds appear even worse.

Look, I don't want to let my father completely off the hook. He did something he shouldn't have done. But he had nine kids and he always took care of us; he was always there for us (well, except when he was in jail). You could leave a hundred-dollar bill on the table in front of George Ward and he'd never take it. He'd hand it back to you. In fact, he'd chase you out into the street to make sure you got it back. He was a flawed man with an interesting and fluid code of honor, and I missed him terribly when he went away. It ain't easy to be thirteen years old and suddenly lose your dad. We'd visit once or twice a week when he was in jail, and he'd always try to put the best face on things. He was pretty tough that way, trying to make us feel like things would be okay.

But they weren't okay. Not for me.

In fact, they hadn't been okay for quite a while.

———————

In a family of nine kids, life sometimes washes right over you. Bad things can happen without anyone taking notice. You're all too busy just getting by, surviving from sunup to sundown. The great thing about a large family is that there is a network of support and love, and you tend to look out for one another. The unfortunate thing, at least in my case, is that the sheer enormity of the living arrangement sometimes results in complacency. There is evil in the world, and if you're not watching closely, it can slip right into your home.

I was about nine years old the first time I met him. His nickname was "Hammer" and he was a friend of my brother's. They'd gotten to know each other ostensibly through boxing (Hammer was an undistinguished fighter of limited ability and ambition), but really through their shared fondness for drugs and alcohol. Hammer was a couple years older than Dicky and ten years older than me. He was a little Italian guy with the taut musculature of a jockey, a jagged scar that ran from his left ear to his collarbone, and an assortment of tattoos splattered across his neck and upper arms (all of which made him appear tougher than he really was). I don't even know exactly how they met; I only remember that my brother brought him home one night, and suddenly he was in our lives, sleeping under our roof, sharing meals with us, tagging along with me and Dicky when we went to the gym. The guy had no job and no money. Even at that age I could tell he was a bum, sponging off our family and trying to take advantage of Dicky's modest success.

At first he seemed pleasant enough. He was polite and respectful around my mother, could flirt a little with my sisters, and, of course, he was Dicky's running mate after hours. So he quickly ingratiated himself with the whole family, eventually becoming a supposed ally of our family, someone who could be trusted to babysit a little kid, and to protect him from all the shit you'd run into on the streets of Lowell. But that was only what he pretended to be. In reality he was an alcoholic, a drug addict and a sexual predator who abused me for the first time when I was just nine years old.

I can't tell you how much it still hurts to write those words. I'm forty-five now, and I've kept this mostly to myself for more than three decades. My wife knows about it, but hardly anyone else. I never told my mom or dad. Shit—my father would have killed the guy with his bare hands. Never told Dicky, either. I don't think he could have handled it; the guilt would have sent him into a tailspin. So I've carried the burden quietly all the way into middle age.

I'm not trying to be a hero or anything. The truth is, for the longest time I was too ashamed to say anything at all. When it started I didn't know what to think. I mean, I was nine years old! I didn't know anything about sex; in fact, there wasn't even anything sexual about it to me. I didn't understand it. This was a man I trusted, a family friend, and he wanted to see part of my body. So I showed him. It seemed vaguely weird and creepy, but I didn't comprehend the despicable nature of the act until some time later.

I was a quiet and naïve little boy. Like most kids, I suppose, I thought adults were put on the planet to protect children, not to take advantage of them. On a fundamental level I understood that something unusual had taken place. But I couldn't explain it, and I sure as hell couldn't tell anyone—Hammer had made me swear to keep it a secret, as though it were some sort of healthy bond between us, instead of a perverted, criminal act, which is exactly what it was.

And it wasn't an isolated incident. A few weeks would go by, maybe a month, and then we'd find ourselves alone together, and it would happen again. Whenever the opportunity presented itself, Hammer would take advantage of me. On some level, I suppose, I was fortunate: He never asked me to do anything to him; rather, I was always on the receiving end of his advances. It wasn't every month or every week, but it happened, and it happened many times.

The abuse went on for nearly three years, with this scumbag deliberately infiltrating my family and creating situations where he knew the two of us would be left alone . . . where I'd be put in his *care*!

I wanted to say something, of course, but I was too frightened. I was ashamed, and yet I didn't even know why I was ashamed. I don't know what I was thinking, really. How can you expect a little kid to deal with something like that? It's just not possible.

"This is our thing, Micky," he'd say, putting a finger to his lip. "No one else has to know."

So no one ever did. It ended around the time I hit puberty and the revulsion and confusion escalated accordingly. I can remember being in school one day when a counselor came to deliver one of those state-mandated lectures on sex education. A component of the discussion was sexual abuse.

"If anything like this has ever happened to any of you," she said, "please don't blame yourself. It's not your fault."

I kept that in my head for a long time; and it helped give me the strength to pull away from him and put an end to the abuse on my own. I'd lie in bed at night sometimes, hormones raging, thoughts of girls in the neighborhood running through my head, and then suddenly I'd see an image of Hammer standing over me, undressing himself, and I'd feel as though I was about to get sick to my stomach. The signals were horribly mixed; none of this made sense to me. I didn't know what I was supposed to feel, what was normal or abnormal, right or wrong.

It ended when I was twelve years old, and not for any particular reason that I can recall. There was no epiphany, no specific act of degradation that sparked my defiance. We were alone, as usual, with Hammer once again having generously offered to keep tabs on me while everyone was out of the house. I stared at the floor as he quietly moved closer to me on the couch. It was a dance I'd endured countless times before, wordlessly, without refusal. This time, though, as his hand touched my shoulder, I pulled away. We sat there for a moment, separated by a distance of no more than two feet. I could feel my heart racing, the pulse beating in my temples. Hammer smiled, then inched his way toward me.

Instantly, I jumped off the couch.

"You get the fuck away from me!"

He froze. The smile thinned into something . . . not uglier, but sadder. Almost pathetic. He didn't seem scared or angry, but almost disappointed. As if he'd been rejected.

"What's wrong?" he finally said, his words barely more than a whisper.

I just stood there, trying to hold back the tears.

"No more."

Hammer stood up from the couch and slowly backed out of the room, never taking his eyes off me. It was only after he disappeared that I felt the blood rush from my head and I looked down at my own hands, which were balled into hard, little fists.

And that was it. He never asked again, never tried to force himself on me. As quickly and unexpectedly as the abuse had begun, it came to an end. All it took was a single act of defiance. I realized then that it's true what they say about the size of the fight in the dog being more important than the size of the dog in the fight. I was twelve years old, stood less than five feet tall and weighed about seventy-five pounds. But I had successfully defended myself against a grown man. Against someone who, I would come to realize, was the embodiment of evil.

What was there left to fear?

For years afterward I'd find ways to avoid Hammer, and to make sure no one left me alone with him. But he never disappeared. Not completely, anyway. He'd move in and out of our circle, never really holding a job or anything. Each time I saw him, I felt a little less intimidated, a little less queasy. The whole time I was growing up, I never mentioned anything. The few people who know what happened have suggested I should get therapy to deal with any lingering issues, but I've never seen the point. I know right from wrong. I was abused by a pedophile, and there was nothing I could have done about it. I didn't invite the abuse, didn't provoke it. The burden of guilt is on Hammer; he deserves whatever karmic retribution awaits him.

I will never understand people who do things like that: abuse women or the elderly or little kids. Or even animals. I despise people who take advantage of the weak and undefended. I don't get it. I know there's a line of psychological reasoning that identifies abusive behavior as being learned behavior. You know—if your father smacked you around, then years down the road you're more likely to smack your own kids around.

I don't buy it.

It's a cop-out.

I can honestly say that I never felt guilty about what happened to me. Did I feel sick about it? Did I feel anger? Did I want retribution?

Yeah.

But I never blamed myself. Not once.

I'm talking about this incident now, after all these years, not so much for myself, but because I think others might benefit from the story. I'd like to work with abused kids someday. There are a lot of them out there, and they might be struggling with what happened to them. I want them to know it wasn't their fault. I want to tell them, "Don't quit. Don't give up."

I want them to know that there are people in our lives who are supposed to protect us from predators, but sometimes they fail. Sometimes I still get mad at Dicky for bringing Hammer into our lives, and for not recognizing what a dirtbag he was. Same with my mother and father. How could they not have seen it? How could they not have known? The answer, of course, is that no one is perfect. So you forgive them and move on. You let it go.

That sounds simpler than it really was. In actuality I benefited from a form of closure that few victims of sexual assault ever get the chance to experience.

By the time I summoned the courage to push back against Hammer, I was already an accomplished boxer. Diminutive, yes, but successful, nonetheless. I fought in the New England Silver Mittens championship when I was twelve, losing in the finals. In 1980, at the age of fourteen, I won the Silver Mittens title. The following year, 1981, I won the novice title at the New England Golden Gloves tournament.

This set the stage for my first amateur fight in the open (adult) division. I was fifteen years old, working with several different trainers out of a handful of different gyms in and around Lowell—the Bullseye Boxing Club, the South End Gym, the West End Gym and the Billerica Boys Club. One day Dicky told me about an upcoming pro-am show in Portland, Maine. My brother-in-law Beau Jaynes was scheduled to fight on the card, so they figured it might be a good opportunity to make my official amateur debut. Today that never happens. The open division has been divided into subgroups that effectively prevent adolescents from facing grown men. In 1981, though, there was nothing to prevent a fifteen-year-old from boxing a forty-year-old.

Or a twenty-five-year-old.

"Sure," I said. "Who do I fight?"

Dicky paused.

"How about Hammer?"

I held my breath for just a moment. Hammer and I had sparred a few times; by now I was quite capable of pushing him around the ring. So I didn't fear him. From a matchmaking perspective, it kind of made sense. We were roughly the same size and training out of the same gym (although "training" implies a level of seriousness that Hammer hadn't earned). He was a logical first opponent, someone I'd be able to box and beat without too much trouble. Still, there was something about the idea of getting into the ring with him that felt strange.

"You all right?" Dicky asked.

"Yeah, fine."

Dicky looked at me hard, like he sensed something was wrong.

"You want to fight him or not?"

I nodded. "Yeah, I'll fight him. I'll take his fuckin' head off."

Dicky laughed.

"That's my little brother."

We met in a convention hall, in front of maybe a couple hundred people, none of whom understood the personal nature of this confrontation. To them it was just a meaningless three-round bout between a journeyman and a skinny little fifteen-year-old kid making his open amateur debut. To me, obviously, it was much more than that. And yet, I had to be careful not to let my emotions run rampant. During introductions I stared into Hammer's eyes, saw nothing that betrayed a hint of regret or embarrassment. We didn't say a word to each other, just tapped gloves, waited for the opening bell and began to fight.

I'd like to tell you I knocked him out in the opening minute . . . that I exacted some sort of sweet revenge, but it wasn't like that. The curious thing is that after the first few punches we settled into a rhythm, and suddenly Hammer became just another opponent. Someone to outbox, outmaneuver and outscore. It wasn't a great fight by any stretch of the imagination. I was much more of a "boxer" at that point than I became later in my career, and Hammer was the same frightened, unwilling fighter he'd always been in the gym. So there was a lot of dancing and minimal action. I was the superior fighter, though—younger, fitter, more skilled—and came away with a unanimous decision. There were no knockdowns, no cuts, no blood.

In the end they raised my hand and we both went back to Lowell. No words were exchanged.

A few more years would pass before I finally confronted Hammer about what he'd done to me. He was still occasionally coming around the house at the time, although by then he'd pretty much given up on boxing. He was just an alcoholic contributing to Dicky's downward spiral. We ran into each other one afternoon on the street, and Hammer smiled at me and tried to say hello, like nothing had ever happened. For some reason I cut him off. After all those years, out of nowhere, the rage returned, stronger than ever, surging through my veins.

"You motherfucking piece of shit!" I said, getting right in his face. "Don't try to be friendly. You know what you did to me."

He seemed more surprised than scared.

"What . . . ?"

I don't know. Maybe he'd buried it, put it out of his mind completely. Maybe that's what people do when they've committed acts so vile they can't live with the truth of their behavior.

"I should kill you right now," I said.

I could have done it, too. I was big enough, strong enough, angry enough. The age difference no longer meant a thing, except to the extent that it provided me with an advantage. Hammer was a little taller and now substantially heavier. But I was a legitimate national-class boxer. I was a fighter.

He was a bloated, boozing bum.

With Hammer standing there in shocked silence, I walked away, my heart pounding, the bile rising in my throat. I could have ripped his head off. I could have put an end to his miserable life right there, that day. Maybe that's what I should have done. But I realized that if I did that—if I took justice into my own hands, and wound up spending the rest of my life rotting in a prison cell . . . he would have won.

And I would have lost.

CHAPTER 4

Physically speaking, I was a very late bloomer. When I won the New England Silver Mittens title at ninety pounds, I was already fourteen years old and still waiting for my first growth spurt. It came within a few months, thankfully, and that same year I won the New England Junior Olympic title at one hundred pounds. The following year, at age fifteen, I won the New England Golden Gloves championship at 112 pounds. By sixteen I was 5'5" and took the 125-pound New England Golden Gloves championship. At seventeen I lost in the finals at 132 pounds. From that point on, for the remainder of my career, I fought at approximately 140 pounds, competing primarily as a light (or junior) welterweight. I was 5'8", with good hand speed and quickness, and for those reasons I fashioned myself as more of a boxer than a puncher.

The truth, though, is that I wasn't a great technical fighter, the kind who can fire off a dozen punches in a matter or seconds; who can slip every blow that comes his way, and thus pile up the points that result in medals and championships at the highest levels of the amateur ranks. I mean, I did okay as an amateur—better than that, really. But it's a rare boxer who possesses the skills to succeed as both an amateur and a professional. Although they may appear similar to the casual observer, the two are actually very different sports. In the amateurs, every punch that finds its target is rewarded on the scorecard, regardless of whether any damage is inflicted. Headgear and officiating, combined with the fact that most fights are limited to three rounds, render the knockout punch virtually meaningless, especially at the lighter weight classifications. By necessity, anyone who hopes to be successful as an amateur boxer must learn the *art* of boxing. It really is a sweet science at that level, with strategy an essential component of every fight.

Boxing in the professional ranks often evolves (or devolves, depending on your point of view) into a battle of brute strength and power, of endurance and pain tolerance. Fights are often long (although not as long as they once were, when fifteen rounds was the standard for a championship), and headgear is not allowed. You can put it any way you want, choose flowery language that makes you feel better about it, but the truth is this: Professional boxing is about trying to inflict as much damage as possible on your opponent. Sure, there are scorekeepers whose job it is to tabulate punches thrown and landed, but every fighter who steps in the ring understands his mission: Hurt the other guy. Open a cut along his eyebrow, deliver a paralyzing left hook to the liver or an uppercut to the jaw. Hit him so hard, so precisely, that his brain sloshes about in its own juices, creating a short circuit that renders him temporarily unconscious.

Knockout.

Fight over.

Accomplish that simple, inelegant goal, and you don't have to worry about the score or the vagaries of judging—whether you might get screwed over because you're fighting in someone else's town or because the judges are in the promoter's pocket. Kick the shit out of the other guy. Turn out his lights. Put him on his back, on the canvas. If you do that, you win. There is no debate.

I was both boxer and fighter in my career. Started out as the former, learned how to move and stick, accumulate goodwill with the judges by getting off a ton of punches, partly because I was in such good physical condition. By the end of my professional career, however, I had morphed into a very different type of fighter—one who banged incessantly in close quarters, and who was willing to absorb significant punishment in the process. The best professional fighters are skilled athletes, of course. They have speed and strength and stamina; they are quick on their feet and in their minds, capable of changing directions, both literally and figuratively, as a fight progresses. But it's unusual to find a champion who doesn't possess that most fundamental of characteristics: a sturdy chin.

Simply put, it's not enough to have a heavy punch; you have to be able to take a heavy punch as well. Unable (for whatever reason) to develop a truly powerful head shot, I adapted by cultivating a sledgehammer of a body punch. And I was willing and able to absorb a lot of punishment while waiting for an opportunity to deliver that blow. I was lucky—I generally didn't bleed a lot, didn't cut quickly (until much later in my career, when the accumulation of scar tissue became something of a problem) and my lights weren't easily turned out. That, too, is a gift, just like any other athletic trait. Of course, it came with a price: Fighters who are inclined not to be knocked out tend to take a lot of punches and suffer more concussions than those who either run for cover or get dispatched quickly. I've paid the price.

Not through choice, but instinct.

We're all built a certain way. Dicky was a mover. All that nervous energy that made him such a bundle of twitches and tics outside the ring (and surely contributed to his addictive personality), helped make him an elusive target inside the ropes. Over the course of a fight, Dicky could slice you up, and he had the potential to be one of the great welterweights. But he was no knockout artist, and he was no brawler. Me? I became marketable and ultimately a champion by demonstrating a willingness to fight. Up close and personal.

My skill set and personality were perfectly suited to the professional game. I did all right as an amateur and I'm proud of my accomplishments, but I was never going to win an Olympic medal. I understood the difference. While there have been Olympic champions who went on to have terrific professional careers (Muhammad Ali, Sugar Ray Leonard and Oscar De La Hoya come to mind), there have also been some great pros who never even made it to the Olympics.

Like Mike Tyson.

I first met Mike in the summer of 1983, when we were both seventeen-year-old amateurs fighting our way through a variety of tournaments designed to winnow the field of Olympic hopefuls. I fell into that category at the time, not only having been a New England Golden Gloves champ, but also having been to the National Golden Gloves championships the previous year in Kansas City, when I was sixteen. That one was an eye-opener, incidentally. I remember being extremely nervous and humbled by how much talent there was in one arena. Every fighter at every weight class seemed to have an abundance of skill. I'd done almost all of my boxing within a three-hour drive of Lowell. Everyone I faced seemed to say "wicked" or "chow-dah," just like me. Now, though, the building was filled with kids from Los Angeles and Philly and Chicago. From New York and Miami. And they all knew how to fight. Every one of them.

I didn't medal at the nationals in Kansas City, but I felt like I had a better chance in '83; I knew what to expect. But even then it wasn't like I was considered a can't-miss prospect. It wasn't like I was Tyson. I tried to keep everything in perspective.

The interesting thing about Mike, even then, was the way he would adopt a different personality in the ring. We all do that to a certain extent, but I think Mike took it to another level. I got to know him a little when we were competing together at the regional championships in Lake Placid, New York, and then, a short time later, when we all went to Colorado Springs for the nationals. I was eliminated from the tournament in my second fight, losing to Zack Padilla, a tough nineteen-year-old kid from California. There was no shame in that loss—Zack went on to become a world champion as a light welterweight (his career, sadly, was cut short in 1994, when he suffered a concussion, subsequently diagnosed as a traumatic brain injury, while sparring with Shane Mosely). Mike, meanwhile, lost by disqualification to a relatively unknown boxer named Kimmuel Odom. I don't remember much about that fight, except that Mike wasn't crazy about losing. He was a vicious fighter back then, so thick and strong and fast. He fought hard, took no prisoners. But he could also be a really gentle, fun-loving guy. He'd come to my room every day and joke around. He looked like a grown man, scary as hell. But when you got to know him a little bit, you could tell he was just a big kid. People looked at him the wrong way, you know? I've always liked Mike. I think he's actually a very soft and sensitive man. I don't think he ever really wanted to be a boxer. It just so happened that he had talent, and the people around him nurtured that talent and helped him become a champion. But all the other stuff that went along with it? The fame and money? The leeches always reaching into his pocket? Mike wasn't equipped to deal with any of that stuff.

What a fighter he was, though. For a while, in my opinion, Mike was as good as anyone who ever laced up a pair of gloves. He fought in Lowell the next year and knocked a guy out in the first round. I'd never seen anything like it, just put the kid out cold in the first couple minutes. It was like the poor bastard wasn't even wearing headgear. Hardest punch I'd ever seen. I mean, it's true that while headgear is designed primarily to prevent cuts and to soften shots to the temple or forehead, it won't prevent concussions. Hell, football players get concussions, right? And their heads are encased in fiberglass. So it does happen. But that kind of knockout, explosive and instantaneous, is rare in the amateur ranks. Like I said, the premium is on scoring, so most guys just stick and move, even at the heavyweight division. Not Tyson. He was an underrated defensive fighter, in constant motion, but he also looked for the knockout blow. And when he found an opening, he threw punches with devastating force.

I never saw anyone else whose very presence in the ring could make another heavyweight look like he was going to shit his pants. Mike could knock you out with any punch, at any moment. He was a different breed of fighter, and destined for greatness. People seem to forget, though, that Mike didn't even make the U.S. Olympic team. Lost in the 1984 Olympic Trials to Henry Tillman. Didn't matter. Within two years he'd become the youngest heavyweight champ in history. Some guys are just better suited to the professional game. Mike was one of them.

So was I.

It just wasn't nearly as obvious in my case.

The commitment to boxing came slowly for me, and more out of necessity than anything else. By the time I turned seventeen, when I should have been a junior in high school, I'd already dropped out. I'd like to say it was a conscious decision based on some master plan, but that wouldn't be true. An indifferent student to begin with, I began to fall woefully far behind when I started missing school because of tournaments and other boxing commitments. Ultimately I just figured there was no point in hanging around when I was failing so many courses anyway. So, like Dicky, I called it quits.

What could have been a desperate existence actually was kind of fun. I didn't mind working for a living. I'd been helping out my uncle Gerry Greenhalge since I was fourteen years old. Gerry owned a company called Ideal Paving, and whenever he needed an extra body I'd go down and put in a day's work. Uncle Gerry was not only family (my mother's brother), but a boxing guy as well, and more than happy to let me arrange a schedule that allowed for time off when I was preparing for a fight. Sometimes I'd help with my father's roofing business as well (which persisted even in the wake of his various legal problems).

So money wasn't a major issue. I had a fairly comfortable, carefree life, one that revolved around training and work and hanging out with my buddies, most notably a carpenter named Tony Underwood (Ricky's cousin), with whom I shared an apartment for several years. We were just two young guys, living together, having fun, trying to figure out what we wanted to do with our lives.

Admittedly, hanging out and having fun in Lowell wasn't without its risks. In *The Fighter* I was depicted as a pretty straightlaced guy, intensely serious and mature. Compared to a lot of the kids I knew in Lowell, that's accurate. Honestly, though? I was no saint. Even as an adolescent, I was a casual drinker, for sure, and sometimes a bit more than that. Although I never showed up at the gym for a training session with a hangover, and always abstained completely in the runup to a fight, I had nothing against going out and having a few beers with my buddies. Shit, that was what we did in Lowell; that was what we did in my family.

When it came to partying, I generally exercised greater restraint than the people around me, but there were times when things definitely got out of hand. I didn't go looking for trouble, but it wasn't hard to find. Sometimes trouble would find me, simply because I'd chosen to be in a certain place, under certain conditions. From the time I was sixteen years old, I'd routinely get involved in street fights. Well, they weren't really street fights, since usually they took place at someone's house, after many gallons of beer had been consumed. This was Lowell when I was growing up—a tough city populated by a large number of legitimately tough kids, as well as posers who thought they were tough. When enough of those kids got together in one place, fueled by alcohol, violence ensued. You'd be at some house party, talking with your friends, trying to hit on chicks, and all of a sudden fights would just erupt, seemingly out of nowhere. It was like jailhouse shit, the way guys would go at it over the slightest transgression. (I know what I'm talking about, since I also worked for a while as a corrections officer).

"What did you say to my girl?"

"Uhhh . . . I said, 'Hello'?"

"Yeah, well, who gave you permission?"

"I don't need no fuckin' permission."

Bam!

Next thing you knew, bodies were bouncing off the walls. Then the cops would show up. Many of my friends knew what it was like to be arrested—multiple times. I got pinched a few times myself. The thing about Lowell cops, though, is that they typically didn't want to make anyone's life miserable. Most of them had grown up in town and experienced the same sort of thing themselves when they were kids, so usually they would just break up the party or the fight and tell everybody to go home. Unless, of course, you behaved like a punk, in which case the night was bound to end badly. If the cops showed up, I'd just leave—of course I might sneak back later—but I wasn't looking for trouble. I was generally respectful of people, especially cops and adults, but I went through a time in my late teens when I was a handful. I didn't start problems, but I didn't mind a fight.

Didn't mind that at all.

Sometimes the limited fame I had achieved as an amateur boxer allowed me to get off with nothing more than a warning. Other times the cops would be a bit more aggressive precisely because they knew who I was. I'm sure it didn't help that I was the little brother of Dicky Eklund, who by then had cultivated a reputation for unruly, sometimes criminal behavior. Most of the time, though, I was treated exactly like anyone else. And so there were a handful of violations and arrests. I was frequently around trouble, and I got into fights, and sometimes I wound up getting arrested for disorderly conduct. One time I got pulled over for a stop-sign violation. Upon investigation the officer discovered an unopened six-pack in the car. I was only nineteen years old at the time and hadn't even been drinking (although I was going to drink it, as soon as possible!), so they gave me a citation for "minor transport." Sounds like an abduction, doesn't it? But it simply means the driver is not of legal age to have alcohol in his automobile. That the beer hadn't been opened was irrelevant.

I guess you'd say I was kind of a weekend warrior. I was in the vicinity when a lot of shit went down, but for the most part it wasn't serious shit. It's all a matter of perspective. In my world, virtually everyone drank and brawled. Hell, there were times when I'd walk into one of the local pubs to buy a pint, and my mom and dad would be there at the bar, tossing them back, having a good old time with their friends. I was maybe sixteen, seventeen years old, well below the drinking age, but what could my parents say?

As for the fighting, well, Lowell was (and is) a hard town, and if you were going to drink, you had to be prepared to use your fists. One might think that few guys would have any interest in challenging a Golden Gloves champ, but that wasn't the way it worked. Most people didn't know who I was, and I never talked about it very much. At 130 pounds (give or take) I sure as hell didn't look like someone you'd be wise to avoid. In fact, hanging out in street clothes, with my baby face and diminutive frame, I'm sure I looked like the kind of kid who would run from a fight. But I never did. Never started one, either.

There was, for example, the time I went to a party in Chelmsford with Tony Underwood and Richie Bryan, and a few other friends. There was a big kid there talking trash, drinking a ton, and generally driving everyone nuts. He was a Chelmsford kid, as were most of the people there. Stupid as it might sound, there was always some tension between kids from those two towns. If you were from Lowell, you had a little bit of a chip on your shoulder; you knew instinctively that the kids from Chelmsford (just one town over) were softer, spoiled. And, of course, the Chelmsford kids looked down on the kids from Lowell. Class warfare on a very limited scale.

Anyway, at some point the loudmouthed kid started taunting me. I don't remember how it started, or what he had against me. I just remember that he was much bigger (probably close to two hundred pounds) and older. And that he'd also bought the beer for everyone! I was sixteen, maybe seventeen, and he was in his early twenties. We were standing around a campfire when he approached. No longer satisfied to curse me out from a distance, he got in my face and challenged me to a fight. I dropped him with one punch—a left hook to the jaw. Then we left.

We used to fight like that all the time when we were growing up. Interestingly, though, I have never been in a true bar fight. Not one. Probably because my street brawling days were just about over by the time I could legally enter a bar. By the time I turned professional, I'd gotten a little better at turning the other cheek. There was too much at stake. I couldn't afford to bust up my hands on the face of some drunken idiot. So I learned to walk away.

Maturation takes time, though, and for a while I'll admit that some people probably worried about where I was headed—following in Dicky's footsteps, perhaps. The thing is, I was actually a pretty easygoing guy most of the time. I usually kept my temper in check, but once I went off, I'd fight like a pit bull. Even at a stupid beach party, by a campfire, I was willing to fight to the death. If you poked me long enough, or hard enough, you'd get a reaction. I didn't care if you were a three-hundred-pound monster. I wouldn't cower or acquiesce. I always figured that I'd been through worse than anything you could do to me. So if you wanted to fight, you had to understand something: The fight wouldn't end until one of us was unconscious. And it wasn't likely to be me, because I was always in shape, and I'd outlast you. I could take the punishment. Most important, of course, I knew what I was doing.

I was a boxer . . . a fighter.

When I see bar fights now, it's all I can do not to laugh—guys drunkenly flailing away, eyes closed, heads tilted back. These people have no idea how to fight. And it's always been that way. I'd been properly taught and trained, and that's worth a lot of points in a street fight. It helped, too, that I was usually accompanied by other kids who knew how to take care of themselves. Richie and Tony weren't competitive fighters, but they both were exceptionally good athletes. And a few of our other buddies, while not classically trained, were seriously intimidating guys. One of my friends eventually did prison time for murder. Even when we were teenagers, this kid scared the shit out of other people. Not exactly a model citizen, but I got along with him just fine, and it was reassuring to have him around when things got ugly.

People assume that just because you're a professional fighter, you've gone through life without ever taking lumps in the real world. In fact, the opposite often is true. I think most boxers have a history of personal pain and suffering, and I certainly fall into that category. Boxing provided an outlet for dealing with some of that in a relatively healthy and controlled environment, but it didn't stop me from getting hurt, or from making bad decisions. More than a few people have asked me whether I've ever lost a street fight. Well, that's a tough one to answer. I suppose it depends on how you define the word "lost." I'll say this much—I know what it's like to get my ass kicked.

There was, for example, one incident that occurred after a night of drinking at the Foxtail Lounge. I was nineteen years old at the time, just about finished with my amateur career and preparing to turn pro. In other words, I wasn't doing any serious training. It was always during those interludes—when structure and discipline were absent—that I seemed to drift toward trouble. I left the Foxtail with a girl, and while driving home we passed some kid who began yelling at us from the sidewalk. I don't even remember why he was yelling. Probably been drinking—just like me. It was a Saturday night and he was looking to unleash a bit of aggression; I was only too happy to oblige.

I slowed the car to a crawl and began exchanging words with the kid. He was roughly my age, but substantially bigger. Eventually, the conversation grew heated.

"Why don't you pull over and we can settle this thing right here?" he suggested.

I smiled, yanked the car to the curb, and threw open the door. The kid—and to this day I have absolutely no idea who he was—didn't move an inch. He had at least fifty pounds and a few inches on me, so I'm sure he wasn't exactly intimidated by what he saw. And neither was I.

Appropriately enough (given the juvenile nature of our behavior), the brawl took place right in front of the high school. I hit him hard several times within a span of about ten seconds—punches that usually put an opponent on his heels even in a boxing ring, and on the street almost always brought the fight to a swift conclusion. Not this time. The kid took everything I threw at him and still wasn't dissuaded. He kept moving forward, until finally he was close enough to wrap me in a bear hug. Suddenly we were on the ground, and that was when I knew I was in trouble. No longer was this a boxing match, where I held the obvious advantage. Now it was something more like mixed martial arts, with a combination of grappling and boxing and plain old street fighting. In that environment my advantage melted away. Big and strong, and clearly no novice in this sort of thing, he pinned me to the ground and began beating on me. Without the benefit of space and speed, there wasn't much I could do other than ride out the onslaught. My strategy became one of survival . . . of endurance. Eventually, I figured, he'd wear himself out.

And that's precisely what happened.

"You can't hurt me!" I yelled, even as the kid continued to rain punches down on my head. "You can't fucking hurt me!"

After a while the blows lessened in both frequency and intensity, until finally they just stopped and the kid merely tried to hold me to the ground, his breathing so labored that I thought he might vomit or pass out. Sensing an opening—a weakness—I summoned whatever strength I had left to throw him off me. Then I jumped on top of him.

Reversal! Two points!

That should have been the end of it, but for some reason, after having been pummeled so badly, I felt the need to humiliate the kid, to let him know that he hadn't prevailed. Once again, I felt compelled to teach the bigger guy a lesson.

"You give up?" I said, holding him tightly, squeezing him so hard he couldn't move.

There was no response, just some subtle, pained moaning.

"Tell me you give up!" I yelled.

"Okay . . ."

"Okay, what?"

"I give up . . ."

Exhausted, I released my grip and rolled off the kid, leaving him there on the ground, curled up in the fetal position, too tired to move. I walked to the car, turned on the light and looked in the rearview mirror. My face was covered with purple welts. My lip had been split open. Nothing too serious, but I sure didn't look like someone who had just won a street fight. The girl I'd picked up at the Foxtail smiled as I settled into my seat.

"You should see the other guy," I joked.

She laughed nervously, probably because she *had* seen the other guy, and frankly he looked a lot better than I did. I mean, I forced him into a submission and I walked away, leaving him on the ground, so I guess, in that sense, I won. But the truth is, this kid had kicked the piss out of me until he got tired. And it works that way sometimes in boxing, too. It isn't always the guy who starts quickly or inflicts the most damage who ends up winning the fight. It's the guy who refuses to surrender. I had a headache for several days after that fight. I was all busted up.

But I didn't quit.

In the days and weeks afterward, though, I started to question the wisdom of being a guy who took no shit. There was no single moment of enlightenment when I realized that I was getting too old for street fighting, or when I suddenly saw the foolishness of reckless behavior. It was more a matter of practicality. If I was going to be more than just a part-time boxer and full-time laborer, I had to commit myself fully to the cause, and that meant adopting a more professional attitude toward the sport and toward my life in general.

Interestingly enough, it was Dicky who convinced me to make the transition. My style, he reasoned, was better suited to the pros. By then I had developed a good left hook to the body (although it hadn't yet become a "signature" punch), and I could box, as well. That combination was much more effective in the professional ranks than in the amateurs, where the lightning-quick boxers tend to dominate. I was a more balanced fighter, and balance, especially in the lighter divisions, would never be fully rewarded in the amateurs. I simply didn't have the speed or style to make it to the Olympics. If I was ever going to make anything of myself as a boxer, it would have to be as a professional.

"Look, you're not getting paid to fight right now," Dicky reasoned one day. "Losing in the amateurs ain't gonna buy your groceries."

Dicky wasn't always the most logical guy in the world, and his own personal transgressions often compromised his credibility when it came to dispensing advice. But on this particular subject, he had a point.

"You gotta be practical, Mick. Let's give it a shot and see how far we go."

We . . .

The implication, of course, was that Dicky and I were a team. And for better or worse, I guess we were.

CHAPTER 5

We were, from the very beginning, a family business. I was the fighter, Dicky was the trainer and my mother was the manager. Well, that's not quite true. Mom did not officially become my manager until I'd fought several times, and even then there was some legal wrangling involved. On paper, my first managers were Ralph Bergeron and Don DiRocco, business partners (they owned a bar together) who had known our family for years, dating all the way back to those crazy summers at the lake. Ralph and Don did their best, but they didn't really know the game, or enough people in the game (the same criticisms had been leveled at my mother, of course, when she was handling Dicky), so I got out of the contract after maybe a year or so. After that, my mother served as my manager, although I was really sort of an independent, with Mom watching over me.

My first professional fight was on June 13, 1985, at a public roller-skating rink in Lowell. This was exactly two weeks after Dicky fought for the very last time (although I don't think he realized then that his career had come to an end). My opponent was a kid named David Morin. Actually, Morin was a last-second substitution, corralled by the fight promoter when my scheduled opponent backed out on the day of the fight. That kind of crazy shit happens all the time in boxing, especially at the lower levels. Matches are made, contracts are signed and they prove to be worth less than the paper on which they're printed. You train for weeks with a specific opponent in mind, and suddenly, on fight night, a different guy is staring at you from across the ring.

Not that it mattered to me. I knew nothing about the guy I was supposed to be fighting; nor was I familiar with David Morin. I knew only that the promoter was so desperate to keep the fight from being postponed that he drove all the way up to Portland, Maine, to pick up Morin after he got out of work.

Unfortunately, my scheduled opponent wasn't the only no-show that night. I can vividly recall sitting in the dressing room with Johnny Dunn, the two of us staring at the clock, wondering whether Dicky was going to show up. Johnny was a legendary Boston trainer who had worked with Dicky throughout much of his career, and so he was well aware of my brother's strengths and weaknesses. Johnny, who never served as my trainer but did work my corner for a number of years, was as reliable as Dicky was unpredictable. Good thing, too, since Dicky never did make it to the roller rink that night.

As was his habit in those days, he was out getting banged up. So when the bell sounded for my first professional fight, my trainer—my brother—was nowhere to be found. Funny thing, though: I don't remember feeling any anger about it. Disappointment, yes. Frustration, no doubt.

But anger?

Not really.

"Don't lose your focus," Johnny said. "You gotta take care of business here."

And I did. Pretty quickly, too. I remember being so excited that I practically ran to the center of the ring when the fight started. It seemed so strange to be fighting without headgear, and to be using eight-ounce gloves rather than ten-ounce gloves. But I liked it. For some reason, rather than feeling vulnerable, I experienced a sensation of having been liberated. I felt lighter . . . faster. Within seconds I had the kid backed against the ropes, ripping his body. The first left hook took his breath away, and I could hear him let out a little groan. I knew then the fight wouldn't last long. Dicky and I had been working hard in the gym to develop my body shot, and this was the first opportunity to test it in battle. And it worked beautifully. The fight ended on a technical knockout at 1:20 of the first round, when I landed another shot to the torso, this one hard enough to break the guy's rib.

A month and a half after fighting in front of a few hundred fans at the roller rink, I jumped to the big-time—or what felt like the big-time, anyway: the Lowell Auditorium. This time Dicky was in my corner and I was fighting under a nickname that seemed to have been plucked from a bad gangster movie.

The Baby-Faced Assassin.

I don't even know where that came from, or who signed off on it, but there it was, on posters and other promotional material for the fight. I suppose they were playing off the fact that I looked very young (hell, I was still getting carded when I was thirty), and yet had the ability to win fights by knockout (well, one fight anyway). What can I tell you? Promoters do what they can to sell a fight, and this made sense to them. Sounded ridiculous to me, and I told them as much. That's why the Baby-Faced Assassin had such a short career: He very quickly became "Irish" Micky Ward, which was still kind of silly (I was born in the U.S., of course, and I'm actually of both English and Irish descent), but a big improvement nonetheless.

Man, the Lowell Auditorium was rocking that night. Talk about a place where they love their boxing. The building routinely would sell out for the Golden Gloves championships, and for top professional cards. This was only my second professional fight, a scheduled four-rounder against a New Yorker named Greg Young (who had fought only three times), but we still managed to sell about 1,500 tickets. I fed off the crowd, got off to a good start and pushed Young around for the better part of four rounds before the fight was finally stopped.

Any celebrating, however, was short-lived, since I immediately signed to fight again just two days later, in Atlantic City. When the offer came down, I never considered the possibility that someone might frown upon a boxer taking two fights in such a short period of time. After all, it wasn't like I'd suffered any serious damage against Greg Young. If someone wanted me to fight, and they were willing to pay me, then I'd fight.

When I arrived in Atlantic City, though, and began filling out the required prefight paperwork, I knew something was wrong. As part of the licensing process I was required to divulge the date of my previous fight. Now, all of this might sound ridiculous to anyone unfamiliar with the shadowy world of professional boxing. In most sports a single governing body oversees operations, ensuring that all participants are aware of and adhere to all rules and regulations. Boxing is different. There is a multitude of governing bodies; rules vary by state and country. Unscrupulous promoters and managers can and do take advantage of these discrepancies.

And the fighter usually gets caught in the middle.

Still, I have to take responsibility for my own role in this particular fiasco. Instead of saying I'd fought just two days earlier, I reported a gap of *fourteen* days. When the New Jersey State Boxing Commissioner, former world champion Jersey Joe Walcott, got word of this indiscretion, he slapped me with one hell of a penalty: an indefinite suspension. In other words, I might never have the opportunity to fight in the state of New Jersey. Given that Atlantic City was one of the busiest boxing locales in the country, second only to Las Vegas, the sentence might have been construed as a career killer. From my admittedly naïve vantage point, the punishment seemed not to fit the crime. I'm older now, and I've suffered enough concussions to understand the need for extremely tight regulation when it comes to protecting the health of boxers. But the legislation must also be uniform, and the fighter shouldn't even have the opportunity to report this information on his own. Again, though, that was the way the system worked at the time, and I was justifiably slapped around for not playing by the rules.

Four months passed without a fight. On January 1, Joe Walcott was succeeded as boxing commissioner by Larry Hazzard, who immediately lifted the suspension, clearing the way for me to box in New Jersey. When I heard that Mr. Hazzard had been appointed commissioner, I kind of thought my luck would change. He'd known me since I was a kid, understood that I wasn't a devious or irresponsible young man.

I just wanted to fight.

Larry knew better than most that shit happens in boxing—eager kids try to sneak in an extra bout here or there, especially when they've not yet graduated to the bigger stages of Atlantic City and Vegas. I had made a mistake and Mr. Hazzard, thank goodness, decided I'd paid enough of a price. Even today he likes to tell the story of how he was inundated with phone calls, letters and personal visits from people advocating for my reinstatement.

"Man, that Micky Ward must be something," he said at the time. "His mother is calling me, his doctor is calling me, trainers are calling me. Seems like everyone in the state of Massachusetts is saying, 'Enough already! Let this kid fight!'"

Atlantic City became my second home. I fought there seven times in the next six months, a brutal and frenetic pace that would not have been suitable for a lot of guys, but which was ideal for me. I'm compulsive by nature, and easily distracted—back then I thrived on the routine of the gym: training every day, fighting once a month. Assuming none of the fights turned out to be epic battles (which require a good deal of recovery time), this was the perfect schedule for a young, eager boxer.

It was important to get away from Lowell for a while, too. There was no shortage of hard-nosed kids in southern New England, but they weren't like the fighters you found in Atlantic City. Jersey attracted the cream of the crop: tough, seasoned boxers from Philly and New York. These were guys who had trained and studied at some of the best gyms in the world, and who had risen out of pools thick with talent and ambition. You could find yourself in Lowell or Boston, fighting a kid with a perfect record, and discover just two minutes into the ring that he lacked some of the most basic, fundamental skills. Conversely, you could fight a guy in Atlantic City with a sub-.500 record and get your lights turned out.

I became almost as comfortable in Atlantic City as I was in Lowell. They adopted me as one of their own, at a time when both the city and the sport of boxing were enjoying resurgence. Mike Tyson's youthful demolition of the heavyweight ranks coincided with my first couple years as a pro—just about everyone who fought at that time benefited from Mike's presence, and I was no different. Didn't even matter if you were on the same card with Mike; he brought new fans to the sport, resurrected old ones. It was an exciting time to be a fighter, especially in Atlantic City. The sport was popular and the town was hot. I fought at just about every resort in the city: the Sands, Caesars, Trump Plaza, and especially Resorts International.

The majority of my Atlantic City fights were televised on ESPN. Every time I stepped into the ring I expected a battle. These guys knew their way around the ring. Years of sparring and training, facing world-class competition on a daily basis, had made them gladiators. They knew how to fight, and they were willing to fight. Granted, I wasn't facing the best of the best. The idea was to stay busy, train every day and get in the ring against a legitimate opponent as often as possible.

And keep winning.

This, of course, is where strong management comes into play. It takes balls and business sense to skillfully guide a fighter's career. My mother, working in conjunction with Top Rank Boxing, one of the sport's premier promotional entities, was shouldering much of the burden in those days, and I think she did a pretty good job. I won all seven of those fights in Atlantic City, including four by knockout or technical knockout. I developed a reputation as a fighter who could both deliver a punch and take a punch. It was a fun and exciting time, and I tried to enjoy it.

One of the things people don't know about me is that I'm kind of a practical joker. For example, when I fought Luis Pizarro in May of 1986, at the Trump Casino and Hotel, I played a little trick on my buddy Dave Mendoza. Dave was one of my best friends, came to a ton of my early fights, usually traveling down with me and Richie Bryan and Tony Underwood. On this particular occasion, though, Dave got stuck late at work and ended up driving from Lowell to Atlantic City in the middle of the night. He got into town early in the morning, around the time I was heading out for a prefight weigh-in. I knew Dave would be exhausted, so I told him it was okay to crash in my room for a while.

After I left, though, I called security.

"Hello, this is Micky Ward. I'm in room three-fourteen. I'd like to report a break-in."

"Yes, sir. Go ahead."

"I just checked my room and there's someone sleeping in my bed. I have no idea who he is or how he got there."

"Don't worry, Mr. Ward. We'll send someone right up."

"Thank you," I said, trying to stifle the urge to laugh.

Not long after that, poor Dave was roused from his slumber by a team of security officers and dragged out of the room, which is basically what I hoped would happen. But the joke went a bit too far. The security guards were going to call the police and have Dave arrested. In the end, I had to go back up to the room and admit that the whole thing was just a prank, and that in fact I had given Dave permission to sleep in my room.

Needless to say, the hotel manager was not happy. And neither was Dave. But he didn't hold it against me. To this day he's one of my best friends.

I relied on Dave and Richie and Tony not just for friendship, but for support and consistency both in and out of the gym. Looking back on it, I'd say it was one of the happiest and least complicated periods of my life. I was twenty years old, fighting every month, working hard in the gym. Success did not immediately produce monetary rewards. Shit, when you're a rookie fighter from Lowell, with no Olympic titles in your background, you take what you can get. The going rate in those days was roughly a hundred bucks per (scheduled) round. So I'd pick up four hundred dollars here, six hundred dollars there. It wasn't a lot of money, but then again, I didn't need much. My mother's management fee amounted to virtually nothing, and Dicky would take maybe fifty bucks a fight. To help pay the bills, I'd pick up paving jobs with Uncle Gerry, whose support and understanding were unwavering. If I needed a few days of work, he'd give them to me, always paying in cash. If I needed time off, no problem.

"Anything you want, Mick," he'd say. "I'm glad to help."

In all honesty (and it still hurts to say this), a big distraction was Dicky. By now his boxing career was long dead, and he'd begun to cultivate a second career built around criminal activity. Like most addicts, he didn't have enough money to feed his habit, and he wasn't clearheaded or reliable enough to hold a real job. Most of the time he'd still manage to get to the gym to help me train; and after that first fight, he didn't miss another one (until he went into the joint for a prolonged period). But when it came to daily training sessions, he was hit-or-miss, no question about that. He'd show up, but he'd be late. And when he got there, he'd want to spar.

"Hey, Mick, let's get to work," he'd say, smacking his gloves together.

I'd look at him in wonderment. The guy's eyes would be bloodshot, his hair matted, his face covered with stubble.

"Yo, Dicky, I don't know, man."

"What, afraid you can't keep up with your big brother? Let's go!"

The amazing thing is, I'd do it. No, actually that's not the amazing thing. The truly incredible thing was that Dicky could actually spar in that condition. Not just a little bit. I'm talking about a formidable foe. The guy would stagger into the gym, straight from a crack house, or off a three-day drunk, slap on the headgear and gloves . . . and . . . *wow!* I don't know how the hell he did it. After *The Fighter* came out, a lot of people asked Dicky and me if that part was really true—the part about Dicky being able to spar despite being in questionable physical condition. Well, yeah. It's absolutely true. That's the way Dicky was—quick and dangerous even when he hadn't slept for seventy-two hours. Dicky actually did worse things than the movie showed. He was crazy. But when it came to training or boxing, he could still get the job done. Especially running. I was in tremendous shape and I'd be trying to lose him on a morning run, churning up hills, pushing as hard as I could, and the whole time I'd hear Dicky breathing down my back. Then the road would flatten out and he'd pull up alongside me, laughing and spitting through the pain. And then he'd pull ahead of me, his stride long and smooth, as elegant as an antelope's.

Are you kidding me? How the fuck does he do it?

Sometimes I think Dicky is indestructible. After all the damage the guy has done to his body—all the drugs and alcohol—he can still get in the ring and spar (which is more than I can say for myself). And he'll hold his own against kids half his age. No bullshit. You know what'll kill Dicky? Something totally random and seemingly benign. He'll choke on a piece of chewing gum or something. And everyone will have a good laugh at the funeral.

Not that there was anything funny about his behavior when it was at its worst. Frankly, I didn't know how to handle it. I was the little brother, the smaller, quieter personality. I never lectured Dicky, never gave him any ultimatums. I didn't have to. He knew he had a problem; and like any addict, he had to embrace the notion of change on his own. I'd hear him talking to people sometimes, dropping hints about the guilt and sadness he felt. He'd never come right out and say it, but I knew what was in his heart. Those days when he'd come into the gym all banged up? And then ask me to knock him around a bit? I'd see it in his eyes:

Don't blow it, Mick. Don't be like me.

I don't know whether Dicky truly worried about me or not. He knew we were fundamentally different, that I'd never shown anything but disgust toward the crackheads and whores and dealers who took up so much of his time. Then again, he also knew that we shared a bond: We were brothers, fighters, kids from Lowell. Maybe, on some level, Dicky felt like his behavior served as a deterrent to me.

Who knows?

Compared to Dicky, I've led a pretty clean life. But then, who hasn't? You're talking about a bar that's been set fairly low (or high, depending on how you look at it). But I'm no choirboy. It's a practical impossibility to have grown up in my house, and in my social circle, without having experimented with a bit of risky behavior. I did a fair amount of drinking and fighting and fucking when I was younger. When I got a little older, and my career went into the tank for a while, and I stopped caring so much about whether I needed to be fit or healthy, I tried a few other things. There is no point in lying about it. I've smoked pot, I've done cocaine. But I never got seriously involved with any of that stuff. I did it for a few years, here and there, during a depressing time in my life. Unlike Dicky, I was able to pull back from the abyss. I never failed to train my heart out. Boxing gave me structure and meaning; it gave me purpose. I didn't want to jeopardize any of that.

For whatever reason, Dicky wasn't able to exercise the same degree of control and restraint, and he paid a terrible price for his reckless behavior. Unfortunately, as often happens in those situations, the people around Dicky paid a price, as well. No one exists in a vacuum. If you're drinking too much, if you're using drugs, you don't just hurt yourself. You hurt the people who love you the most.

Officially, Dicky was my trainer for the majority of my professional career. But even when he held that title, he didn't always show up for work, and if not for the contributions of a handful of others, I might never have been more than a local hero. Although I was more focused and driven than most people you'd come across in the gym, I still needed someone there every day to help oversee workouts and provide impartial observations. Some boxers mistakenly believe they can train themselves. Even if you're capable of pushing through a two-hour workout alone, you still need someone who can tell you what you're doing right and wrong. A smart trainer can observe the slightest shift in technique, correct errors before they become unmanageable. He is a mentor, coach, father figure, advisor, friend.

Boxing is too hard to go it alone. You need someone you can trust in your corner. Someone smart and savvy and reliable.

Dicky was all of those things.

And none of them.

When Dicky was relatively sober and clearheaded, he was one hell of a trainer. Knew as much about boxing as anyone I've come across. We worked well together, and I wanted him on my team. But I couldn't always count on him to be there for me, and everyone knew it, which is why I turned to others at various points in my career. Arthur Ramalho, Leo Lydon, Gardner Brooks, Ouchie McManus and Mickey O'Keefe were all there during my amateur days; some of them (especially Mickey) helped me out as a professional as well. David Ortiz, who worked out of the West End Gym, was a big help in the first year or two of my professional career, when Dicky was still very much involved but also beginning his descent into drug addiction and crime.

It always seemed that people were willing to lend a hand, to give me whatever support I needed. I don't know that I've ever adequately expressed my appreciation for what they did. It wasn't always easy being around the Ward clan. Mom was a handful, as were my sisters (although they weren't much of a presence in the gym). And Dicky? Well, Dicky sometimes didn't deserve the title of trainer, but he held it anyway. I loved him and needed him, and I knew that he needed me, so I accepted him on his own terms. I don't know that it would be fair or accurate to say that Dicky held me back early in my career. He knew his shit and was more than capable of guiding a workout and getting the best out of a fighter. But he was a distraction, no question about it.

There were so many times that I'd leave the gym after Dicky failed to show up for a training session, and not only would I be pissed at him, I'd be worried, as well. See, that's the problem with hiring family. If Dicky hadn't been my brother, I'd have fired his ass in the first year. But what could I do? We were bound by blood.

So I learned to live with the chaos . . . the uncertainty. In some weird sort of way, I suppose, Dicky's unpredictability forced me to become even more focused, to tune out everything around me. When I look back on it now, it's remarkable that everything went as well as it did in that first year. A casual observer might glance at the record and see one victory after another, a string of knockouts and impressive performances, and presume that Team Ward was running like a well-oiled machine. If, by oil, you're referring to alcohol, then I suppose it was. By the end of 1986, Dicky had been arrested roughly a dozen times, on charges ranging from assault to larceny. To that point he managed to avoid serious jail time, but we all knew where he was headed, and that his story seemed unlikely to have a happy ending.

Each time Dicky went on a binge or got arrested, he'd bounce back impressively, returning to the gym without even bothering to issue an apology or an explanation. That wasn't his nature. He was much more likely to either say nothing or dismiss his transgressions with a joke. I never knew from one day to the next what was going to happen, which really kind of sucks when you're in serious training. But whether Dicky was there or not, I trained as hard as I possibly could.

You don't need anyone.

That was what I'd tell myself, even though I knew it wasn't true. I never used Dicky's absences as an excuse for slacking off. That, to me, would have been a sign of weakness. I never had to have anyone wake me up for my morning runs, never needed anyone standing over me, exhorting me to work hard in the gym. Shit . . . Dicky would tell me to hit the speed bag, then he'd go out and have a beer, and I'd still be working the bag when he got back! Ask him, it's true. I'd kill myself in that gym, like nobody else. If I was going to lose a fight, I didn't want to have any regrets. I could handle getting beat by a better man. I could even handle getting screwed by the officials.

I could not accept cutting corners. With or without Dicky, I was determined to be prepared.

It was the end of August before I completed the string of Atlantic City fights and returned to the Lowell Auditorium for another bout in front of the hometown fans—the first of my local fights televised on ESPN. The opponent was Johnny Rafuse, a light welterweight from nearby Malden, Massachusetts. Rafuse would be the biggest challenge of my early career. Strong and tough, he was five years older than me and had a professional record of 12–2. The most recent loss had come at the hands of John Wesley Meekins, who, like me, was part of the Top Rank stable and one of the more promising young fighters in the division. Although undefeated, with a 9–0 record, I didn't think I was special or anything. Boxing is weird that way. You can run up a record that seems, on the surface, to be impressive, without it actually meaning much of anything. And anyway, I wasn't the type to think I was unique. I was just a blue-collar boxer, a worker. I mean, there was some buzz locally, but outside of New England I was basically an unknown commodity. I mean, I was known on ESPN and a little bit within Top Rank, but it wasn't like they were grooming me to be a star. Rafuse was probably ahead of me, in that regard. So I suspected this would be no walkover, and I was right.

Dicky, as I recall, was lucky to make this one, as he'd recently been arrested yet again. (By now Dicky had become intimately familiar with the Lowell Police Department, and his reputation would ultimately prove costly to both of us.) Our team, however, was not entirely intact that night.

I remember sitting in the dressing room, getting my hands taped, when someone walked in. He was looking for Richie Bryan, who had been a fixture at each of my fights. Outside of my family, I was probably closer to Richie than I was to anyone else. I watched the guy talk with Richie and knew right away something was wrong. They left the dressing room, Richie listening intently, the other guy talking. A few minutes later the door opened again, and in walked this same guy, only without Richie. He huddled with Dicky for a moment.

"What's wrong?" I asked.

"Nothing, Mick," Dicky said. "We'll talk about it later."

Now I was getting aggravated. I wasn't a child. If something had happened to Richie, I wanted to know about it.

"Bullshit," I said. "Just tell me now."

The reason for Richie's sudden departure was that his father had passed away, and Richie had just received the news. It wasn't really a surprise, as his dad was quite old and in failing health. Still, they were close, and I knew Richie was devastated by the news. I started thinking about my friend, and how he was hurting, and suddenly I lost the concentration you need before entering the ring. I was supposed to have three people in my corner that night: Dicky, Johnny Dunn and Richie. Now I would have two, and one of them wasn't fully there himself.

"You all right, Mick?" Johnny asked.

I nodded.

"Just do your job. Richie will be fine."

Johnny and Dicky were understandably concerned. Few sports demand as much focus as boxing. It's so important to be in the right place, mentally, before you climb through the ropes. There's no room for distractions, no place for sentiment. You have a job to do, and the job is inherently dangerous. You lose focus in a basketball game and maybe someone steals the ball from you. Lose focus in a boxing match and the consequences can be deadly. At any moment, in any fight, you can be killed. Not just knocked out, but knocked *dead*. It's rare, of course, but it does happen. Your intensity wanes, you drop your hands and suddenly—*bang!*—blood clot on the brain. Every knockout punch is potentially lethal.

At the very least, your career is at stake. In football, if you get your bell rung, you just go to the sideline and recover, maybe take a few weeks off. But in boxing? There are no time-outs. You take a shot that rattles the brain, you're suddenly in survival mode, trying to make it to the end of the round. If you get knocked out, your career is sure to take a turn for the worse. You're damaged goods, literally and figuratively. Once your brain gets scrambled like that, you're more susceptible to further deterioration down the road. For some reason the brain never fully recovers. With each concussion there is residual damage.

And everyone in the business knows it.

See, there's something else that happens in the wake of a knockout, something less tangible. People look at you differently. And you look at yourself differently. Once you lose in boxing—and this is particularly true following a knockout—you feel vulnerable. Suddenly you know that you can lose. Okay, sure, everyone understands they're going to lose at some point. Not since Rocky Marciano a half century ago has a boxer retired as an undefeated champion. But you lie to yourself.

I can't get hurt.

I can't get knocked out.

I . . . can't . . . lose.

But you can, of course, and eventually it happens to everyone. How you deal with that first loss, that first knockout, determines what type of fighter you really are. Look at Tyson. No one could beat that kid; hell, no one even wanted to get in the ring with him! Then Buster Douglas came in and knocked him out, and that was that. Suddenly guys weren't afraid of Tyson. His image—that aura of invincibility—had been shattered. For thirty-seven fights Mike was as good as anyone who ever set foot in a ring. He was unbeatable. And then suddenly he's crawling blindly around the canvas, trying to scoop up a dislodged mouthpiece through the concussive haze of a knockout, and . . . well, let's just say that image followed him forever. If you're fighting Mike Tyson, you don't want to go into the ring thinking about the time he nearly decapitated Trevor Berbick. You want to go in there thinking about the guy who wound up on all fours in Tokyo.

Why?

Because the first guy scares the crap out of you; he's a monster, impossible to beat. The second guy is merely human. Just like you.

Really, though, it's all about gamesmanship. I've known Mike a long time. He's a teddy bear. Always has been. But he had that mystique about him—that ability to get mean and convince the other guy he was going to kill him or eat his kids or whatever. Come on, man. That wasn't Mike. It was an act. I'd see him doing that and I'd think, *Who is that guy?* People would sometimes get in my face about it, too.

"Why do you defend him, Micky? He's an asshole."

No, he's not. See, I understand the mental games Mike played, the way he tried to convince himself he was something he's not just so he could get in the ring and survive. We all do that sort of thing; Mike just took it to an extreme level. And I think the drugs and alcohol changed him, as well. But I got that, too, because I'd seen the same thing with Dicky.

Here's the truth: Boxers are among the strongest, most well-conditioned athletes on the planet. They're also among the most fragile.

So you can't blame Dicky and Johnny Dunn for worrying about me before the Rafuse fight. If I walked into the ring thinking about my friend, rather than my opponent, I'd be in trouble. In the end, though, it wasn't an issue. Before we left the dressing room, I told everyone that I was dedicating the fight to Richie's dad. That helped me recapture some of my focus and motivation. By the time I got to the ring, I was ready to battle. Good thing, too, since Rafuse was the toughest guy I'd ever fought. He was more experienced than me, and he was every bit as much of a warrior. I knew by the third round that Rafuse wasn't going to go away. And he didn't. We brawled and boxed for the full eight rounds. I threw everything at the guy—body shots, combinations, even tried switching from an orthodox stance to southpaw. He didn't wilt.

And you know what? I was okay with that. As the fight went on I gained confidence. I didn't mind trading punches. I wasn't afraid of getting hit. If I had to take a shot to the head in order to get off a nice two-punch combination, well, so what? I was willing to pay that price.

And in the end I was rewarded with a unanimous decision.

––––––––––––––––

The pace slowed somewhat over the course of the next year, but Top Rank ensured that I was fighting regularly, usually on ESPN, and always against credible opponents. When you're with Top Rank, you're busy, but the Rafuse fight had been both a blessing and a curse. It indicated that I was not only a promising young light welterweight, but an athlete capable of putting on a pretty good show, as well. Let's be perfectly candid here: White guys are a rarity in the sport of boxing; white guys who can brawl without bleeding profusely are almost unheard of. So I was marketable. But I wasn't about to get handed any easy opponents. Top Rank wanted competitive fights, and so did ESPN. You can't blame them for that. It's just good business.

Like I said, though, boxing is weird. Until you're at the very top of the heap, fighting for titles against well-known opponents, you never really know what you're going to face inside the ring. Sometimes you just shake your head and say, "Who the hell is this guy and where did he come from?" You learn to expect the unexpected. Carlos Brandi, for example, was undefeated but also untested when we fought on October 24, 1986, at the Lowell Auditorium. I didn't know much about him, except that he was from Argentina and supposedly had a 10–0 record. What I discovered, roughly one minute into the fight, was that Brandi was a wild and careless boxer.

This guy was like the Tasmanian Devil, flailing away from the opening bell, throwing one haymaker after another, wading in with his chin as well as his fists. Now, I suppose that sort of approach looks good on television, and maybe it catches the eye of a promoter; if the competition is weak, you win your first ten fights. But I'd been in the game long enough to know that while a guy like that could be very dangerous, he was never more than one mistake away from getting flattened.

All I had to do was wait for an opening.

So I spent most of the first round in a defensive posture, covering up, moving around the ring, letting Brandi do all the work. I could tell right away that while he was fit and athletic, he lacked discipline and technique; he was almost like a street fighter. I kept my composure, waited for him to lower his guard. The opening presented itself late in the round, after Brandi threw a couple more wild punches. A well-timed left hook caught him flush on the jaw and put him down. Brandi survived the round, but not much more. He came out for the second round with exactly the same sort of suicidal fury. I had to admire the kid's guts. But his inexperience really showed. I put him down with a right hand midway through the round, and then knocked him out with a left at 2:55.

A split decision over Hilario Mercedes on February 24, 1987, in Atlantic City served as a tune-up for my first fight in Las Vegas, in April of '87. This was a big deal. I had a 12–0 record and an opportunity to fight at Caesars Palace on the undercard of the World Boxing Council middleweight championship fight between Sugar Ray Leonard and Marvin Hagler. In retrospect, it was a fight that served as a line of demarcation in my career—the border between everything going well, and everything turning temporarily to shit.

My original opponent was a Puerto Rican fighter named Alfredo Rojas, but he withdrew just a couple weeks before the bout and was replaced by Californian Kelly Koble. I remember Dicky being more upset about the substitution than I was. Rojas was a left-hander, and Dicky had done a good job of lining up southpaw sparring partners while we trained for the fight. Koble, though, was a righty.

"It don't matter, Dicky," I said. "I'll be ready."

I could be a bit of a hardhead about these things, sometimes to my own detriment. In all fairness, when the occasional curveball came our way, Dicky was always quick to look out for me. But once a fight was put on the calendar, I was committed. Didn't matter if they changed the venue, the purse or the opponent. In this particular case I was so excited about fighting in Vegas, on one of the biggest cards in recent history (the entire show would be broadcast to a pay-per-view and closed-circuit television audience estimated at four hundred million) that I didn't even care who I was facing.

We went to Vegas about a week before the fight, just to get acclimated to the heat and the three-hour time difference. Richie and I flew out together. On the way Richie must have eaten something that didn't agree with him, because that night he came down with a pretty nasty case of gastric distress. The poor guy was up all night, running from his bed to the bathroom (I know because we shared a hotel room). The next morning, while Richie slept in, I went for a jog. When I got back to the hotel, a maid was cleaning our room, and Richie was nowhere to be found.

"Morning," I said to the housekeeper.

She said nothing, just made brief eye contact and then shook her head disapprovingly. I could hear her muttering something in Spanish under her breath.

I shrugged and went into the bathroom, figuring she was just having a bad day. By the time I came out, the housekeeper was gone. A short time later, Richie returned. I told him about the maid, and the icy reception I'd received. Richie tried to stifle a laugh.

"What's so funny?" I asked.

"Sorry, man. She probably thinks you're sort of a pig."

Now I knew something was up.

"Richie, you bastard. What did you do?"

Apparently, during his night from hell, Richie had accidentally messed the sheets on his bed. So when I left in the morning to go for my run, Richie called housekeeping and asked to have the beds changed and the room cleaned as quickly as possible. When the maid arrived he was quick to plead innocent and pin the blame on his friend and roommate.

"Poor guy had an accident," Richie had said. "It happens to him a lot."

No wonder she'd treated me like a bum!

Anyway, I guess I had it coming after all the practical jokes I'd played on some of my buddies over the years.

The atmosphere on fight night was incredible. Leonard-Hagler was one of the biggest fights of the decade, maybe one of the biggest in history. Held in a 15,000-seat stadium constructed in the parking lot of Caesars Palace, this was a classic Vegas card, starting in the late afternoon and running well into the night. There were eight fights in all, and I was early enough in the card that it was still light out when I walked into the ring (I actually had to shade my eyes from the sun as I entered the ring). I wasn't as starstruck as you might expect. Stuff like that—the surroundings, the television cameras, celebrities—didn't affect me very much. Once you're standing in the ring, looking at your opponent, it's no different from being at the Lowell Auditorium. There was a lot of hoopla surrounding the Leonard-Hagler card, but at the end of the day the job was the same: Beat the other guy. Don't get me wrong—I knew it was a special night, and I was thrilled to be there. But when the bell rings, you have to put all of that stuff out of your mind.

I'm sure there weren't many people at Caesars that night who had any interest in watching Micky Ward and Kelly Koble. Folks were meandering in as we were introduced to the crowd, which probably numbered only a couple thousand (most of whom weren't even paying attention). It would be several more hours before Leonard and Hagler took the stage, and the celebrities who typically come out for the big fights had yet to show up. Who could blame them? Kelly and I were merely an appetizer.

I didn't know a lot about Koble, except that his record was 12–5, and despite the fact that he was coming off a bad loss, he was considered a "gamer," the kind of boxer who would not be easily intimidated. And he wasn't. Kelly actually took the fight to me. I got off to a slow start, probably lost the first two or three rounds before finding my rhythm. Once engaged, I was able to hit Kelly with relative ease. I can still remember thinking that the gloves that night felt unusually small and tight. They were eight-ounce Reyes gloves, nothing out of the ordinary, but for some reason, while putting them on in the locker room, I got the sense of being almost bare-handed. When I caught Kelly with a shot to the right eye in the fourth round, I knew I'd done some serious damage. This rarely happens, but I could actually feel the flesh separate as my fist drove into his eyebrow. The blood began to flow almost immediately; as I watched it spill down his face, I knew the fight was over. Referee Richard Steele, one of the best in the business, summoned a ringside physician to examine Kelly's eye. The doc took one look, shook his head and signaled an end to the proceedings.

I hung around long enough afterward to see Sugar Ray put on one of the most amazing performances of his career. Although he was only thirty-one years old, Ray had been inactive for a long time. He'd retired in 1984 with both the WBC and WBA welterweight titles to his credit, as well as an amazing legacy that included a pair of incredible battles with Roberto Duran and another with Thomas Hearns. He had nothing left to prove, but there he was, fighting at 158 pounds (more than ten pounds above his usual weight), against one of the greatest middleweights in history. If Leonard was rusty, you never would have known it. Lightning quick and in spectacular shape, he outboxed Hagler for twelve rounds and came away with a split decision.

I wondered how Dicky felt watching Ray that night, given the different paths they'd chosen. But I didn't get to ask him. You see, Dicky loved Vegas, maybe a little too much. Open and uninhibited, with access to just about every vice known to man, Vegas was Dicky's kind of town. When we'd go out there, he'd be a ghost. You'd barely see him before the fight, and you wouldn't see him at all afterward—not until you got on the plane, anyway.

I had a couple beers after the Leonard-Hagler fight, just hanging out in my room with Richie and some other guys. Very low-key. Dicky? I don't know where he went, but he showed up at the airport the next day looking like dog crap. Our whole camp was moving a little slowly, mainly because Johnny Dunn had taken a fall the night before while leaving the arena. The poor man was eighty years old, and he'd made the mistake of trying to climb over a small barrier to avoid the crush of the postfight crowd. In the process he'd fallen hard enough to cut his chin and bruised just about everything else. We had to strap him to an upright dolly just to get him back to the hotel. The next day Johnny was so sore that he still couldn't walk, so we found a wheelchair and took our time getting to the airport. As we were waiting for curbside check-in, Dicky pulled up.

A few minutes later, so did Ray Leonard.

He arrived with his entourage in a big stretch limo. They all got out slowly, Ray demonstrating that exhausted postfight shuffle that every boxer recognizes. He wore dark glasses to shade his eyes from the sun and no doubt to conceal the bruises from the previous night's war. Dicky, who looked almost as bad as Ray (despite not having been in a fight), walked right over and offered his congratulations.

"Hell of a fight, Ray."

Leonard said thanks, keeping his hands at his sides, a gesture that might have seemed rude to anyone other than a fellow boxer. To us, though, no explanation was necessary. You don't shake hands with a fighter the morning after he's gone twelve rounds with Marvin Hagler . . . when every knuckle is so sore that he couldn't even hold a pencil. The small talk lasted only a few seconds before we went our separate ways. Nine years had passed since Dicky and Ray had faced each other in Boston, and their lives could not have unfolded more differently. I think Ray always respected Dicky as a fighter—he even hired him as a sparring partner before the first Duran fights in Montreal, in the summer of 1980. But that, too, was a lifetime ago. Dicky's career was now long dead, Ray's had just been resurrected, and mine was beginning to take flight.

It had to have been a little awkward for Dicky. A little sad.

But he never would have admitted it.

CHAPTER 6

I should have known better.

In Lowell, as in any city, there are places it's best to avoid if you want to stay out of trouble. High on that list in the mid- to late 1980s was a nightclub called the Cosmopolitan Cafe. The Cosmo, located on Market Street, had a hard-earned reputation for attracting trouble. It was the kind of place where the toughest folks in town liked to congregate. They drank too much, shared lines of coke off bathroom sinks and fought at the drop of a hat. A nasty place, all the way around, and not the kind of bar for amateurs. No one ever started out at the Cosmo on a Saturday night. It was the sort of club that got busier and more problematic as the night wore on, since a large percentage of the clientele was often shitfaced by the time they arrived.

Only a few weeks removed from the victory over Kelly Koble in Las Vegas, I felt pretty good about how things were going in my life at this time. Actually, I felt great about how things were going, despite the fact that the usual chaos persisted, both in and out of the ring, most of it revolving around Dicky, who by this time was starting to get into some fairly serious trouble on a regular basis. His reputation had deteriorated to the point that being Dicky's little brother was practically an occupational hazard. The guy could still fill a room with his personality, and he continued to walk and talk like he was the mayor of Lowell or something. It was almost as though by continuing to skate through life with a smile and a bit of patter, Dicky felt like he could get away with anything.

Most of the time he was right. Even when he was getting into trouble with the law, Dicky would make excuses or minimize the seriousness of his behavior. By the time I was seventeen or eighteen I knew Dicky was into some really bad shit—you don't stay up for three straight days if you're just a drinker. Nobody does that, unless they've moved on to cocaine and crack, which Dicky clearly had done. For the most part, though, I stayed quiet about it. When I did say something, Dicky would just growl or laugh, depending on his mood.

"I'm fuckin' fine. Just leave me alone, all right?"

It wasn't like you could reason with Dicky, the way you can with most people. He was smart and charming and funny. He knew how to lie, which made it even harder to pin him down. But, then, that's a characteristic shared by most addicts: They're elusive. I'm sure my mother knew that Dicky was much more than a drinker, but she never really admitted it—not even when he was in jail. I don't think she could bring herself to acknowledge the depth of his problems. It was just too painful. And maybe she blamed herself for some of it. Who knows? I'm a proponent of personal accountability, but I have to admit that anyone who grows up in a culture of alcoholism, in a city thick with drug traffic and other crime, has a better-than-average chance of screwing up his life.

I could have gone down that path myself. For a while, in my late teens, I seemed to be headed that way. But I'd been careful and well-behaved for a couple years now, ever since turning pro. I trained and fought and worked. I tried to keep my nose clean. Between fights I'd relax and enjoy the occasional night out on the town, but rarely, if ever, did I allow myself to get sloppy drunk. There was too much at stake. I knew myself well enough to know that under the right circumstances, in the wrong place, I could get into big trouble. A few too many drinks could easily lead to a bar fight, a busted hand or nose, an arrest and a quick demolition of my career. All that hard work down the drain.

It just wasn't worth the risk.

So how do I explain what happened on this particular night? Well, I can't. Not really, other than to say that I fell victim to a serious lapse in judgment. And I paid dearly for it.

The Cosmo, as usual, was our last stop of the night. I'd been out having a few beers with some of my buddies, and we wound up on Market Street around one o'clock in the morning. The Cosmo, with a line of motorcycles parked out front, was just getting heated up. Not long after we arrived at the bar, one of my buddies, Mike, spotted some-one he knew. I could tell Mike was agitated by the guy's very presence, so I asked him what was wrong. Well, it turned out that Mike's mother had been dating a man, and at some point, according to Mike, their relationship had gotten abusive: The guy had supposedly hit his mom. Well, Mike wasn't the kind of kid to let something like that slide, espe-cially when he was fueled by several hours of drinking. So he went right up to this guy and got in his face. They exchanged words for a few minutes, and then headed for the parking lot, presumably to settle their dispute.

The rest of us, including Dicky and some of his friends who were also at the Cosmo, followed them outside to get a ringside view. That was when things got really complicated and convoluted. The brawl went on for only a few minutes, with Mike easily getting the best of things. He was younger, stronger and bigger, and quickly put the other guy on the ground and then pounced on top of him and continued to kick the shit out of him. I think he might have killed this guy if someone hadn't intervened. But someone did.

That someone was Dicky.

"Come on, that's enough!" Dicky yelled. "He's a friend of mine."

Now, I really don't think Dicky was close to this guy, but I also don't doubt that they were acquaintances. Like I said, Dicky knew just about everyone in town.

As Dicky tried to help the man to his feet, I could hear sirens wailing in the distance. My buddy Mike, meanwhile, had the good sense to get the hell out of there, using a nearby canal path to put some distance between himself and the melee. As the cops pulled up, Dicky was in the process of hoisting the losing fighter to his feet, an image that was bound to be misinterpreted by the Lowell police officers who had come to regard Dicky as one of the biggest troublemakers in town.

I can still see the look in Dicky's eyes as the cops rushed toward him, brandishing nightsticks—a look that reflected not so much fear as astonishment. Like he couldn't believe what was about to transpire.

Here I am, trying to do the right thing, and look what happens. I still get arrested.

But that's the lesson, right? You do enough bad things and people just presume that's all you have to offer anymore: trouble.

After a brief scuffle, Dicky was on the ground, his hands cuffed behind his back. By now more than a dozen police officers had arrived on the scene, probably a smart move considering the size of the crowd, the hour of the day and the venue. If I'd been one of those cops, I might have reacted the same way. This was neither the time nor the place to utilize whatever they might have learned in sensitivity training.

Of course, I wasn't one of the cops. I was just a guy standing outside a bar in the early-morning hours, having had a few too many drinks, watching my brother get dragged down the street to a waiting paddy wagon. Probably should have kept my mouth shut, but I felt the overwhelming urge to come to Dicky's aid. Not just because he was my brother, but because, on this occasion at least, he'd been wrongfully accused.

"Why are you arresting him?" I shouted. "He was just trying to help."

At first they ignored me, but as they approached the back of the wagon, one of the cops shoved Dicky forward and onto the ground, face-first. With his hands shackled, he couldn't even break his fall. When I saw that, I ran over to the wagon and tried to intervene. Not the smartest move, as it turned out.

"What are you doing?!" I yelled. "Leave him alone."

I barely got the words out before I felt the sting of something hard against my ribs.

Whump!

A nightstick, I presume, or maybe one of the foot-long flashlights the cops were carrying. Whatever it was, it hurt like hell, instantly took my breath away. And then another shot, this one to the side of my head.

As the blood poured down my face, the cops wrestled me to the ground. I don't know how many of them there were—it felt like an army. They kept hitting me, even after they had me cuffed and subdued. By now there was a big crowd in the street, people shouting at the cops, some of them identifying me by name, thinking perhaps that this would somehow quell the violence.

"Hey, don't you know who that is? It's Micky Ward!"

The cops didn't give a shit. If anything, this only served to stoke their anger. You don't get preferential treatment from the cops—not in the middle of a brawl at one o'clock in the morning. Not at a place like the Cosmo. And let's be honest: It wasn't like I was a world champion or anything. I was just a good young fighter who also happened to be the brother of Dicky Eklund, a relationship that did not work in my favor on this night. Dicky, unfortunately, was on a first-name basis with half the Lowell Police Department, and not because they thought he was such a great guy. Dicky was a fighter, too, and on more than one occasion he'd gotten into physical altercations with the cops. It's human nature to paint with a broad brush, and I don't doubt for a second that the officers figured I was guilty by association.

The cops kept beating on me long after I'd been subdued. As they dragged me to the wagon I could feel the sting of the nightsticks hammering against my body. I was flat on the ground, two or three cops pinning me down, hands shackled. I was utterly helpless and still the hits kept coming. The last few did the most damage, three or four solid shots across my hands and arms. I don't remember yelling or screaming; I don't remember saying anything at all. I just remember thinking, *Christ, why won't they stop?*

Finally they lifted my broken body off the ground and tossed me into the back of the paddy wagon alongside Dicky and my sister Gail.

That's right—Red Dog was there, too! For better or worse, the Ward/ Eklund clan stuck together—whether drinking, fighting . . . or getting arrested. Gail, you see, had been drinking at the Cosmo, as well, and she'd actually jumped into the fray when the cops were going after me and Dicky, screaming, "You're gonna arrest them? Take me, too!"

So they did.

And now here we were, the three of us together in the police wagon, disheveled, drunk and humiliated. And, in my case, bleeding like a motherfucker.

You know who wasn't there? My friend Mike, who had instigated the whole episode. He'd left at the first sign of police intervention and didn't look back (smart move, actually). He was never apprehended, never charged with a crime; neither was the guy with whom he fought. But Dicky and me? And Red Dog? We got our asses kicked.

Eventually we went down to the precinct house, where Dicky and Gail were formally booked. I was arrested, too, of course, but because of my injuries, I was allowed to stay in the wagon. Then I went to the hospital. Six stitches and several X-rays later, I was released to my parents and allowed to go home. But the fallout from that night would be felt for many years to come.

Officially, the diagnosis was a hairline fracture in my right hand, where one of the cops had hit me with his nightstick. Funny thing about that term—*hairline fracture*. It sounds so innocuous, as if the injury isn't all that severe. Tiny, narrow. Easy to fix. In reality, though, a hairline fracture can be worse than a clean break. With a clean break there's a standard protocol for recovery and rehabilitation. With a hairline fracture, everything is kind of murky and unsettled. You think you're better when you really aren't. The pain starts to subside, range of motion returns, and so you get back in the gym and start working the bag, maybe sparring a little. Then, all of a sudden . . .

Crack!

It happens all over again.

I went through that cycle more times than I can remember. For the better part of a dozen years, until I finally had reconstructive surgery to get the damn thing fixed properly, I fought with a bad right hand. The pain and swelling, symptoms of deteriorating bone disease, were constant reminders of that night at the Cosmo. I never let it heal properly; I just learned to live with the discomfort. Every day I'd train, and then stick my hand in a bucket of ice. It became a normal and accepted part of the routine.

I was supposed to fight just a few weeks after that incident. The injury forced a cancellation, but it didn't stop me from getting back in the gym to train. I ran while wearing a half cast. Within three or four weeks I was hitting the bag. By two months I'd begun sparring. I knew even then that the injury was bad, and that I probably hadn't given it sufficient time to heal. But, hell, I was only twenty-one years old, and I felt like I could bounce right back. Who thinks about long-term consequences at that age? Boxers are trained to ignore the odds, to look past the probability of injury or impairment. We all know the possibility of brain damage or death awaits each of us; by comparison, a hairline fracture of the hand seems like a minor annoyance.

But it's not. It's much more than that. From the day I returned prematurely to the gym, I was on a roller coaster. I should have taken at least six months off from any contact at all. Instead, I was training within a matter of weeks, and fighting within four months. I have no one to blame for any of that. It was my decision to go to the Cosmo that night; it was my decision to intervene when Dicky was getting cuffed.

And it was my decision to resume training even though my hand was killing me. No one pushed me. No one tried to make me feel guilty.

It was all on me.

The comeback fight, if you want to call it that, was uneventful, a fourth-round TKO over Derrick McGuire on August 25, 1987, at Bally's hotel and casino in Atlantic City. McGuire wasn't a bad fighter, but neither was he as polished or impressive as his record might have indicated. Like I said, though, that's a common theme in boxing, and I knew enough to take both the fight and the fighter seriously. McGuire was 13–4, but had lost three of his previous four bouts. In fact, though I didn't know it at the time, this poor guy was well on his way to becoming nothing more than a punching bag, one who would lose twelve of his last fifteen fights. No matter. I focused on my job, which was to recapture some of the sharpness that had naturally eroded during my time off. Since turning pro I'd gotten accustomed to fighting every month, maybe every couple months, and the layoff had left me restless and uncomfortable.

With the victory over McGuire I remained undefeated, but that was about to change. Exactly one month later, on September 25, I suffered the first loss of my professional career, at the hands of Edwin Curet, a journeyman lightweight from Puerto Rico who now lived and trained not far from me, in Brockton, Massachusetts. Like Derrick McGuire, Curet was in the midst of a rough stretch, having lost his two previous fights. Unlike McGuire, Curet was a hell of a fighter whose resume included respectable performances against two champions, Livingstone Bramble and Greg Haugen. Curet was a smart and effective boxer who didn't tire easily, and his strategy of constant movement proved effective. It didn't help matters any that my hand ached throughout the fight (a precursor of things to come). The swelling that had been merely bothersome in training was now seriously inhibiting my ability to generate power. In the end I came up short, losing a ten-round split decision.

I remember feeling somewhat depressed after that fight. Having never lost before, and knowing how easy it is to lose momentum—how quickly a hot fighter can turn cool—I fretted over the possibility that Top Rank and ESPN would now look at me with a little less enthusiasm. There's something special about being undefeated. It doesn't mean much when you've only fought four or five times, but when you get up to 14–0, and you've faced a handful of legitimately challenging opponents, then people start to talk about you. There's an air of excitement surrounding anyone with that kind of record. Once you lose, though, things can change very quickly. You're no longer "unbeaten," and you never will be again. Losing your first fight is like losing your virginity—you can't ever get it back.

It's a rite of passage.

The only reasonable strategy was to get right back in the gym, and then start winning again. In mid-January of 1988, after taking a little time to let my hand heal, I fought Joey Ferrell in Atlantic City. Ferrell, whose nickname was "Bugsy," was a typical Philly fighter: tough and technically proficient. Although his record was unimpressive (7–7–2), Bugsy was not to be taken lightly. Far as I was concerned, the Philly credential was all he needed to be considered a worthy opponent. But there was more. Having faced the likes of former world champion Buddy McGirt, as well as John Meekins and Mike Mungin—a pair of contenders in the welterweight and light welterweight divisions (they were a combined 25–0 when Bugsy had the misfortune of running into them)—Ferrell obviously wasn't going to be intimidated by me. Hell, the guy had beaten Mungin and had lost by decision to McGirt. Must have had a pretty good chin, too, because he'd never been knocked out.

I didn't expect to be the person to change that. My goal was simply to get busy from the opening bell, to make sure that I didn't make the same mistake I'd made against Edwin Curet, which was to let the fight drag on and turn it into an endurance contest. I prided myself on being one of the fittest athletes in the game, but I also knew that with each passing round, the swelling on my right hand would increase, diminishing the power of my punches. By necessity, I had to strike early and often.

"Jump all over him," Dicky said before the fight. "Don't waste any time."

That was the plan, and it couldn't have played out any better. I caught Bugsy with a left hook to the body early in the first round, a shot that clearly hurt. I could hear that distinctive "Uhhhhh . . ." that happens when you catch someone with a clean punch to the ribs. Bugsy retreated. I caught him again with a body shot, and this time he went to a knee. Sensing the potential for a quick exit, I threw everything I had at him, until I could barely lift my arms. It was a withering flurry, and too much for Bugsy to survive. He hit the canvas again late in the round, prompting the referee to stop the fight.

Just like that I was back on track. I was 14–1, with an impressive first-round knockout over a guy who was known to be a formidable opponent. Afterward I couldn't wait to get back in the gym. I didn't want to take any time off. I just wanted to keep fighting. So that was what I did—four times in the first six months of 1988, a pace similar to my first year as a pro. Yeah, I was putting my health and career at risk by fighting so often with a bum hand, but I didn't know any other

way. Time off was time that needed to be filled, and that had the potential to create problems. As long as I was busy, and winning, I was happy.

By July I was 17–1, and my name was at least in the conversation
when boxing people started talking about the best light welterweights
in the world.

"Keep 'em coming," I told anyone who would listen—my mother,
Dicky, the folks at Top Rank and ESPN. "I'll fight anybody, anywhere."

That was the truth, unfortunately. As I'd soon discover, sometimes
it was best to say no.

I'd been offered a chance to fight Saoul Mamby in Atlantic City in
September, and quickly accepted the invitation. Mamby was a former
world light welterweight champion. His best days were well behind him,
but even then, at the age of forty-one, he could still hold his own against
most of the best guys in the division. He was a household name (well,
in houses where they followed boxing, anyway) who would continue
to fight for another thirteen years, before finally retiring at the age of
fifty-four! And if that weren't enough, he came out of retirement in
2008, fighting once and losing a ten-round decision. He was sixty years
old at the time. So, looking back on it, I guess you could say I was a
mid-career fight for Saoul Mamby.

Except the fight never took place. Mamby came down with some
sort of virus shortly before the fight and was still running a fever on the
day of the bout. This guy was about as hard as they come, fearful of
nothing, so naturally he didn't want to back out. But the docs wouldn't
allow it. This sort of thing happens on occasion in boxing, and when it
does, promoters are left with only two options: cancel the fight, or find
a new opponent.

Not surprisingly, they chose option number two.

Working against the clock, Ron Katz, a matchmaker for Top Rank, focused his efforts on the Philadelphia area, since it was only about an hour and a half away from Atlantic City. There he tracked down Mike Mungin. I knew a little bit about Mungin. We'd been on the same card a few months earlier, and he had a reputation for being a strong fighter, but I can't honestly say I had paid attention to his performance. And I didn't know that he'd been out of commission for a while.

"The kid's a tough fighter," Mom said. "Got a 17–2 record. But he's only fought once in the last three years."

"Why's that?"

"He's been in prison."

That caught my attention. It wasn't like I was scared to fight against an ex-con—I'd faced enough of those guys both in the gym and on the street—but it did seem likely that a Philly fighter who had just gotten out of jail would be more than a little hungry. I also discovered that in his last fight he'd lost a ten-round decision to John Meekins. And guess what? He'd taken that fight on roughly twenty-four hours' notice as well!

"Guy's no slouch, huh?" I said.

Mom shook her head.

"No, he's not."

I was okay with all of this. I had trained particularly hard for this fight—so hard, in fact, that I weighed only 136 pounds, about four or five pounds less than usual. I felt fit and well-prepared. Mungin was supposed to be a heavy puncher, but I couldn't help but believe that all that rust accrued while sitting behind bars would be too much to overcome. Simply put, I was confident.

Unfortunately, nothing about that day went as planned.

Although at 5'7" Mungin was an inch shorter than me, he was actually a bigger, stronger fighter. He'd been a natural welterweight, comfortable within a range of 140 to 150 pounds. I figured he'd be on the lower end of that scale, but he wasn't. Not even close. Mungin weighed in a few hours before the fight, tipping the scales at 154 pounds! When I heard that, I was legitimately shocked. It happens sometimes that fighters fail to meet the weight contractually established for a particular fight. On those occasions it's up to the fighters (and managers) to determine how best to proceed. I was well within my rights to back out of the fight. They'd thrown a new, unknown opponent at me, and it was revealed that the opponent had eighteen pounds on me.

If you've never been in a boxing ring—if you've never sparred with anyone nearly twenty pounds heavier—you probably can't appreciate just how big a difference that really is. It's basically a lightweight fighting a middleweight. And I don't care how talented the lightweight might be; he's going to have trouble with any experienced middleweight. It's a recipe for disaster.

I didn't know about any of this until the afternoon of the fight, when my mother and Ron Katz came into the dressing room and told us. Dicky's response was immediate and emphatic.

"Fuck this! We're going home."

I sat there quietly for a few minutes while Dicky and Mom argued with Katz. I tried to focus, but the noise and the bickering made it virtually impossible. I'd come to Atlantic City expecting one thing, and now here I was, preparing for something else entirely. Suddenly, the risks outweighed the benefits. And I knew it. Then again . . . the show must go on.

Right?

"Look, Dicky, I want to fight," I said. "I trained, I'm ready. And

Me (age 16), Tony Pavone and my brother, Dicky, after I won the New England Golden Gloves championship, 1982

Me, in fighting stance (center front), with Mike Tyson (second from left) and Marty Foley (center back row), 1983

Atlantic City, 1986

PHOTO COURTESY OF MICKY WARD

My manager, Sal LoNano; his wife, Darlene LoNano; me; Charlene; Dicky;
Rhonda Burke; and Al Valenti after the Shea Neary fight in London, 2000

Me and my mom

My wife, Charlene, and me on our wedding day in Las Vegas, May 27, 2005

My nephew Sean Eklund fighting Golden Gloves, with me and Dicky

Actor Holt McCallany; my agent, Nick Cordasco; me;
and MMA legend Bas Rutten

PHOTO BY DARREN PRINCE

Arturo Gatti, Chuck Zito and me at my retirement party in Connecticut

PHOTO COURTESY OF CHUCK ZITO

Me and Dicky with the actresses who played our sisters in *The Fighter* at Spike TV's Guys Choice Awards. From left: Bianca Hunter, me, Erica McDermott, Kate B. O'Brien, Dicky, Dendrie Taylor, Jenna Lamia and Melissa McMeekin.

PHOTO BY NICK CORDASCO

anyway, we got all these people coming down in buses from Lowell. I can't disappoint them."

Dicky scowled, waved a hand dismissively.

"Hell with them! Doesn't matter what they think. They don't have to get in the ring."

He was right, and I want to make that perfectly clear. It's been suggested in the past that no one was looking out for me the night of the Mungin fight—that a better manager and more clearheaded trainer would have held me out of the ring. I suppose I've lent legitimacy to that notion by failing to set the record straight. So I'll do it now. My mother was uncomfortable with the whole situation. I know she was worried and would have been perfectly fine if I had turned down the fight. As for Dicky, well, he was adamant that I not fight Mungin. I can remember it vividly. Dicky's instincts as a fighter and big brother told him that everything about that night was wrong; he did his best to stop me from fighting. Ultimately, though, it was my decision to make, and I chose to fight. Pride and ego got the best of me. I was too concerned about how it would look if I backed out. I couldn't stand the idea of people being disappointed.

I couldn't stomach the thought of anyone calling me a coward.

"Don't worry," I told Dicky. "The weight won't make a damn bit of difference."

Hah! Famous last words.

As part of the deal, my mother negotiated an increase in my share of the purse. I was supposed to get ten thousand dollars. By agreeing to fight a last-second replacement who outweighed me by almost twenty pounds, I earned an additional twenty-five hundred bucks. Hazardous duty pay, I guess. And let me tell you—it wasn't enough. Nothing against Mungin. He was a good fighter and I don't hold him accountable in any way for what happened. The man got a call and he accepted the fight. What was he supposed to do—turn it down? I'm sure he needed the payday. And, at the time, I was a career-making opponent for him.

In his shoes, I would have done the same thing.

Within the first few rounds I knew I was in trouble. Well, before that, actually. Like, as soon as Mungin took off his robe, revealing the kind of thickly muscled, chiseled physique you see on a middleweight.

Holy Christ . . .

Mungin's announced weight was 145. I have no idea where they came up with that one, since he'd been 154 earlier in the day. If the guy had sweated out nine pounds in a few hours, I don't want to think about what he would have looked like with the additional weight. Anyway, we all believed 145 was a fabrication designed to make the fight seem fair and reasonably in line with the terms of the contract.

Despite the difference in size, I doubt anyone in the arena that night, or watching the fight on ESPN, expected Mungin to win. I was the hot young prospect. He was damaged goods, an ex-con trying to resurrect his career. But as soon as the fight started I could tell Mungin wasn't nearly as rusty as I expected him to be; and he was every bit as strong as he appeared. Those are underrated weapons in a fighter's arsenal: physical strength, brute power. Not just the ability to throw a heavy punch, but to lean on an opponent and push him around. The casual observer thinks of boxing as merely the trading of blows, but a huge part of every bout is spent in close quarters, banging foreheads, clinching, using weight and muscle to gain every possible advantage. This is true of junior welterweights as well as heavyweights.

With that in mind, I decided to keep my distance from Mungin in the early going, try to move and stick, make him wear himself out. The guy was a physical specimen, but I figured since he'd only fought once in the past few years, he'd be unable to run with me all night. By the third or fourth round, though, Mungin had cut down the ring considerably, and every time he got off a clean shot, I was surprised at the force behind it. The guy knew how to fight, and he was beating me at my own game. So I closed the distance a bit, tried to get off a few body punches. Each time, though, I felt like I was pushing against a concrete wall—I couldn't move him, couldn't hurt him. By the fourth round my nose was bleeding. Then, in the sixth, Mungin caught me with a big uppercut that snapped my head back and momentarily scrambled my brain. It was the hardest I'd ever been hit, and the effect was startling. I backpedaled, trying instinctively to escape the onslaught. Mungin bore right in, popping me above the left eye, in that sensitive spot along the eyebrow, where blood pools and tissue is easily damaged. I'd already begun to swell, and the force of this particular punch was enough to create a fissure along my eyebrow. Like a boil getting lanced, the swollen eye popped open, spraying blood and sweat into the first row of the crowd. It didn't really hurt, didn't affect my vision or my ability to fight. But I knew from experience that it probably looked very bad. Those are the kinds of cuts that scare ringside physicians and horrify both fans and broadcasters. When a fighter sustains a gash above the eye, and crimson pours down his face, boxing looks less like a sweet science than a blood sport.

The importance of a good cut man can't be overstated at a time like this. These guys are freakin' wizards, and very few people appreciate the work they do. When you watch a fight, you see them for only a few seconds at a time, dashing through the ropes, cotton swabs tucked behind their ears, a bag full of tricks at the ready. They work feverishly to close cuts and reduce swelling, and in the process they bring sanity and hope to the sometimes chaotic atmosphere of the corner. You'd be amazed at how often a boxer will stumble onto his stool, his face a pulpy mess, his confidence shattered, and somehow the able cut man restores him to fighting shape within sixty seconds.

I was fortunate to have one of the all-time great cut men in my corner, Eddie Aliano. They called Eddie "The Clot" for reasons that ought to be self-explanatory. On this night I needed all of his expertise, and he gave it willingly, as he always did. It just wasn't enough. I mean, Eddie kept me in the ring; his expertise was probably the only thing that prevented the fight from being stopped. But there were other issues well beyond Eddie's control. Like the fact that I just couldn't get close enough to Mungin to do any damage—not without getting seriously pummeled in the process. The guy was just too big and strong. Late in that same sixth round, he caught me with a hard right, flush on the chin. It was like no other punch I'd felt, and it sent me reeling across the ring. Suddenly everything seemed to be moving in slow motion. I could feel my legs wobbling, my feet getting tangled. And there was nothing I could do about it. Next thing I knew, I was flat on my back on the canvas, staring up at the ceiling.

It's always a strange feeling when you get knocked down, whether in sparring or in a real fight. But the very first time it happens? That's not just a physical setback; it's a jarring psychological blow. I knew I was far from invincible, but the shock of getting knocked down for the first time, combined with the nagging sense of futility I felt against Mungin, was almost overwhelming. I got to my feet pretty quickly, but there was no denying that I was hurt. Sometimes it's the force of the blow that puts you down; sometimes it's a matter of balance and timing. And, once in a while, the knockdown is primarily the result of a perfectly delivered punch, one that short-circuits the brain for a few seconds.

That was what happened in the sixth round. Instinct lifted me off the canvas; I rolled my shoulders, tapped my gloves together and feigned indifference to the blow. Total bullshit. I wasn't thinking straight. I was in deep trouble. God's honest truth? I was a little scared, too. It's embarrassing the first time you get knocked down, but that comes only after your head has cleared. Initially, though, there is a feeling of helplessness, which is scary.

With Dicky shouting encouragement from the corner—"Hands up! Hands up!"—I went into survival mode, moving and protecting myself from another onslaught. Eventually the fog lifted, without Mungin landing another serious shot, and I was able to survive the round. But I looked like a bloody mess. To anyone watching, it had become obvious that Mungin was not there to simply serve as an opponent.

He was there to win.

Although I remained upright for the rest of the fight, I took a pretty good ass-kicking. No point in sugarcoating it. Mungin controlled the action from start to finish, and his size advantage was more than I could handle. By the end of the fight he'd opened another cut (this one below the eye), and had earned the unanimous decision he was awarded. Another strange thing about boxing: Sometimes you walk into a dressing room after a match, and the winning fighter looks like the loser: cut, bruised, hands bathed in ice, every muscle aching. That was me after the Mungin fight, except I hadn't won. I looked every inch the loser.

As for Mungin, I didn't see him. But I'll bet he looked just fine.

CHAPTER 7

There were multiple consequences in the wake of the Mungin fight, the most obvious of which were physical. Ten rounds with a guy that big and strong had left my injured hand in a state of perpetual recovery. I took some time off after the fight, but as soon as it started to feel better, and I went back to the gym, the pain and swelling would return. After a while I grew accustomed to it, but chronic pain plays tricks on your mind. You become irritable. And if you're a fighter, you not only worry incessantly about aggravating the injury, but you start to question whether you've lost the ability to box effectively. To some extent, all fighters have sore hands. It's an occupational hazard. But a hand that fractures easily, or one that hurts so much you can't deliver a solid punch, is essentially useless.

Which leads to the second consequence of the Mungin fight: my emotional state, which had become increasingly fragile. It's easy looking back now to recognize the Mungin fight for what it was: not merely a physical mismatch over which I had no control, but the beginning of a downward slide that would end only with a temporary retirement. That fight hurt in so many ways. It made me question my own ability as a boxer (which always happens when you get beat); more important, it provoked feelings of doubt and frustration about my entire career. I wondered whether the people around me—manager, trainer, promoters— really had my best interests at heart. It wasn't that I questioned the love or loyalty of my family; I didn't. But I couldn't help but feel that maybe I wasn't being properly cared for.

Was my mother the most effective or qualified manager?

Was Dicky the best (or most reliable) trainer?

The answer to both of those questions, in all honesty, was no. Mom was limited by her lack of connections and influence, and Dicky was hampered by his self-destructive nature. I'd been comfortable with both of them in my corner, but now I had doubts. And that's a tough position for any fighter to be in.

The damage wasn't immediately apparent to anyone who might have been watching from the outside. Three months after the Mungin fight, on December 13, 1988, I returned to the very same venue where I'd fought Mungin: Resorts International in Atlantic City. My opponent was Francisco Tomas Da Cruz, a former Brazilian super featherweight champion who had recently moved up in weight class. Da Cruz was a good fighter whose best moment had come two years earlier, when he met Julio Cesar Chavez for the WBC championship. Now he was ten pounds heavier, but lacking the strength of a true junior welterweight. I hit him often and early—after what had happened against Mungin, it was reassuring to discover that I hadn't lost power. In fact, I threw some of the best body punches of my career in that fight, eventually stopping Da Cruz in the third round with a series of hooks to the ribs.

Confidence is such a fragile thing for a boxer, and mine was now temporarily restored. Because the fight had only lasted three rounds, I hadn't suffered any serious damage to my injured hand. Oh, it hurt afterward, but not so badly that I had to stop training for any length of time. Maybe, I thought, this was just the fight I needed. The folks at Top Rank, mainly Bob Arum, seemed sold on the notion that my career was still on the upswing. To ensure some much-needed consistency in the gym on a daily basis, I'd reached out to Mickey O'Keefe, a Lowell cop and onetime Golden Gloves champ who had trained both me and Dicky during our amateur days. He'd actually worked more closely with Dicky, and their relationship had been somewhat volatile (no great surprise, given their respective backgrounds), but I'd always liked and respected Mickey and thought he'd add stability to my camp. I'm not sure exactly what I was thinking at the time—whether I viewed O'Keefe as a replacement for Dicky, or merely an insurance policy. Regardless, it was great to have him in the gym, even if it rubbed Dicky the wrong way. I figured they'd work it out, and if Dicky's problems escalated (which they did), I knew I could rely on Mickey. The man was a friend and mentor, with a terrific and profane sense of humor (a natural performer, Mickey even played himself in *The Fighter*), and a work ethic that was second to none.

I needed Mickey O'Keefe, and he was more than happy to join the team.

Both Mickey and Dicky were in my corner on January 1, 1989, at Caesars Hotel and Casino in Atlantic City, when I met Frankie Warren for the United States Boxing Association light welterweight championship. Now, granted, the USBA title did not carry the same weight as some of the other more global alphabet titles: WBC, WBA, IBF. But for me, at that point in my career? It was a very big deal. Hell, just a few

months earlier I'd gotten hammered by Mike Mungin, and now I was
getting a chance to fight for an American title, against one of the top
guys in the division.

Frankie Warren was the real deal, 28–1, with the lone setback coming against Buddy McGirt one year earlier in the IBF light welterweight
championship. Frankie was eight years older than me and, as it turned
out, nearing the end of his career, but the guy was hardly over the hill.
He was thirty years old and in spectacular physical shape. He also presented some interesting challenges from a technical standpoint. You see,
Frankie was only 5'3", with a body that looked like a fire hydrant. His
low center of gravity, combined with quickness and punching power,
made him an elusive target, especially for someone who relies so heavily
on body punches. I'd be looking down at him the whole night, and trust
me, for someone who is only 5'8", that's an unusual occurrence.

Warren was a ferocious competitor. I was accustomed to being the
aggressor in fights, someone willing to put his neck on the line in order
to get the job done. But Frankie was a tiny, whirling beast of a fighter,
the kind of guy who'd probably spent his whole life with a chip on his
shoulder. Small boxers are like that sometimes (I know from firsthand
experience), but Frankie was an extreme example. He backed down from
no one. That's taking nothing away from his skill as a boxer. He clearly
knew how to fight, had a game plan and executed it to perfection. More
than anything, though, he brought superior energy to the ring. By the
time I figured out how to effectively fight against him, I was well behind
on the scorecards.

"Micky, you gotta get busy in there," Dicky had repeatedly said
between rounds. His thoughts were echoed by Mickey O'Keefe.

I have no excuses. Frankie was the better fighter that night—busier,
stronger, hungrier, smarter. He came away with a unanimous twelve-

round decision and retained his USBA title. I left the ring with aching hands, a badly bruised ego and serious doubts about whether I'd ever become a champion. As always, though, there was only one thing to do—get back to work.

Easier said than done. My hands were all fucked-up, which made training difficult and inconsistent. My personal life was a challenge as well. By now I'd moved in with my girlfriend Laurie. We'd known each other for a long time—started dating when I was only fifteen years old and she was just thirteen. Laurie was my first girlfriend, the first person I ever fell for. But we didn't exactly have a fairy-tale relationship. Laurie and I broke up after a few years together, and then reunited when I turned professional. We were both looking for something more stable and permanent. Unfortunately, there's nothing about the life of a fighter that offers much in the way of stability or permanence. Unless you reach the highest level of the sport—championships, pay-per-view broadcasts, sold-out arenas—money is hard to come by. And it's not like there's a fat pension waiting for you at the end of your career. By its very nature, a boxer's life is unpredictable and volatile.

It's not exactly the best environment in which to raise a family; nevertheless, that was what we tried to do. When I entered the ring on May 23, 1989, to face Clarence Coleman at the Showboat hotel and casino in Atlantic City, I had a lot on my mind. I needed a victory to get my confidence back and demonstrate that I was still a legitimate contender. I wasn't just fighting for myself anymore; I wasn't just fighting for the Ward family. Now I was fighting for Laurie and the child to whom she'd give birth in just a few short months. And let me tell you— that's a whole different kind of pressure.

It wasn't easy, but I did the best I could. I stopped Coleman in the fifth round to run my record to 20–3. Less than one month later my daughter, Kasie, was born. That was the happiest day of my life, a thrill unmatched by anything I ever experienced in the ring. I fell in love with Kasie instantly, and wanted nothing more than to protect her and provide for her. Whether I could accomplish that goal as a professional boxer, though, remained questionable. After each fight—even the short ones—my hands felt as though they'd been cracked by a sledgehammer. The momentum you need as a working fighter proved elusive. I'd train, fight, take time off, and then start the cycle all over again. Along the way I began to acquire the kind of reputation that can destroy an athlete.

I could hear the whispers.

Micky Ward is damaged goods . . .

Who could blame them for feeling that way? Fact is, I was damaged. I was supposed to fight for the North American Boxing Federation championship in August of 1989, just a couple months after Kasie was born. I was in great shape, training hard, fully prepared to meet Harold Brazier, the reigning champ. In the weeks leading up to the fight, though, I hurt my hand again. Now, I suppose I could have taken the fight anyway, just kept my mouth shut about the injury and given it my best shot. But that would have been career suicide. Brazier was a tough son of a bitch (as I'd later find out firsthand), and to fight him at less than full strength would have been risky, if not downright dangerous. Still, after watching Brazier get beat by my replacement, Livingstone Bramble, I couldn't help but wonder whether I'd made a mistake.

The layoff eventually stretched out over nearly nine months, time filled by hanging out with my daughter, training sessions and the occasional paving job to help pay the bills. I finally got a chance to fight again in February of 1990, against David Rivello, at the Hynes Convention Center in Boston. I dedicated that bout to Johnny Dunn, who had passed away after suffering a heart attack shortly before Christmas. I'd never fought professionally without Johnny in my corner, and I missed both his wisdom and his sense of humor. Like me, Rivello was a local kid (from nearby Attleboro), but the crowd was clearly on my side. Good thing, too, since this was yet another long and difficult fight. I earned a ten-round split decision that left my hands aching but my title hopes still very much alive.

The opportunity came on April 26, 1990, in Atlantic City, and once again the scheduled opponent was Harold Brazier, one of the busiest and most fearless fighters in the game. I'd fought only twice in the previous year, and once in the last nine months; Brazier, meanwhile, had fought eight times, including a stretch in May of 1989 when he'd fought three times in less than a month. Brazier was known to be a throwback to an earlier era, when boxers took fights on little or no advance notice, and seldom worried about the consequences. A lot of guys like that end up with no money and no career. They lose more fights than they win and get the shit kicked out of them on a regular basis. They're among the saddest people in all of professional sports.

Harold Brazier did not fall into that category. He was thirty-five years old when we met, with a record of 67–10–1. By the time he retired, in 2004, at nearly fifty years of age, he had compiled an incredible record of 105–18–1. The guy was a friggin' tank when we fought in '89, and I'm sure he was no different even at the end of his career. At thirty-five or fifty, he was a man who could hurt you. And he was utterly fearless.

On the line that night at Resorts International was the IBF Inter-Continental light welterweight championship. Again, this was not considered a major title; nevertheless, it was an important fight for me. Any title looked good on the resume, and Brazier was a quality opponent. More than that, actually. Like Frankie Warren, he was among the best fighters in the world at this weight class. No, he wasn't a world champion, but he clearly was in that stable of fighters—an exclusive group of maybe five to ten—who were capable of beating anyone on the right night.

This was one of those nights.

Taking a page from my playbook, Brazier worked the body hard from the opening bell. He was a little heavier and stronger than I was, and the punches took their toll. A low blow in the fourth round, followed by a nasty head shot, left me momentarily dazed, and from that point forward I felt like I was playing catchup, trying to get back in the fight. Something else was happening as well, something I'd never experienced before.

I was exhausted.

Like I said, I always put tremendous emphasis on physical conditioning, always prided myself on being in the best shape possible. Coming into the Brazier fight I felt like I'd prepared exceptionally well. I was a little light—137 pounds—and that might have given Brazier a bit of an edge in terms of strength, but I thought I'd have the advantage in stamina. For some reason, though, I was having trouble catching my breath. I'd never felt anything quite like it, not even in some of the ten-round wars I'd fought. Here we were, in the sixth and seventh rounds, and I was running out of gas! Maybe it had something to do with the fact that I'd had only one fight in the better part of a year. Maybe it was a by-product of the heart murmur that would not be diagnosed for several more years, a condition that sometimes took my breath away and left me feeling panicked and spent. Regardless, Dicky shouted at me from the corner to get busy.

"You're behind, Mick! You don't knock this guy out, you're gonna lose."

Well, what the fuck, Dicky?! You think I'm not trying?!

I didn't say that, of course. The corner of a boxing ring, in the middle of a brutal fight, is no place for two brothers to settle old scores. That wasn't my style, anyway. When it came to Dicky, I was nonconfrontational. Half the time we worked together I was pissed at him, always doing a slow boil. Pissed because he wasn't there for me, pissed because he was killing himself and hurting my mother in the process. But I rarely let him know how or what I was feeling. I worried about Dicky, felt sorry for him, wondered what would become of him if he didn't have boxing in his life. And the truth is, by the early 1990s, his only link to boxing was as my trainer. I couldn't kick the guy to the curb—he needed me more than I needed him. Somewhere along the way it was like our roles had gotten all tangled up and reversed. I'd become the big brother, with all the responsibility that entails . . . and Dicky had become the baby boy. I had to take care of him, and if that meant putting up with his bullshit, then so be it. We'd find a way to muddle through.

But not against Harold Brazier. By the end of the fight I was spent and bleeding from my nose and an assortment of cuts. The announcement—Brazier by unanimous decision—was merely a formality. I'd been beaten in every way possible, and I knew it. What I didn't know—but would soon figure out—was that the landscape had shifted. I'd now lost two of my last four fights. Granted, Frankie Warren and Harold Brazier were good fighters. It wasn't like I was a heavy favorite to beat them. But by losing both fights, and getting knocked around pretty good in the process, I'd slipped from the upper tier of fighters—the ones who are considered title contenders—to the next tier. That's not a place you want to be. Before I knew it, I'd become an *opponent*. You know—the guy used by promoters as a barometer to measure the progress of young, talented fighters.

"Hey, let's put him in against Ward. If he can stop Micky, we know he has potential."

I'd never thought of myself as that kind of fighter, but the evidence was hard to refute. It wasn't like I was in over my head, but I wasn't getting any easy fights, either. Every time I went into the ring, I could expect an almost epic battle, one followed by weeks or months of recovery and rewarded with a meager paycheck (maybe five to ten thousand dollars). That's not the way you handle a rising star or someone you expect to be a world champion. It's the way you treat a banger.

I was twenty-five years old, and I felt like I was over the hill.

I kept at it for another year and a half. Three more fights, each of them against a legitimate title contender. And three more losses. First came Charles Murray. We fought for the USBA light welterweight title on Murray's home turf—the War Memorial in Rochester, New York. Murray wasn't nearly as experienced as I was, but he did have a 17–0 record and he was well on his way to a respectable career in which he'd later capture a more legitimate crown: the IBF light welterweight title. The Murray fight, in which I lost a twelve-round unanimous decision, was probably the first in which I realized that something was missing. The fire and fury I'd always brought to the ring was lacking, and I couldn't get it back. Hell, I didn't even know where to look.

Seven months later I lost a ten-round decision to Tony Martin, and five months after that, in October of 1991, I found myself yet again on the short end of a ten-round unanimous decision, this time to a Ricky Meyers. Do the math. That's forty-four rounds of boxing in a year and a half, with very little to show for it. I'd lost four consecutive fights to opponents with a combined record of 121–14–1. Whatever progress I'd made in the first five years of my career had eroded. By this point no one thought of me as a solid investment.

I'm still not sure exactly how it happened, but I will say this: I don't blame anyone but myself. The kind of men I was fighting—Frankie Warren, Harold Brazier, Charles Murray? Those aren't the kind of boxers you face when you're trying to get your confidence back, the way I was after getting beaten up by Mike Mungin. But I hold no one else accountable. Some people blamed my mother; others blamed Bob Arum and Top Rank for putting me in with certain fighters. Nah . . . it was all me. My mother was my manager, so obviously anyone who wanted me on a fight card had to go through her. But I signed off on every one of those fights. She never forced one down my throat. And Bob? He was a businessman, and his job was to create good, competitive fights. He gave me opportunities. Same with ESPN. Obviously they weren't going to put me in with cupcakes because they wanted tough, entertaining fights; competitive fights. They wanted ratings. I don't fault them for that. While it's true that they take care of certain fighters—they're more careful with the matchmaking process when dealing with a star—it's also true that I hadn't really earned that status. And you know what? I think Bob Arum, for a while, anyway, honestly believed I was a really good fighter. He thought I could take these guys, and that's why he authorized the fights. He wanted to give me another chance.

The bottom line is that I wasn't exactly a victim. I realized what was going on. It wasn't like anyone was taking advantage of my naïveté. I was well aware that I'd fallen out of favor with Top Rank, but I wasn't bitter about it. If you're a professional, you deal with that kind of shit. You're in the meat line, waiting for someone to yell, "Next!" and that's just the way it is. You want it to change? Then start winning.

I kept losing.

And not losing easily or painlessly. I was going through ten, twelve rounds at a clip. Every time I finished one of those fights, I could barely move or breathe. That kind of punishment will take its toll on anyone—I don't care how strong you think you are. I suffered one concussion after another, and I was still in my early twenties. Looking back on it now, it's almost like it was a blur, the rounds seeping into one another, forming one long, continuous, dizzy slide toward retirement. I can't even remember when it started. For most of 1990 and 1991, I was sick or injured. My hands hurt all of the time, and I suffered continually from post-concussion syndrome. That's the thing a lot of people don't understand about boxing: It's the accumulation of blows that does the real damage. Critics of mixed martial arts are nauseated by the apparent viciousness of the sport. Well, you know what? Fighters in MMA do a lot of "leaking" (bleeding), but they rarely suffer long-term damage. Why? Because the fights are so short—typically, three five-minute rounds—and because it's acceptable for the combatants to "tap out," or surrender.

Not so in boxing. Championship fights are twelve rounds. And only a quitter quits. You fight long enough and often enough, your brain pays the price. For weeks after each of those ten- and twelve-round decisions, I'd lie in bed at night, the room spinning, my stomach churning. Endless, relentless waves of nausea, like I was out on a charter boat fishing for stripers in four-foot swells. I rarely got headaches, and their absence fooled me for a while into thinking I was all right. Maybe I just had the flu. Maybe I was nervous or upset. Only much later did I learn that nausea and vertigo are common symptoms of post-concussion syndrome, and every bit as alarming as the crippling headaches endured by some fighters.

Eventually it was too much to overcome. By the time I fought Ricky Meyers I was a different fighter (and person) than I'd been a couple years earlier. Not coincidentally, my relationship with Laurie had deteriorated at almost precisely the same rate as my career. Not that I'm blaming Laurie for our problems. I'm sure I wasn't the easiest man to live with. I was frustrated, hurt, angry. Money was tight, and we had a young daughter. Not exactly an ideal scenario. I guess it's no great surprise that we split up a short time later.

The fight against Meyers was a low point, and perhaps the only performance that actually left me feeling embarrassed and guilty. I had nothing to give that night, didn't really even care whether I won or lost. I mean . . . I *cared*. Just not enough. The announcers broadcasting the fight for ESPN criticized my performance, as did reporters for various newspapers. And they were right to do so. I wasn't *fighting*; I was just trying not to get hurt. It was as if I'd forgotten or ignored everything I believed in—everything that had defined me as a boxer and as a man.

I was no longer a warrior. I was . . . not a quitter, really, but something less than I wanted to be. Meyers was a tough kid, a good boxer, but he shouldn't have beaten me. I went in there and started fighting defensively from the get-go. My mind wasn't in the right place. There were so many distractions. I couldn't focus, couldn't concentrate. I'm not saying I took the fight just to take it (and certainly not for the money, because there wasn't all that much of it), but I wasn't there for the right reasons.

The hunger was gone.

And afterward, so was I.

"Fuck it," I said to Dicky as he tried to console me in the dressing room. "I'm not going to be a punching bag anymore. Let them find someone else to pad their record. I'm done."

CHAPTER 8

"Yo, Micky! What are you in for?"

The question came from a muscular little Hispanic kid whose face I recognized, but whose name I could not recall. He was hanging out on the second-floor of the Middlesex County House of Corrections, in Billerica, Massachusetts, killing time with a bunch of other young inmates.

"Nah, it ain't like that," I said with a smile. "I'm gonna be working here."

The kid laughed, waved his hand in disbelief.

"Bull . . . shit! How much time you get?"

I shrugged. That was a damn good question.

"I don't know, man. Guess we'll see."

This was the winter of 1992. Nearly six months had passed since I'd hung up my gloves, presumably for the very last time. I'd gotten a little thick and lazy, spent too much time hanging out at the Highland Tap and other local watering holes, feeling sorry for myself about all the shit that had gone wrong in my life. I'd been filling my days and paying the bills the same way I always had—by working highway construction. Although I was grateful for the work, it was sporadic and inconsistent, and not the kind of thing I wanted to do for the next twenty or thirty years. I'd invested a number of years in preparing for one thing and one thing only: being a professional boxer. I was going to be a champion. I'd have wealth and fame (not that I ever boxed primarily for the money). Now everything had changed. As it does for a lot of athletes, retirement came quickly and rather unexpectedly for me. One moment my career was on a nice, steady climb; the next moment I was sitting in a dressing room, after getting my ass kicked for the fourth consecutive time, coming to terms with my own indifference.

Retirement is hard for everyone, in every field, I think. I mean, it's so final. I suppose that once you reach a certain age, with a boatload of accomplishments and few regrets, retirement isn't such a terrible thing. But when you're twenty-six years old and calling it quits . . . with a lot of unfinished business?

That can be devastating.

More than anything else I needed stability—and the reassurance that I had something to offer. Laurie was gone, and there was nothing I could do about that. But I was determined to provide for my daughter in the best way possible, and if I couldn't do that as a boxer . . . well, then I had to think of something else. I had a couple friends at the time who had worked as corrections officers. Richie Bryan had worked at the Billerica facility, and Mike Ryan was currently holding down a supervisory position there.

"You should apply, Mick," he said. "It's good money and the benefits are great."

Benefits.

Jesus . . . I'd never even thought about any of this stuff before. Health insurance, pension plans, life insurance, disability. Grown-up, real-world stuff. The boxer's life is incredibly hard and unrewarding in some ways, but there is a simplicity to it that I found comforting. It's such a narrow and neatly defined existence: eat, sleep, train, fight. I missed the routine. I missed the austere beauty of the gym. I didn't want to admit any of this, of course. I'd had it with boxing, knew in my heart that my best days were behind me and that I had to get on with the business of life. I'd gotten my high school equivalency degree, but my options were still limited. What was I qualified to do, other than drive a piece of heavy equipment on a road crew or knock another man into unconsciousness?

Valuable skills, admittedly, under the right circumstances. But useless in most circles.

Truth is, I wasn't all that thrilled about working as a corrections officer. Then again, I wasn't thrilled about much of anything at this particular point in time. Most of the decisions I made were based on practicality and limited options. I had to think about Kasie; I had to think about our future together.

"Okay," I told Mike one day. "I'll fill out the application and we'll see where it goes from there."

Where it went, rather quickly (since some guys wait months or years to get a CO job) was to an offer of permanent employment. That's how I ended up at the county jail that day, getting my balls busted by convicts from the old neighborhood. Prior to wearing the uniform and carrying a nightstick, every new corrections officer is given an extensive tour of the facility, along with an explanation of basic duties and scheduling. It's not an easy job, by any stretch of the imagination, but it's not a complicated job, either. I figured out right away that the best approach was to simply do my job, quietly and with as little emotion as possible, especially since I knew some of the kids in this joint. We'd grown up together in Lowell. In some cases, we'd hung out together at the West End Gym, done some sparring and training together. I'd gotten to know a lot of the Hispanic and black kids in town, and some of those kids had ended up here, in county jail.

Upon seeing me walking the tier, they just naturally presumed that I'd fucked up in some way. Just like they had. Wasn't that the story for most boxers? Hadn't that been Dicky's story? He'd been in this very facility. To these guys, I suppose, it made sense that Dicky's little brother would be following in his footsteps.

"Come on, Mick . . . what'd you do? Bust someone up?"

It wasn't until I returned a few days later for my first official shift, wearing a crisp navy blue uniform, that they were finally convinced.

"Motherfucker! You're on the wrong team, Mick!"

I never felt scared or even particularly uncomfortable as a corrections officer. The fact is, a lot of white guys who enter the profession bring racism and fear to the job. All of those misconceptions and biases had been wrung out of me by middle school. Boxing is predominantly an ethnic sport, populated primarily by people of color. Decades earlier boxing had been the sport of choice for working-class Irish and Italians, but that had changed by the time I walked into a gym as an eager seven-year-old. It remained a sport for the downtrodden; the Italians and Irish, the Poles and Jews—they'd moved up the socioeconomic ladder and left boxing behind. I got used to being a minority in the gym. Didn't bother me in the least. I was always one of the few white kids who could fight, so I got to know the black kids and the Puerto Rican kids.

I was one of them.

In the gym I never saw color, and I brought that same philosophy to my work as a corrections officer. I also tried to bring a sense of fairness and respect to the job. I knew enough about some of these young men to understand how easily I could have fallen into the same trap, made the same mistakes, and ended up right there alongside them, just like they expected. I'd been in street fights, I'd been arrested. I'd seen what drugs had done to Dicky. I came from a hard-drinking family. There were a hundred ways for me to fuck up, and somehow, through the grace of God or just plain dumb luck, I'd avoided most of them. So it was unnatural for me to look at the inmates in this joint and think of them as evil.

I don't know where I got my moral compass. I just knew, instinctively, the difference between right and wrong. I knew if I wanted to get somewhere in life, there were certain things I couldn't do. Some of those lessons were taught (or at least voiced) by my parents, even as they were making bad choices themselves. Some were modeled by the men who taught me how to box, when I was still young and impressionable enough to absorb the lessons. I respected people—always did. Even as a kid I felt that every person who crossed my path deserved to be treated with dignity and fairness and compassion. So long as they were nice to me, anyway. I ain't no angel. That's fairly obvious. There's a part of me (and I think this is true of most fighters) that wants to rip your head off. Sometimes it's a challenge to keep that aspect of my personality in check. But that's different from wanting to sell drugs or hold up a liquor store, or pick on the defenseless. I never felt the urge to do anything like that, probably because I had avoided much of the behavior that would have led inevitably to more violent and dangerous criminal activity.

It's a simple and undeniable fact: Like most people who end up in jail, Dicky's problems stemmed from his drinking and drug use. The guy never hurt anyone when he was sober. Twenty-seven times he was arrested, and every one of those collars was related in some way to drugs or alcohol. That's not an unusual story. Go to any jail in the country—any jail in the world, for that matter—and probably 90 percent of the cons are doing time for crimes connected to drugs and alcohol. They're selling crack or carrying weed. They're getting high or drunk and then going out and ripping someone off or getting in a fight or a car accident. Maybe, like Dicky, they get so hooked that they don't care about anything else but getting high. And the pursuit of that high consumes every waking moment. They're smoking crack or trying to come up with ways to pay for the next hit. Since they can't hold down a job, and they don't have any money, they invariably end up waving a gun in someone's face, or breaking into a cash register.

And then they're here, at the county jail. If they're lucky, that is. Billerica was not, generally speaking, a place for hardened criminals. They were short-timers, mostly, with less than a couple years on their sentences. Some were repeat offenders on their way to state prison. What many of them had in common, though, was a taste for drugs and alcohol. Eliminate those two vices from their lives, and most of these guys would not have been in prison. The saddest part was, they didn't really know any better. Most of them had been reared in a culture of crime and addiction.

They had no shot.

I probably sound like a bleeding-heart liberal, huh? Well, I'm really not. I believe in personal accountability, and paying for your mistakes. But I come from a family of trouble, so maybe I'm a little more open-minded when it comes to the criminal justice system and whether it ought to be simply warehousing (and punishing) inmates, or offering them a chance at rehabilitation.

I tend to believe everyone deserves a second chance.

Which is not to suggest that I was a pushover as a CO. No friggin' way. First day on the job I had inmates in my ear, trying to work me, soften me up, see if I could be used to their advantage. See, that's how it goes in jail. There really aren't all that many fights (although they do occur, and a CO must constantly be aware of the potential for violence), but inmates will do whatever they can to gain some sort of edge. As a guard, you spend a lot of time just pushing people along, making sure they follow the rules and adhere to a schedule. But you also face an exhausting amount of manipulation—inmates asking for favors, offering small bribes, nagging like preschoolers.

And you can't ever show the slightest degree of vulnerability on this subject. A corrections officer has to be hard, even if it's not in his nature. You can't give anyone even the smallest of favors; once you give in—once you display the slightest weakness—they own you. They can use it against you forever, or at least as long as you work there. I was fortunate. No one ever came right out and asked me to do anything for them—not even the kids I knew from our days in the gym. I'd like to think this was a consideration that grew out of respect for our previous friendship, but I doubt that was the case. I think it was more a matter of my demeanor. I was relatively easygoing, but I wasn't *easy* . . . if you know what I mean.

There are a lot of ballbusters among the ranks of corrections officers; a lot of men who would love to crack the skull of an inmate, or at least write them up for every possible infraction. You can do that, too, if that's the way you want to operate, but I figured out pretty quickly that the guards who ruled by threats and intimidation were generally the most insecure guards. They were miserable pricks, hated every minute they were on the job. And they were hated by the inmates, as well.

Me? I gave most people the benefit of the doubt. I tried to be calm but firm. I'd see other guards—guys who'd never been in a bar fight, never witnessed trouble of any kind—handing out tickets left and right, jamming up inmates like they were high school hall monitors. That wasn't me. An inmate had to really do something serious to get a ticket from me. At the same time, I never allowed any of them to trade on the fact that they knew me when. So it was a matter of mutual respect. We were all doing time in there. The difference, of course, was that I got to go home at the end of the day.

There was no boxing allowed in the jail. That's become a widely accepted prohibition at correctional facilities throughout the country. Used to be that inmates who were so inclined could work out their aggression (or simply make the most of their talent) in jailhouse boxing programs. For a while, in fact, it seemed like prisons and jails were spitting out contenders and champions on a monthly basis. Sonny Liston learned to fight behind bars while serving time for armed robbery. Dwight Braxton took up the sport at Rahway State Prison (also while serving time for armed robbery); he later was paroled, turned professional, changed his name to Dwight Muhammad Qawi, and became the WBA cruiserweight champion in 1985. James Scott was a heavyweight contender in the 1970s whose career was interrupted by a robbery conviction. Like Qawi, he was incarcerated at Rahway State Prison, where he continued to hone his boxing skills. Scott even fought Eddie Gregory (who later became Eddie Mustafa Muhammad) in a nationally televised bout held within the walls of Rahway.

Back then boxing was, for some reason, viewed as a worthwhile rehabilitative tool. Inmates could train and fight, and prison tournaments were not unusual. Over the years, however, public sentiment has shifted. Seems like most people fail to see any benefit from boxing or other recreational opportunities for inmates. Money is part of the issue, of course. Taxpayers hate to see their hard-earned dollars allocated for what they consider to be the coddling of society's lowest form of life. I think a lot of people would just as soon forget that prisons even exist. And fuck anyone who happens to get convicted of a crime. Toss the scumbags in jail and let them live like animals. On some level I understand where they're coming from. But having worked in a jail, and having grown up with a lot of kids who ended up in prison, I can tell you with absolute assurance that ignoring or mistreating this segment of society doesn't do anyone a damn bit of good. These guys are all getting out someday, so why not at least make an effort to help them become better people once they're released? In every way imaginable, prison sucks. Anyone who thinks it's a country club, just because you get to watch TV or work out, has never spent any time inside the walls. Trust me when I tell you this: There's no such thing as a pampered convict.

I only spent a little more than a year as a corrections officer, but in that time I thought it was fairly obvious that sports and recreation were key components to maintaining order and sanity in such a volatile atmosphere. Most of the inmates at Billerica were young, practically children. They were naturally aggressive and energetic, and the more opportunities you provided for them to burn off some of that aggression, the better it was for everyone involved. Made my job easier, I know that. By then, though, the options were limited. Inmates could lift weights, run, play basketball. But no boxing. You could work out on the heavy bag, but that was about it. There were no rings, no headgear, no gloves. Practically speaking, boxing didn't exist within the jail.

There were boxers there, nonetheless, and sometimes when I walked through the yard, one of them would try to get my attention as they leaned into the heavy bag.

"Hey, Micky, you got a second?"

"Not really."

"Come on, man. I heard you were pretty good at this. I just want some advice."

Sometimes, if no one was watching too closely, I'd step up to the bag, show them how to position themselves properly . . . how to rotate their hips (the power of any punch comes from the core, not from the arms or shoulders) and drive through the bag. Again and again. Circling, pivoting, punching.

Whump! Whump! Whump!

"Damn, that's some nasty shit, CO!"

Technically speaking, this demonstration was not part of my job description, and I suppose I could have been reprimanded for it. The administration naturally frowned upon the guards offering any advice that inmates could later use in a show of force against us. In the unlikely (but not unthinkable) event of a riot, you wanted the inmates to be as limited as possible in terms of weaponry and force. But I figured if they knew what I was capable of doing with my fists, maybe they'd be even less inclined to give me any grief. And some of them were decent enough people, respectful and hardworking. Why not show them how to work out on the heavy bag without breaking their hands?

My personal feeling is that boxing is no different from any other recreational opportunity in prison. If you're going to let these guys lift weights for hours on end, and get all jacked up, you might as well let them box. In my experience, boxers cause less trouble than most folks, especially if they're seriously devoted to their training. So use the program as a carrot. Make it available to those inmates who are well-behaved. I think it's good and appropriate for the guys who earn it and stay out of trouble. The inmates who get in trouble are denied the privilege. To me, that's the most sensible solution. But I don't ever see it happening again. I think the days of jailhouse boxing programs are long gone.

Funny thing, though: I kind of liked it when one of the inmates asked me for advice. Not because I missed the fame; not because I craved recognition. But simply because I realized that I was, for better or worse, a boxer. That was all I really knew, all I'd ever wanted to be, and the simple act of walking past a guy haphazardly slapping at a heavy bag provoked a sense of longing.

Much as I wanted to walk away, much as I tried to tell myself that I wanted nothing to do with the sport, and that I was better off without it, there was no denying what I felt in my heart.

I missed the hell out of it.

After about a year or so, I started going back to the gym on a semi-regular basis. My life was kind of a mess at the time. I was living alone, staying out too late, drinking too much, dabbling a bit in cocaine. The CO job was steady but undemanding work, and I found that at the end of the day I had all this pent-up energy that needed to be released. So, in the summer of 1993, I began to train. Not with any real purpose or plan—not at first, anyway. Mike Ryan was the first person to offer encouragement. In addition to being a CO, Mike had a small gym up in Tewksbury, and I started hanging out there a bit, seeing how it felt to work the bags, skip rope, put on the headgear and spar.

"You know what, Mick?" he said one day. "I think you've got a lot left in the tank."

"Ah, I don't know, Mike. I feel so slow."

He laughed.

"That's because you're an old man."

This was a joke, of course. I was not quite twenty-nine years of age, and already I'd been retired for nearly two years. I'd pissed away some prime time, but I didn't feel any regret about it. I needed to get away from boxing. I needed a break—physically and emotionally—after so many years in the gym. Yeah, I was young when I walked away from the sport, but I'd been at it for two decades. I was tired. I was burned out. But now, working out in the evening, after a long day walking the tier at Billerica, I felt the hunger returning.

Maybe Mike Ryan was right. Maybe it wasn't too late, after all.

I know now that taking time off was the best thing I could have done. It didn't feel good at the time, didn't leave me with a sense of fulfillment or success. But it was necessary, and it was the right thing to do. I had so much more energy after that, so much more drive and ambition. For several months I worked with Mike. He was one of the first people to realize that I was actively training again, and not merely with the idea of getting back in shape. With each gym session I felt sharper, more connected with the fighter I'd once been. And here's the other thing: My hands didn't hurt anymore. Not even my massively fucked-up right hand. I could hit the bag for hours and not feel more than a twinge of discomfort.

I remember Richie Bryan coming to the gym one day and watching me work out. Richie had remained one of my closest friends. He'd been right there with me when I called it quits, offering unconditional support when I'd needed it most. A lot of other people around me felt that my retirement had been premature, that I'd simply lost confidence and quit. They didn't understand. At that time in my life, I had nothing left to give. But Richie was different. He got it.

"Fuck them," he said. "They ain't the ones fighting. You do what you think is right."

And that's what I did. Now, nearly two years later, after healing up and realizing how much I missed the sport, I was ready to give it another try. And once again Richie was right there with me.

"You think I'm nuts, huh?" I said to him.

"Nope, not at all. You look good. Let's give it a shot and see how it goes."

I didn't really care what anyone else thought. As far as I could tell, people in Lowell hadn't exactly been devastated by my retirement. Life goes on, right? They had their own problems to worry about. Anyway, it wasn't like I was this big champion, with the whole town following my every move—I flew under the radar most of the time. I'd thought about retiring even sooner than I did, but concern over what other people would think—Had I let them down? Had I failed to properly represent the city of Lowell?—kept me going for a while. It wasn't until after I'd hung up the gloves that I understood how little an impact my career had on anyone else. Once in a while someone would come up to me on the street and ask how things were going.

"You ever gonna fight again, Mick?"

I'd shrug.

"Dunno. Maybe someday."

That was usually enough to appease them.

One of the first steps on the comeback trail involved leaving my job as a corrections officer, which didn't exactly break my heart. I never did feel comfortable at Billerica. Not so much because of the inmates or any trouble they might have caused (I think I had to break up only one or two fights the entire time I was there, and I was never the target of violence), but simply because it wasn't conducive to training or to my naturally fidgety nature. I hated being inside all day, cooped up in the stale air. And I discovered after a few weeks of training that I needed a job that offered more flexibility and less time on my feet. You see, while the job of CO isn't all that strenuous, it does require a solid eight hours of walking around. The mileage takes its toll when you're trying to train seriously for a comeback.

So I handed in my resignation and went back to the job I knew best: highway construction. It was a comfortable job with decent pay and flexible hours. It was a job I knew well. A safe job.

Or so I thought.

Three days before Thanksgiving, in November of 1993, our crew was repaving a parking lot in front of the local Costco store. My job, as usual, was to operate a massive five-ton back roller. I'd been driving smaller rollers since I was a kid and had gradually moved up in scale and responsibility. I felt totally at ease at the wheel of the roller. My job was to carefully and slowly smooth out the blanket of hot mix as it poured from the back of a moto paver. Some crews utilize additional laborers to help out with raking and tamping asphalt in hard-to-reach places. But extra bodies mean extra salaries, and most crews simply tacked tamping responsibility onto the roller operator's job description. That was the way we worked, and I didn't mind in the least. Twenty, thirty times a day I'd stop the roller, grab the tamper, jump six feet to the ground and finish the job by hand, flattening the pavement into place.

I never even thought about whether the work was safe or dangerous. I just did it. And until this cool November day, I never had a problem.

Here's the way it went down (please forgive me for being graphic— there's really no other way to tell the story). I came to a concrete island in the middle of the parking lot. Unable to reach the edges of the pavement with the drum, I brought the roller to a stop, applied the emergency brake and tossed the tamper onto the ground, all in one smooth move, just as I'd done so many times before. While the tamper sailed downward, I stood up, swung my legs over the side of the roller . . . and jumped.

In the course of hundreds of paving jobs, stretched out over more than a dozen years, I'd probably repeated this exact procedure a few thousand times. Every time it had unfolded without incident. But just as I leapt, I could see something odd, something so strange that at first it barely even registered. Instead of falling flat, the way it always had, the tamper had landed business end first, and somehow remained upright. And I was heading straight for it.

It must have looked like something out of a *Three Stooges* movie—the hapless construction worker impaling himself on the handle of a tamper in an accident so improbable that you almost had to laugh. Except that there was nothing funny about it—and there were no witnesses, anyway. Everyone on the crew was off doing their own thing. I knew while I was in the air, as I saw the tamper rushing up toward me, that I'd made a gigantic mistake. But there was no time to correct it. All I could do was hold my breath.

Oh . . . this is going to hurt.

What an understatement. The tamper hit me square in the ass, like a dart burrowing into a bull's-eye. The tip of the handle pierced my denim jeans, shredded my thermal underwear, and funneled its way toward my anus and rectum, literally ripping me a new asshole in the process. Although this might seem hard to believe, I was actually somewhat fortunate. Had the strike been an inch or two closer to the center, the handle would have roared into my body like a colonic missile, not stopping until it reached the vicinity of my stomach or esophagus. I would have been gutted. Killed instantly. As it happened, the path of the tamper was altered slightly, probably by my clothes, or just through dumb luck. So the tip of the handle missed its target by just a few centimeters, slid into my anus, and then charted its own course parallel to my rectum, gouging a four-inch valley in the process.

"AHHHHHHHH!"

Here's the funny thing: I never even hit the ground. Seriously. I landed on top of the tamper, felt a white-hot bolt of pain shooting through my body, and then the wooden handle fell out of my ass, all in one big motion. I looked around the parking lot. No one had any idea what had just transpired. They simply went about their business. I tried to yell but could barely get out any words—not that anyone would have heard me over the roar of heavy equipment. So I kept walking, lurching forward in short, painful steps. With great hesitation I reached around and felt the back of my pants, poking my fingers through the shredded fabric, horrified at the prospect of what I might find. I couldn't believe what had happened. I mean, the fucking Marquis de Sade couldn't invent something like this. It was like some sick, perverted joke.

I looked at my hand. Blood everywhere. Two more steps, each weaker than the last. My legs were wet, my underwear heavy—it felt like I had shit my pants (which would have been infinitely preferable to what had actually occurred). After what felt like an eternity, I made it to the side of the parking lot, where our foreman was managing the job.

"Mike . . ."

I could barely speak. He gave me a funny look, kind of cocking his head to one side.

"Something wrong, Mick?"

I nodded. Suddenly I was overcome by nausea, along with an overwhelming urge to lie down on the pavement and sleep.

"I gotta go to the hospital."

"What happened?" Mike asked.

"I'm bleeding, man. I'm hurt."

I held up my hand for Mike to see. His face went white.

"Jesus, Micky. What the fuck?!"

I didn't respond, but merely turned around, bent over, and revealed the damage to my backside. I could feel the blood pulsating from the wound, flowing down my legs.

"Holy shit!" Mike yelled. "Somebody call an ambulance!"

He tried to stay calm, but I could tell by the look in his eyes that he was seriously concerned, which meant the damage must have been pretty bad. It was a look I recognized from all my years of boxing. When you're in the middle of a fight, taking a beating, you rely on your corner—your trainer and cut man—to provide calm reassurance in the face of grim reality. You take a shot to the face and feel blood streaming into your eye, you know you're in trouble. The last thing you need is someone on your team freaking out over it. Your corner is supposed to close the wound, pat you on the back and tell you everything will be all right.

Unfortunately, Mike was no seasoned cut man. And the wound was a long way from my eye, and a whole lot bigger than anything I'd ever experienced in a boxing ring.

"Uhhhh . . . You just sit here," Mike said. Then, quickly realizing the lunacy of that suggestion—*Sit?! Really?!*—he put a hand on my shoulder and guided me to the ground.

"Lie down," he said. "Don't move. Try to relax."

I never did lose consciousness. Before long the rest of the guys on the crew had gathered around us. They offered nervous reassurance that help was on the way, and that I'd be just fine. No one made any jokes— a sure sign that they were scared shitless. My cousin Rudy, a raker on this particular job, could barely make eye contact. He looked like he was going to be sick at any moment.

In time I could hear the wailing of sirens off in the distance. I was taken by ambulance to the University of Massachusetts Memorial Medical Center in Worcester, where doctors performed emergency reconstructive surgery. I'd spent enough time in hospitals to know how serious the situation was. It's all a matter of triage in any hospital setting. The faster you're treated, the more likely it is that you've been seriously hurt. I went from the back of the ambulance, to the emergency room, to the surgical suite in a matter of minutes. Once inside, the docs discovered that the muscles holding my sphincter in place had been ripped apart. So they stitched them back together. They also reconstructed my bowels.

I spent four days in the hospital—four of the worst days of my life. I remember coming out of surgery, getting wheeled into the recovery room and feeling pain like nothing I'd ever experienced. The anesthesia hadn't completely worn off, so I was groggy and queasy; there was an annoying itching sensation at the back of my throat—probably left over from the breathing tube that had been inserted during surgery. Instinctively, I tried to "scratch" the itch by clearing my throat.

I'd barely made a sound when one of the nurses noticed what I was doing and tried to intervene.

"Mr. Ward . . . I wouldn't do that if I were you."

Too late.

"Ahem . . ."

The pain was excruciating, and so it would be for some time to come. I was given strict orders to avoid using any of the muscles in my core. Sounds simple enough, until you really start thinking about it. Try to sneeze without tightening your stomach or abdominal muscles. Try to cough or clear your throat. Try to swallow or laugh.

Try to talk.

Hell . . . try to breathe.

All your strength comes from your core, from your abs and glutes. Literally, from your ass. As a boxer, I sort of knew that, but I'd never been faced with such glaring, irrefutable evidence. Lying there on my stomach, I felt utterly helpless. Several months passed before I recovered fully. I was on painkillers for quite a while, along with an assortment of medications designed to prevent infection and encourage proper, clean maintenance of the digestive system. Most patients recovering from surgery face constipation as a likely complication. In my case the doctors were far more concerned with the possibility that I might experience loose or frequent bowel movements, which would naturally irritate the wound and increase the likelihood of contamination. So they pumped me full of something that basically made me shit bricks for a couple months.

Although I had custody of my daughter on weekends, I was living alone at the time. I couldn't take care of myself, of course, so each day a visiting nurse would come to my house and change the dressing in my wound. She'd remove a mile of cotton gauze, irrigate the wound and surrounding tissue with saline, apply antibiotic ointment, and then put the whole shitty mess back together. Talk about embarrassing! Every one of the nurses was incredibly professional and polite. Patient and empathetic. They were also very old, which was another blessing. The last thing I wanted was some pretty young girl staring at my surgically repaired butt.

The whole experience was humbling and horrific. I wandered around for weeks in a Vicodin-induced stupor. Watched a lot of TV (with a padded donut beneath my backside), slept twelve to fifteen hours a day. After a while I started to feel a little better. I could eat small meals, shuffle around the house without feeling like I was going to pass out. I started weaning myself from the painkillers. That was hard at first, although not because I'd built up any sort of physical dependency. The fact is, I was still hurting. But I knew that the longer I avoided getting off the painkillers, the harder it would be.

For three or four months, my comeback was placed far on the back burner. I couldn't even get behind the wheel of a car—the simple act of applying pressure to the accelerator pedal provoked incredible pain. The idea of going to the gym and working out? Sparring?

Laughable.

Frankly, I didn't even care. When you get hurt that badly—when you come so close to getting killed—you stop taking small things for granted. Things like going to the bathroom, or eating . . . or holding your daughter in your arms. I was grateful to be alive, and to be getting a little bit healthier with each passing day.

Everything else could wait.

CHAPTER 9

People wander in and out of our lives unexpectedly, often without any apparent plan or motive. They just sort of happen by, and if you're open to the possibility, they can change everything.

That's the way it was with Mickey O'Keefe and me. Like I said, I'd known Mickey just about forever. He'd been a Golden Gloves fighter in his youth and had long offered his expertise on the sport to local kids who wanted to learn a thing or two about fighting. Boxing wasn't his profession, though. Mickey was a tough Irish cop, had been for as long as I'd known him. But he loved boxing and he believed in the power of sport—this sport in particular—to transform the lives of kids who might otherwise find a way to get into some serious trouble. He'd been there for Dicky in the amateur ranks, and he'd been there for me, on and off, as both an amateur and a professional. He'd never been my trainer, in an official capacity, but if I needed help—like on those days when Dicky couldn't find his way to the gym—Mickey was always there. The guy was a total straight shooter, told you exactly what was on his mind, no bullshit. Ever. You couldn't get one over on Mickey. He was too smart, too hardened by years on the police force.

But Mickey also had a big heart. If he was your friend, and you needed something, he'd be there for you, no questions asked.

I'd heard that Mickey was asking about me during the early stages of my comeback. The boxing fraternity in Lowell is pretty tight—it's not like you can hide in the gym and expect that no one will figure out what you're doing. Me and Dicky—we were the most well-known and successful fighters Lowell had ever produced. Okay, neither one of us had ever won a championship, but most people who followed boxing knew who we were. So when I started kicking around various gyms, working out at Mike Ryan's place up in Tewksbury or one of the other gyms closer to home, word got out.

"I seen Micky Ward in the gym—think he might be fightin' again."

O'Keefe knew what I was thinking probably before I knew it. He was that kind of guy—sharp, intuitive. And I was fine with it, really. Truth is, I was looking for a trainer. More than that, even. I was looking for a mentor. See, 1993 had been one a hell of a year. Dicky had been arrested—again—and this time he'd been sent away for several months. My father had also been jailed after being convicted of fraud charges related to his contracting business.

And me?

I'd been assaulted by a piece of construction equipment and spent the better part of four months recovering. It seemed as though the men in my family were fucked.

Boxing changed all of that for me. Once again, it saved my life. And Mickey O'Keefe deserves a lot of the credit; everything changed when we started working closely together in the mid-1990s. I ran into

Mickey on the street one day, and we began to talk. I'd just started working out again after the accident, and he wanted to know how things were going. He seemed happy to hear that I was serious about fighting again.

"You've got a lot left in the tank," Mickey said. "Don't waste it."

He was right, and I knew it. I was only twenty-seven years old when I'd retired—way too early to give up on my dream. Now I was hungry again. I wanted to give it one more shot while I was still relatively young. I'd been around the sport long enough to know that while some guys keep fighting into their late thirties or even forties, the results are usually unimpressive and even dangerous. For every Bernard Hopkins or George Foreman knocking guys cold in middle age, there are dozens of tired, old boxers putting their lives at risk for one more paycheck. I didn't want to be that fighter; nor did I want to look back on my life with regret twenty years down the road.

This was precisely the right moment. I was stronger, more mature. I saw things differently. The frustration of those last few fights had melted away. The pain was a distant memory. I could accept the fact that boxing was a cold and brutal business, and that in order to succeed I had to get my managerial house in order, and put my body back together. And for some reason it all seemed possible. Reinforcement and encouragement from someone like O'Keefe really helped. I knew he wouldn't lie to me or blow smoke up my ass. He was a cop to the core. If he thought I lacked motivation, or that my skills had begun to erode, he'd say as much. Whether discussing training and strategy, or my personal behavior, there would be no gentle touch from Mickey O'Keefe.

"You been drinking a lot?" he asked me one day, before we'd really gotten into heavy training. "I mean, more than usual?"

I shrugged, nodded sheepishly. It wasn't a question that needed answering. Mickey knew from his work as a cop exactly what I'd been up to. He knew I'd been hanging out in the wrong places and with the wrong crowd, knew I was partying too much. You couldn't do shit like that (or at least I couldn't) without Mickey knowing about it. At one time Mickey had been a pretty hard drinker himself—nothing unusual about that for an Irish cop—but recently he'd put down the bottle for good. Said it was the smartest thing he'd ever done, that sobriety had changed his outlook on life. He didn't preach about it or anything, just talked matter-of-factly about the merits of sobriety, and in particular the positive reinforcement he'd gotten through Alcoholics Anonymous.

"Do me a favor, Mick," he said one night. "Come to a meeting with me. I'm not saying you need it or you don't need it. Just check it out. Then make up your own mind."

So I went home that night and thought about it. The next night I went to a meeting with Mickey. A few nights later I went to another meeting. And then another. I don't remember exactly how many meetings I attended, but it was probably a couple dozen over the course of several months. What I learned is that I had a problem; I'd let my life veer off course, and in order to get it back on track I had to make some fundamental changes. Like so many of the kids I'd grown up with—like Dicky and half my relatives—I was drinking more than I should have. A lot more. And, you know, when you're out late at night, in the city—Boston or Lowell—nothing much good ever happens. If you're drinking enough, and you're out late enough, eventually alcohol gives way to other substances. The party takes on a darker tone. I did cocaine for a while. Not a lot, but I was starting to get involved. The insidious thing about coke, of course, is that once you start doing it, you want to keep doing it. I should have known better. Hell, I did know better. I'd seen what coke and crack had done to my brother, and to so many other people on the streets of Lowell. That shit was a killer. Nevertheless, there I was, doing lines of blow in the car, or on the coffee table of someone's apartment at two o'clock in the morning. There was a pattern to this type of behavior. Or at least there was for me. I never did coke until after the bars were closed. That's when you start looking for a way to keep the party going. Suddenly someone says, "Hey, try some of this," so you take a hit. Next thing you know it's six in the morning and you feel like a fuckin' bum. It's a terrible drug.

I didn't do a lot of cocaine, but I did experiment for a while. And that just wasn't me. I found myself behaving in a way I never imagined I would. Then I'd wake up the next morning with the jackhammers pounding away at my temples, the nausea bubbling in my gut . . . looking and feeling like total shit. Not just physically, but psychologically.

"Oh, man . . . why did I do that?"

I hated that feeling—the awful combination of guilt and hangover. Thankfully, with the help of AA and Mickey O'Keefe, I stopped. Or at least got it under control. I knew if I wanted to go anywhere in my life, I couldn't treat my body like a trash can. There's no way you can train seriously to be an elite boxer while tearing yourself down with alcohol and drugs. Sure, some guys get away with it for a while—Dicky comes to mind—but eventually it catches up to them. They get in trouble, or they get hurt in the ring. Maybe, if they're lucky, they just fail to live up to their potential. None of those scenarios was acceptable to me. Given Dicky's history, it's probably reasonable to wonder whether we ever did any hard-core partying together. The answer is no—we didn't. Truth is, when it came to risky or self-destructive behavior, I was an amateur compared to Dicky. Shit, who wasn't? I don't think he ever had any idea that I'd slipped from casual drinking to hard drinking, and then to dabbling in cocaine. Had he known, he would have been pissed, to put it mildly.

Here's the great irony about Dicky: He was big on lecturing about hard work and clean living—a real "do as I say, not as I do" kind of guy. If he'd even suspected that I was doing coke (and just for the record—I never did crack; that's a whole level worse—maybe several levels), he would have been furious. And if he'd found out who sold me anything, he'd have beaten the shit out of him. That's just the way he was—always looking out for his little brother, or at least acting like he was looking out for me. His intentions were good in that regard; he just didn't always follow through. Maybe I couldn't rely on Dicky, but I always trusted him. As bad as he was on drugs—and he was pretty damn bad—he never took a dime from me, never even asked me for anything. Not money, not favors. Nothing.

"Watch your back, Mick," people would sometimes say to me. "He'll screw you over."

Didn't happen. Not once. I never even worried about it.

Addiction is a strange and powerful thing. In all candor, I never considered myself an alcoholic. And certainly not a cokehead. There are, however, degrees of dependence and abuse, and I'd definitely reached the point where I didn't feel good about myself, and some of that—maybe a lot of it—stemmed from what I was doing at night, after work or after leaving the gym. There were gaping holes in my life, and I tried to fill them through alcohol and, occasionally, drugs. Didn't work, of course. It never does. But each of us has to learn that lesson on his own, and then figure out how to move forward.

Looking back on it now, I feel lucky. Through Mickey O'Keefe's intervention, I was able to get a glimpse into what my life could become, as opposed to what it was. I was just beginning to slide down the slippery slope; Mickey helped me regain control. But I don't want it to sound too dramatic or imposing. When I used the word "intervention," I don't mean to imply that I was cornered or confronted. It wasn't like that at all. It was more like an invitation, and I accepted willingly. I met a lot of good people at those AA meetings; a lot of solid, well-intentioned, intelligent people who had problems and had changed their lives around because they stopped doing what they were doing. I never really talked much at the meetings, because that's not me. But I listened, and I got a lot out of it. In the end I made a decision to change my life, and to stop behaving like a self-destructive, self-pitying asshole. I'd always prided myself on never making excuses, and on outworking everyone else. Somewhere along the way, I'd forgotten the lessons I'd learned. Now I remembered. Now I had a second chance.

You may be wondering where I stand on all of this now. Well, I do not refer to myself as a recovering alcoholic or addict; nor do I abstain entirely from alcohol. I like to have a beer now and then, but I'm not a big partier. Drugs? Nope. Been a long, long time since my last line of coke. See, I think AA and the other twelve-step programs are there for people with all kinds of problems and issues. I'm glad they were there for me when I needed them. I was fortunate. I was able to do some serious reflection and get my life under control. A lot of people, though, rely on the program for the rest of their lives. They attend meetings monthly, weekly, even nightly. But we all have something in common: Alcohol and drugs have caused us great pain and suffering.

Some folks talk about the spiritual or religious component of AA and other recovery programs. I can't speak for anyone else, but that really had nothing to do with why it worked for me. I'm a Catholic; I believe in a higher power. But the main reason AA worked for me was because I couldn't bear the thought of ending up like so many of the people I met at these meetings. Not that I looked down on them; I didn't. Not at all. I just didn't want to have to endure the pain and degradation so many of them had obviously experienced. While sober they were good people. But I'd seen some of them on the street when they weren't sober, all raggedy, doing things they didn't want to do—begging, turning tricks, eating out of Dumpsters. Horrible, soul-sucking shit. Their stories made you want to cry. I knew Dicky had stories like that, and I vowed not to have one myself. So I guess maybe you'd call it pride that lifted me back on the right path. Or maybe fear. I tried to imagine picking up my daughter at her mother's house, and taking her home for the weekend for our usual visit, and exposing her to the kinds of things I heard at AA.

That alone was enough to make me shiver.

I couldn't let that happen. I wouldn't. Having spent a couple years away from the sport, boxing and training only sporadically, I came to understand how much it meant to me, and how it shaped the man I had become. I realized now that if I wasn't training—and training *hard*—my life would get out of control; I'd lose focus and start to drink. So I did the sensible thing:

I went back to the gym. Day after day.

And there, ready to work with me, was Mickey O'Keefe. We started out slowly, committing ourselves to each other, and to the simple goal of getting back in fighting shape. I really can't thank Mickey enough for what he did. He was there for me at the lowest point in my life, just as he'd been there for so many people over the years. This is a guy whose whole life has been all about public service, about giving back to the community, and I don't know that he's ever gotten the credit he deserves. Mickey showed an interest in me when I was just a little guy barely able to hold up my mitts. And he was there for me now, when I needed both a trainer and a friend. Mickey wasn't using me or trying to ride my coattails, or anything like that. He cared about me as a person. He worried about whether I was throwing away my life. He helped me get back on track, both as a man and as a fighter.

"Look at this guy," he'd say, pointing out some news report about a kid who had totally fucked up his life and ended up in jail. "Do you want to be like that?"

"No, of course not."

"Good, because you're better than that, Micky. You're a great fighter. Don't waste your talent."

We started out at the West End Gym, where I'd learned the sport as a little kid. Then Mickey opened his own place in The Acre, called Lowell Boxing, and that became our training center. I was in pretty good shape, better than I had any right to expect, given the way I'd been living and the injuries I'd recently sustained. I really hadn't let it slip too badly. I was never one of those guys who drank every day, or who abused his body in other ways, so the muscle memory was still there. I was rusty, no question about it. My conditioning had deteriorated. But I didn't care. I liked feeling tired, the way my arms ached and my lungs burned after a long session in the gym.

"It feels good to be back," I told Mickey.

"I know."

There was no carefully designed plan for the comeback. Frankly, hardly anyone even knew it was taking place, at least not in the beginning. For one thing, I wanted to do things a little bit differently from an administrative standpoint. First time around, especially at the end, I felt like

I was fighting for all the wrong reasons. I was fighting for the city of Lowell; I was fighting for everyone else. I didn't want to let anyone down, and so I kept taking fights I probably should have rejected, and I got badly beaten up and discouraged. This time I was fighting for myself. I wanted to be in the gym. I wanted to get back in the ring to see what I could accomplish—before it was too late. There would have to be some changes on the managerial end of things, as well, but that wasn't a concern in the beginning. Right then, it was just a matter of getting back in shape and preparing for the battles that lay ahead. I had no great expectations, no sense of entitlement.

"One step at a time," O'Keefe would say. "We'll take it as far as we can."

In some ways the training of boxers remains as primitive as it was a century ago. You build muscle and endurance through endless repetition: speed bag, heavy bag, shadowboxing, sparring. These are time-honored strategies and techniques that few trainers or fighters are willing to reject. I'm a traditionalist, always have been. So was Mickey O'Keefe. But we did a few unusual things this time. As before, it was a family affair in the gym, only now it wasn't my family. It was the O'Keefe family. Mickey's sons, Brian and Timmy, both helped out with training. Timmy was a college student at the time, attending Edinboro University, where he also was a member of the wrestling team. When Timmy came home on break, he would work out at his dad's gym. Mickey watched him one day, and was impressed by Timmy's ability to churn out hundreds of push-ups, pull-ups and dips. The kid's upper body was absolutely ripped, and he credited the physique, and strength, to this type of work. So Mickey wanted me to give it a try.

"Timmy says this is all they do in wrestling practice," he said. "Maybe it'll help you, too."

And it did. I didn't know too many boxers who were doing that sort of training, but I loved it. I felt so much stronger in sparring sessions. I felt bigger. My body actually changed. I was thicker, more well-defined. It gave me confidence. Another guy who helped out was my friend Brian Meade, a postal worker who became my running partner. We'd jog together around the canals almost every day, getting in our roadwork after Brian finished work. These are the people who helped me rebuild my career, and they did it without asking for anything, without any expectation of glory or financial reward. I still think back on those training runs with Brian, or the workouts with Mickey, when we had no promoter, no manager, no contracts . . . nothing. And seven years later I fought for a million dollars.

I am living proof that miracles happen. But they don't happen in a vacuum. You need a network of support.

We started at the bottom, which was entirely appropriate. I'd been gone a long time; and anyway, it wasn't like my first career had ended with a bang. No one was anxiously awaiting the return of Irish Micky Ward. The sport had gone on just fine without me, thank you very much. If I wanted to resurrect my career, I'd have to bring equal amounts of confidence and humility to the table. Fine with me. I deserved nothing, had earned nothing. I was starting all over again. And I was okay with that. A few years earlier I'd made seventeen grand to get beat up by Mike Mungin.

Now?

"You'll be lucky to get a few hundred bucks," Mickey said.

"Doesn't matter," I told him. "I just want to fight."

See, you have to start someplace. Who was I to ask for more than that? Who was I to *demand* anything? I had walked away from the game. Now I had no promoter, no matchmaker . . . nothing. As far as the sport of professional boxing was concerned, I had withered and died. I was just another contender who had failed to live up to his potential and wound up on the scrap heap of ex-boxers. It was on me to prove to people that I wasn't done, that in fact I was in the best shape of my life, and hungrier than I'd been in years. But how do you do that? I'm not a loud person. I don't talk much. I am, however, a good listener. And I heard things in the business and around town while I was training quietly with O'Keefe and his boys.

"Micky Ward ain't got shit left."

"He'll never be what he once was."

"Kid's a loser . . . just like his brother."

I heard all of these things, and I tucked them away, kept them close to my heart, used them as motivation every time I walked into the gym.

"Watch me, motherfuckers. I'll show you . . ."

I knew some of these guys—they'd been drifting in and out of gyms their whole lives, never really dedicating themselves to the sport (or to anything else, for that matter). They'd train for a little while, then fight once or twice, then quit, take some shitty job or collect unemployment. And then after a year or two they'd do it all over again. One look in the mirror should have told them they had no business criticizing anyone else. But I guess some people only feel good about themselves when they're tearing others down. These were the kinds of guys I'd like to get in the gym once in a while, when I needed extra sparring partners.

"Come on, we'll go easy," I'd promise.

Then I'd try to kill 'em.

Well, not literally, but I would make the experience unpleasant enough that maybe they'd think twice about running their mouths again when they were out holding up a barstool at the Highland Tap or the Cosmo.

Here's the thing about being a local hero: half the people who shake your hand on a daily basis? They want you to lose. I know that. It's lousy human nature to want other people to do badly, especially when your life sucks. Frankly, I don't understand how people live like that. How can you stand being miserable all the time? But I'll tell you something: The whispering and the backbiting was a source of great motivation.

I had something to prove.

The road back began with a scheduled ten-rounder against Luis Castillo, on June 17, 1994. We fought in my hometown, in a ballroom at the Lowell Sheraton, before a few hundred people. (Dicky was out of jail, so both he and Mickey worked my corner.) It was a far cry from the undercard of Leonard-Hagler, or headlining a card in Atlantic City, but I was grateful for the opportunity. The fact that I would earn approximately four hundred bucks for the night's work—one of the lowest purses of my entire career—didn't matter in the least. I just wanted to see if all the parts were still in good working order.

As it turned out, they were.

Castillo was hardly made of championship material. He had a 5–10 record, with only one victory in his previous eight fights. The last time he'd been in a ring, two months earlier, he'd been knocked out in the second round. At no point in ten years of professional fighting had Castillo faced the likes of Frankie Warren or Harold Brazier. The kid was no world-beater, that's for sure. He was just a basic fighter, the kind of guy I sparred against all the time. In other words, he was exactly the right kind of opponent. Nearly three years removed from my last fight, the last thing I needed was a war; I wanted nothing more than a good tune-up, and that is precisely what Castillo offered.

It wasn't my best day, but I was satisfied with the outcome. Took me two or three rounds to find my rhythm. In the early going, a lot of punches sailed wide. I felt a little slow, sluggish. Even though I was in terrific physical shape, my breathing was shallow and labored. That's natural, too. The pace of a fight is different from sparring. No matter what you do to replicate the experience in training, fight night is different. Your adrenaline is pumping, your heart racing. It's not unusual to feel fatigue in the opening rounds, a function of nerves as much as anything else. Once I settled down, though, I took control of the fight, began peppering Castillo with lefts and rights, moving him around the ring, pretty much dictating the action.

Then, in the fifth round, I went back to one of my favorite combinations: tap to the head, look for the opening as the hand comes up, and then . . .

Boom!

Left hook to the body.

Castillo left himself open to this combo a couple times, and each time I hurt him with the hook to the abdomen. But I wasn't able to get up under the rib and into his liver, where the punch can stop a man in his tracks; however, the cumulative effect of the body shots was enough to weaken Castillo and leave him open to a short right to the body. The punch caught him just below the sternum and took his breath away. As soon as it landed, I knew the fight was over. Castillo crumpled to the canvas . . . and stayed there.

It's interesting to deliver a punch like that, and to feel the effect that it has on an opponent. Knockout blows are usually concussive, and they tend to look spectacular, especially on television; almost as if the fighter's head has been dislodged from his body. But I'll tell you something. As bad as it is to get knocked out with a shot to the head—as serious as the long-term consequences might be—it's nowhere near as painful as a perfectly placed body shot. Drive a left hook deep into a man's belly, right below that floating rib, and he is instantly incapacitated. Get hit in the head and maybe the lights go out; maybe not. Sometimes they just flicker and you have to go into retreat mode for a while. The fog lifts slowly, but eventually it does lift, and the fight can go on. But watch a man who gets knocked down by a body shot. There is something elegant about it—the delayed reaction, the way the punch lands, and the fight continues . . . until suddenly, after a second or two, the man who has been hit drops to one knee in a display of utter submissiveness.

A display of surrender.

He doesn't tumble or fall over. He doesn't spin wildly out of control, the way he does after an uppercut to the jaw.

He simply gives up.

And he can wait five seconds, ten seconds . . . a minute. It doesn't matter. The paralyzing pain isn't going away.

So that became my signature punch, a crushing shot to the body (usually a left hook), which is kind of interesting considering that as an amateur, and even in my early professional days, I was known as a boxer and mover. I didn't like trading punches, didn't think I had the power to get away with it. I lacked confidence in my power, until I got deep into the pros and then started dropping people. Then I became fascinated with the technique, with setting up the body punch, and delivering it with absolute precision. I would practice in front of mirrors, working different angles and movements. I did hours of shadowboxing every week, and I brought the same energy to these solo sessions that I brought to the ring on fight night. I'd go hard, like I was fighting, because I wanted to mimic the feeling of competition and exhaustion.

Tap to the head . . . move and feint . . . boom-boom-boom!

Some guys just sort of muddle through shadowboxing, lumbering in small circles, flicking off half-assed punches. Not me. My arms ached afterward. I'd be drenched in sweat. I figured if I went easy in training, like shadowboxing, I'd go easy in the fight. So I'd get in front of a mirror and work like crazy, envisioning that moment when the other guy lifts his guard ever so slightly, protecting his head but leaving his body exposed.

That's when you draw the left in tight, and you pivot hard, rotating your hips like a golfer on the first tee. And then you drive right through the man, sinking your fist deep into his tissue, so far and clean that you swear if you weren't wearing a glove, you could grab his liver with your fingers.

You hit someone anywhere in that area, he's going down. I promise you. And yet, you don't see fights stopped with body shots very often. Roy Jones did it. Tyson used to do it. Arturo Gatti did it. But it's rare. Not because it's ineffective, but simply because so few boxers even try to execute the combination correctly, and even fewer have any idea how to do it. As a trainer, though, I teach all of my fighters to master the art of a well-placed body punch, because nothing is more disabling. You can't shake it off. The pain lingers. Remember what it was like when you got the wind knocked out of you playing sandlot football? Well, it's like that—multiplied tenfold. I was once told that when you get hit hard in the liver, it actually interrupts the flow of blood to the brain for a second or two. That's why you see a delayed reaction—the boxer continuing to fight, then stepping back, with a look of horror on his face, and dropping to one knee.

If you're in the ring when that happens, you can almost always hear the victim's response.

"Ooooooph."

Like the air leaking out of a tire.

Hit a man in the head and he says nothing. Hit him in the ribs, or in the liver, just right . . . and he deflates.

Although generally satisfied with the way I performed, I tried not to overreact after the Castillo fight. There was still much work to be done if I had any intention of climbing back into the ranks of the top light welterweights. It's one of the great clichés in sports for an athlete to say he's taking things one day at a time. But that's the way I looked at it. Just stay focused, get to the gym every day, work hard and hope for the best. I tried not to fret too much about things I couldn't control.

Three months later, for example, I was supposed to face a Puerto Rican fighter named Miguel Santana at the Lowell Auditorium. Santana's resume was dotted with some of the division's bigger names: Pernell Whitaker, Terrence Alli, Greg Haugen. He'd lost to each of those men, however, and it had been some time since Santana had been considered any sort of championship contender. If there was a concern about him, it was only that the guy had bulked up a bit in recent years and routinely fought as a welterweight, or even as a middleweight. So when Santana weighed in at more than 150 pounds on the morning of the fight, I couldn't help but have flashbacks to the night I got my ass kicked by Mike Mungin.

This time was different. No one even asked how I felt about giving up ten pounds to Santana. I was simply going through my usual fight-day routine when I was told that Santana was out. Dicky, Mickey and the promoter, a local guy named Johnny Gagliardi, had exercised our right to reject Santana based on the fact that he had come in overweight.

I hadn't even been consulted, which was probably a good thing, since my generally hardheaded nature might have caused me to make the same mistake all over again. (To be honest, I don't know whether my mother was consulted, either; she was still my manager, in name, anyway, but she was no longer making the decisions where my career was concerned.) Instead, I was told to sit tight, relax and be prepared to fight someone else.

The new opponent was a younger kid named Genaro Andujar. Unlike Santana, Andujar tended toward the light side. He'd started out as a pro fighting at 128 pounds. Now, typically, he weighed between 135 and 140. He came in at 141 for our fight (I was 144). Forget about size, though. Andujar was not in my league. The kid was in the early stages of a twenty-fight winless streak; realistically, he had no business being in the ring with me. But you can't think about that stuff when the bell rings. Every opponent deserves respect; every opponent must be considered dangerous; anyone can hurt you.

"Let's make this quick," Mickey O'Keefe said before the fight. "Go after this kid hard."

And that's what I did. Andujar was game, but overmatched. I put him down twice in the second round (he also took a standing eight count); he had to be saved by the bell in order to remain in the fight. The poor kid was still out on his feet when we started the third round, and I quickly put him down and out with a body shot.

I gotta admit—that was a good night. I was 2–0 on the comeback trail, having won a pair of fights in my hometown. I wasn't making any money to speak of, but didn't really care. I figured if I kept winning, opportunities would present themselves. I felt confident, eager. Ten minutes after the fight, I couldn't wait to get back in the ring.

But I would wait. A lot longer than I had anticipated.

CHAPTER 10

The first time Dicky appears on-screen in the HBO documentary *High on Crack Street: Lost Lives in Lowell*, you'd swear he's fifty years old. Gaunt as a corpse, with his eyes bulging out and his teeth all messed up, my big brother looks into the camera between tugs on a crack pipe, and rattles off one joke after another.

"Like Richard Pryor," he says with a startled laugh, pulling back from a sudden flare-up as he presses a lighter to the pipe.

But there's nothing funny about it. Not a damn thing. A few minutes later, when a voice off camera asks Dicky about his boxing career, Dicky explains that he once fought Sugar Ray Leonard . . . on television. The interviewer seems shocked. Could that be possible? Could this one-hundred-pound bag of bones sucking on a crack pipe really have once fought the great Sugar Ray?

Dicky nods.

"What network was it on?" the interviewer inquires.

Dicky takes another hit, smiles awkwardly, uncomfortably.

"Yours truly."

Talk about a fall from grace. But then, that's Dicky's story, right? Local boy makes good, then gets involved with drugs and fucks up big-time. It was only natural that the producers of *High on Crack Street* would want to include Dicky in their project. The idea was to make a film about the devastating effects of the crack epidemic on cities small and large throughout the country in the early 1990s. One of the producers was a guy named Richie Farrell, who was a distant cousin of ours. Richie had grown up in Lowell and was himself a former addict, so when he got involved in this project, he naturally wanted to focus on his hometown. And who better to exemplify the harrowing effects of crack than Dicky Eklund?

Dicky is one of three addicts featured in the documentary. They're all sad and broken people, spending every dime and every ounce of energy chasing the next high, and I suppose if the intent of the film is to serve as a deterrent, it probably works. To me, though, it was just heartbreaking and pathetic; I wish it had never happened. And Dicky? He hated it. I don't blame him. I can't imagine how it must feel to see yourself like that. There's a scene in which Dicky gets a jailhouse visit from his son, Dicky Jr. Our mom supervises the visit, telling little Dicky, who is only about two years old, that "Daddy is in the hospital."

Dicky tries to smile through the visit, but he looks like just about the saddest guy on the planet.

Like most people in Lowell, Dicky doesn't have much good to say about the documentary, and he's claimed in the past that the filmmakers set him up or framed scenes to make him look particularly bad. I don't know about any of that—Dicky did a pretty good job of getting himself in trouble. If you trailed him with a video camera in those days, you were bound to get some interesting footage. I think maybe Dicky believed he was doing something positive—taking part in a project that would show kids the danger of getting involved with drugs. Or maybe he just wanted another shot at fame. Hell, Dicky was so banged up in those years that he couldn't possibly have been thinking straight.

Regardless, I'm no fan of *High on Crack Street*. It made everything look like shit: the city of Lowell, with its abandoned mills and boarded-up row houses; the people who live here; the cops and the politicians. No one comes away unscathed. I have trouble believing that *High on Crack Street* was good for anyone, with the possible exception of the filmmakers. Look, I'm not trying to make excuses for Dicky. I've never done that. He's always been his own worst enemy. But he's still my brother, and I'll always love and support him. Dicky was out of his mind when they were shooting that film, and everybody knew it. I understand what they were trying to do, but it just doesn't seem right.

Maybe I'm too close to it. I mean, I lived through some of that stuff with Dicky, where he'd go missing for two, three, four days at a stretch, leaving me alone in the gym, or (thank God) with Mickey O'Keefe. I don't even know if Dicky remembers some of this stuff, like the time I went looking for him at two o'clock in the morning, after the bars were closed, because he hadn't shown up at the gym for a while. I tracked him down at my sister's house and found him hiding in the bathroom. I can still see him like it was yesterday, as I pulled back the shower curtain to reveal Dicky pressed against the tile, like he was trying to melt into the wall. It was so sad and pathetic. The way he didn't want me to see him, even though he wasn't doing anything wrong. Well, I'm sure he had been doing some bad shit earlier in the night—drinking or scoring crack or whatever—but at the moment? No, nothing.

Nevertheless, he was embarrassed.

"Dicky, what are you doing?" I said. "Get outta there."

He dropped his hands, cocked his head.

"Come on," I said. "We're going home."

And then, just like always, even when he was at his worst, he'd show up in the gym, eager to help me train, sometimes even willing to get in the ring and spar. A few times I'd get so mad that I'd start smacking him around, taking out my frustration on him. And then I'd catch myself and remember:

He's my brother . . .

By the time *High on Crack Street* was broadcast, both Dicky and I once again found our lives on hold. Not that our situations were comparable. Dicky had been arrested in the fall of 1993 (around the same time the documentary was being filmed) and charged with a variety of crimes, including kidnapping, breaking and entering, and armed robbery. Dicky did a lot of stuff to get money to support his habit in those days, including stealing from johns who found their way to the wrong side of Lowell in search of some action with the local hookers. Anyway, it was Dicky's twenty-seventh arrest, and this time he didn't get away with just a slap on the wrist. He was sentenced in March of 1995 to a term of eight years at the maximum security state prison in Walpole, Massachusetts. I felt terrible for him, of course, but I have to admit that some part of me felt like maybe it was all for the best, that prison might be the one place where Dicky could clean up his act.

And that turned out to be true.

On the day Dicky went off to prison, I was working on a road crew, laying asphalt, trying to summon the energy and drive to go to the gym that night, despite having no fight on the calendar. You see, Dicky wasn't the only person in my circle to have problems staying on the right side of the law. A promoter with whom I supposedly had a contract (we really only had a handshake deal) had recently pleaded guilty to drug-related charges (possession and intent to distribute), and was sentenced to a prison term roughly equal to that being served by Dicky. Now, you might think that when a promoter is convicted of a felony and sent away to prison for eight years, he'd lose his license and all clients would become free agents.

You might think that—if you knew nothing about boxing.

As I discovered, it isn't easy to break free of a promoter's grip—even when he's behind bars! In fact, it took me more than a year to earn my independence. And I felt the clock ticking. I'd worked hard to get back in shape after my retirement, won two consecutive fights, and finally felt like I was getting sharp again, only to be sent on another prolonged sabbatical. But what could I do? Boxing is among the messiest of sports—both in and out of the ring. You learn to live with it.

"Just get in the gym," Mickey O'Keefe told me. "Everything will work out."

With Dicky completely out of the picture, I relied even more heavily on Mickey, and I took his advice to heart, training with even greater intensity and purpose. Once again I did roadwork with Brian Meade and trained with Mickey's sons, Brian and Timmy. We would run stairs for hours, do pull-ups and chin-ups and dips. It was quiet, anonymous work, and I know I couldn't have done it without the help of those guys. I think that's worth mentioning—that at so many points in my career people have reached out to offer assistance, even though they had little or nothing personally to gain from it.

Of course, professional boxing is a business, and any fighter who hopes to succeed needs the guidance and support of people who understand that business and can make things happen. I was basically a free agent again, but it wasn't like promoters and matchmakers were beating down the door. When you've been away for a while—and two fights in four and a half years certainly qualifies as a long hiatus—people forget about you. ESPN had no interest in airing any of my fights at that time. Top Rank had no desire to promote me. I was back at the bottom, looking for anyone who could get me a fight and sell a few tickets. Two people helped in that regard: Al Valenti, who had promoted some of my earliest fights, and Joe Lake, who was a respected personal trainer, but also a manager and matchmaker who had worked with some very respectable fighters, most notably Dana Rosenblatt, a local kid (from Malden, Massachusetts) who was a rising star in the middleweight division.

Both Al and Joe, however, were at first reluctant to throw any weight behind the new Team Ward. Each of them had concerns about how much interference there would be from my family.

"Well, Dicky's in prison," I explained, "so obviously he won't be a problem. And my mother will stay out of your way, too. You have my word."

They also had the word of Mickey O'Keefe, who didn't make promises lightly. If Mickey said something would happen, then it happened. Things would be different this time around, he assured Lake and Valenti. There would be no distractions, no infighting.

Both men agreed, and on New Year's Eve weekend, 1995, I was back in the ring. As was the case a year and a half earlier, during my first comeback, the venue was unimpressive, and the opponent virtually unknown. Again, I didn't care. I would have fought just about anyone, and I would have traveled almost anywhere to do it. As it happened, I had just a short trip, to the North Shore of Boston.

Wonderland Racetrack in Revere, where folks bet small money on greyhounds, sometimes hosted local boxing cards. A few years earlier I couldn't have imagined fighting there. Now? I was grateful they'd have me, and I promised myself that I would give everyone a good return on their investment, minimal as it was. And that's what I did, knocking out Edgardo Rosario (who was making his professional debut) in the first round. It was the first of three consecutive fights at Wonderland, each of which carried a purse of a few hundred bucks. Next up, on January 26, 1996, was a kid named Alberto Alicea, who had won just six of his thirty-seven career fights. It's true what I said earlier—that a fighter is sometimes not as advertised, and that records can be deceptive. But sometimes a fighter with a 6–31 record is exactly as strong (or weak) as his record indicates. The fight was stopped in the third round. Two months after that I met Alex Ortiz, who was winless in five fights. He went down in the first round.

Just like that, I was back in the game, as Al Valenti worked with matchmaker Ron Katz and Top Rank to put together a card that would appeal to boxing fans throughout New England. There would be co-headliners: Dana Rosenblatt against 1976 Olympic gold medalist Howard Davis in one fight, and me against Louis Veader of Providence in the other. The card would be held on April 13, 1996, at the Fleet Center in Boston. ESPN would televise the bouts.

For me this represented a very quick and unexpected return to the big-time. I was excited but also somewhat concerned. So far on the comeback trail I'd come across two overmatched opponents. Veader was a completely different story. "The Viper," as he was known, was one of the hottest young light welterweights in the game. He was 31–0, and while he might not have been quite as good as that record would seem to indicate, he was a very impressive boxer. I'd seen the kid fight once, a couple years earlier, when he'd hammered out a ten-round decision over the always competitive and entertaining Livingstone Bramble. Veader was a tough, strong boxer, four years younger than me and on the kind of roll that gives a fighter incredible confidence. I'd been that way once, many years earlier; you think you can't lose.

Things were different now. I'd lost a bunch of fights and took a more pragmatic approach to the business. I understood that anything was possible. I also knew that Veader represented both opportunity and risk. We'd be fighting for the WBU Intercontinental light welterweight championship—a minor title, to say the least. That didn't matter. Veader was a significant hurdle, one I had to clear in order to be viewed as an elite boxer. If I beat him, I'd be right back among the contenders in the light welterweight division. But if I lost (and let's face it—most people expected me to lose), my career essentially would be over. I was thirty years old and hadn't beaten anyone of note in a very long time.

I needed this fight.

There wasn't a lot of time to prepare, so Mickey and I went right to work. This time we were blessed to add a new training partner to the mix: Lou Rosselli, a former All-American wrestler at Edinboro, and a friend of the O'Keefe family. Lou was in the process of training for the 1996 U.S. Olympic Trials (he would make the team, but unfortunately suffered a broken arm during the Atlanta Games that summer), so he was in phenomenal physical condition, with huge shoulders tapering to a thirty-inch waist; the guy was just a ball of muscle. I worked closely with Lou and the O'Keefe brothers, doing a ton of exercises designed to not only increase cardiovascular conditioning but also improve upper-body strength. I can't overstate the impact of training with those guys. By the time the Veader fight rolled around, I was in the very best shape of my career—strong and fit and confident. I was like a bull, with thick muscles along my neck and chest, and the biceps of a middleweight. Call it vain, if you'd like; but the fact is, strength is power. I knew how to box; I was a technically sound fighter who had been studying his sport for more than twenty years. Still, there's something about looking in the mirror and seeing all that muscle, feeling cut and powerful, that gives you added confidence.

There were more than six thousand screaming boxing fans at the Fleet Center that night, and it sure sounded as though most of them were on my side. They hissed and cursed at Veader during introductions and throughout the fight, which kind of surprised me. After all, he was a New Englander, too. I figured a lot of people would have forgotten me by now. Guess I was wrong.

I've rarely started a fight with as much energy as I did that evening. The bell sounded and I practically shot out of the corner, so eager to meet Veader in the center of the ring that I could barely control myself. You have to be careful about using up too much adrenaline in the early going, or getting so excited that you forget all about strategy. In this case, though, it worked to my advantage. I was able to put Veader back on his heels right away, setting the tone for the entire evening. He knew immediately that I was not some washed-up old tomato can there to pad his record.

I had come to fight.

The first couple rounds went about as well as I could have envisioned. I felt quick and strong; my timing was sharper than it had been in the first two fights, and I even opened up a cut over Veader's eye in the second round. Everything seemed to be going my way. In the third round, however, the strangest thing happened. While applying heavy pressure along the ropes, I took a shot to the solar plexus from Veader, a hard jab that burrowed into my chest and nearly knocked me out cold. Not from the force of the blow, but because my heart suddenly began beating furiously, a hundred miles an hour, like I was having a heart attack or something. And then it slowed down dramatically, even pausing for what felt like several seconds between beats.

Holy shit! I'm going to die right here in the middle of the ring.

It was all I could do to ride out the round. I tried to grab Veader, hold on, prevent him from doing any more damage. As I said earlier, I'd felt something like this once before—the sensation of being unable to breathe, despite being in great shape. But this was much worse. This was almost crippling. And it was terrifying.

"What the hell's wrong with you?" Mickey asked me when I got to the corner between rounds. "You had this guy runnin'."

"I can't breathe."

Mickey seemed confused.

"What do you mean, you can't breathe? You're in the best shape of your life. Suck it up!"

"No, I mean . . . I can't catch my breath. There's something wrong . . . in here."

I tapped my chest.

Mickey cupped the back of my head, told me to relax, said everything would be fine. I don't think he had any idea that I was in serious distress.

A physical exam later revealed a slight heart murmur—I'd probably been born with it. Under normal circumstances—including physical exertion—it wasn't much of a problem. Occasionally, though, the murmur could be provoked into something more mischievous, something closer to cardiac arrhythmia. That was probably what happened on this night, although the docs couldn't say for sure. Basically, the shot to my chest, coupled with the fact that my heart was already racing from so much exertion, led to a slight disruption of normal rhythm.

And I freaked out. Shit, who wouldn't?

_____

When the heart jumps around like that, the worse thing you can do is panic. If you just relax, take a few deep breaths, the rhythm almost always returns to normal. But if you panic, the arrhythmia will continue, maybe escalate, and you could end up having a full-blown heart attack. I didn't know any of this at the time. All I knew was that my heart felt like it was doing flip-flops in my chest—in the middle of the most important fight of my life.

Instinctively, I tried to slow the pace of the fight, and in so doing I allowed Veader to gain confidence and control. I didn't throw many punches in the next few rounds. Pretty soon I fell behind on the scorecards. By the sixth round, though, my heart rate seemed to have returned to normal; the fear melted away, and I began fighting furiously again, just as I had in the opening round. In the eighth round, I caught the guy with a hard left hook. He hit the canvas and got up slowly. Although he survived the round, I knew he was in trouble. Midway through the ninth I caught him with a body shot against the ropes.

And that was that.

I heard the telltale moan of a boxer who has been incapacitated as Veader doubled over and then went to one knee. I figured it was over right there, but Veader, a game kid, tried to get up and continue, even though he was clearly in a lot of pain. Fortunately, the referee, Gerry Leone, stepped in front of Veader and stopped the fight. As the crowd went nuts, I jumped into Mickey O'Keefe's arms. My mom came into the ring, crying. This, I thought, was what it felt like to be resurrected.

In the summer of '96, following a second consecutive victory over Veader (whose bicycle strategy—keep moving and try to avoid contact—was designed to prevent another knockout, but merely resulted in a lot of inactivity on his part and my earning a lopsided decision), I went looking for a new manager. Technically speaking, my mother had still been managing my career to that point; in reality, though, Mickey and I had been calling the shots. Nevertheless, my feeling was that we needed someone else to handle the business end of things, while Mickey and I focused on training and competition. That's how Sal LoNano came on board.

Sal was a local businessman and an acquaintance of my father's. They'd gotten to know each other in the joint. Now, you might reasonably wonder why I'd choose an ex-con to take over as the manager of Team Ward. But past indiscretions didn't really factor into the decision. Hell, most of the people I knew—friends, casual acquaintances, enemies—had experienced brushes with the law at one time or another. If I refused to associate with anyone who had been arrested or done time, I'd have been a mighty lonely guy. I liked Sal, knew he was good with money and wouldn't easily be pushed around. While it's counterintuitive, I actually liked the fact that Sal had virtually no experience in the sport of boxing—aside from having been a fan. Admittedly, though, most people didn't share my opinion.

"Guy doesn't know shit about boxing" was the refrain I heard. "He'll ruin your career."

I didn't feel that way. I think I'm pretty good at reading people, and something told me I could trust Sal. My dad's recommendation played a part in it, of course, but it was also the way Sal responded when I first approached him with the prospect. He didn't jump at the chance, didn't try to sell himself. In fact, he did just the opposite, instead pointing out his own inexperience.

"Honestly, Mick, I don't know if I'm the right guy for the job."

He wasn't the only person who had doubts. As a lifelong cop, Mickey O'Keefe had a natural distrust of ex-cons, and in the rehabilitation process in general. I was a big believer in second chances; Mickey was more likely to say something like, "A leopard don't change its spots." So he and Sal butted heads almost from the get-go. Mickey didn't trust Sal, always figured he was trying to work some angle; and Sal felt threatened both by my close relationship with Mickey, and Mickey's obvious antagonism. But I was in charge and I wanted both of them in my corner. So that's the way it was . . . for a while, anyway.

Sal wore Mickey down by apparently getting off to a great start. Working with Top Rank (primarily Bob Arum) and HBO, he helped arrange what would have been my biggest and most lucrative match: a one-hundred-thousand-dollar payday against Julio Cesar Chavez. While Chavez was thirty-four years of age and slightly past his prime by this point, he remained one of the top draws in boxing. Arguably the most talented light welterweight ever to lace up a pair of gloves, Chavez went 89–0–1 in the first fourteen years of his professional career. The guy fought everyone, beat everyone, backed away from absolutely nothing. Even now he was a terrific fighter, having only recently given up his WBC title, in a fourth-round TKO to Oscar De La Hoya.

Chavez was still one hell of a talent and able to command a seven-figure payday. I didn't begrudge him that. He'd earned it. I was perfectly happy with one hundred grand. Shit, I'd never made more than seventeen thousand; less than a year earlier I'd been willing to fight for little more than cab fare. To me, this was the opportunity of a lifetime.

Too bad it never happened.

The fight was supposed to be held in Reno, Nevada, so we set up training camp at Big Bear Lake, in the San Bernardino Mountain Range of California. Reno is at an altitude of nearly 4,500 feet, which may not sound like all that much, unless you're a city kid from the East Coast accustomed to training at sea level. Big Bear sits at nearly seven thousand feet, so we figured that after a month of getting acclimated to the higher elevation, fighting in Reno would seem comfortable by comparison.

I liked Big Bear, enjoyed the fact that all I had to do was train like a madman. No job, no distractions. Just focus on getting in great shape. Get up every morning and run through the mountain passes. Then have a big breakfast and hit the gym. Train and eat, train and eat. Then go over strategy and game plans. It was one of the few times I'd felt like a full-time boxer, as opposed to a part-time boxer and full-time something else (like construction worker). But it wasn't all peace and harmony. There was some tension in the camp, thanks to the presence of a second trainer by the name of Jimmy Connolly, who had been brought in by Sal to help Mickey work the corner. Mickey didn't like Sal as it was, and he naturally viewed the addition of Connolly as an insult and a threat to his authority. But as long as Jimmy understood his place—one step behind Mickey—I figured things would be okay.

Less than a week before the fight, though, Sal delivered the news that Chavez had pulled out. There were a lot of rumors floating around at the time—that Chavez's camp had heard about the way I was destroying sparring partners, and had therefore decided the fight was too big a risk; or that Chavez was simply having trouble making weight. Knowing what I know about Chavez, I have a hard time believing that he would have pulled out without a valid reason. Who knows? I'm sure he wasn't scared; shit, no one has ever accused that guy of being scared of anyone. But managers and promoters take things out of your hands sometimes, and maybe they didn't want to take a chance on his losing to someone like me. They probably assumed they'd wipe me out, but after seeing me train, they thought, "Wow, this kid is the real deal."

Regardless, the fight was off, and I was heartbroken.

"You've gotta be kidding me!" I said to Sal. "What do we do?"

Mickey O'Keefe wanted to pack up camp and immediately get the hell out of town. But Sal offered another option: a fight against this kid named Manny Castillo, out of East L.A., a tough son of a bitch with a modest record (13–6–2), but enough talent and guts to give me trouble if I wasn't careful. And here's the really bad part: Instead of earning one hundred thousand dollars (as I would have against Chavez), I'd have to settle for about a tenth of that amount.

Mickey was adamant that we reject the offer.

"Tell Top Rank to go fuck themselves," he said.

But apparently the situation was a little more complicated than that, since we'd run up a pretty big expense bill in Big Bear. The promoters, of course, wanted a return on their investment. And I gotta be honest here: I wanted to fight. I needed the money and I knew I was in great shape. It's always risky to fight a last-minute substitute, but I knew there was no way Castillo would be a more formidable opponent than Julio Cesar Chavez. I was sure in my own mind that I could beat Chavez. No fuckin' way I was going to lose to Manny Castillo.

"Let's take it," I told Sal, overruling Mickey O'Keefe in the process, and probably driving a wedge even further between him and Sal.

Because of the way things went on fight night, December 6, 1996, Mickey ended up looking like the only guy in the room with half a brain. Not because I lost (I didn't), but because of the toll that fight took on my body and our friendship.

We weren't two minutes into the first round when I threw a left hook to the body. A signature punch, just to see what Castillo was made of. Well, the guy must have done his homework, because he saw the punch coming and dropped his arm just slightly, enough to cover his ribs. Instead of landing a sharp blow to the liver, I got hung up on Castillo's elbow, the thumb of my left hand separating from the rest of my fist with an explosive force.

Bam!

I don't know if the injury actually made any noise or not. They say sometimes that when you tear a ligament or tendon, it actually sounds like a gunshot. I do know that it felt like someone had blasted a hole in my hand—it was one of the most painful things I'd ever experienced. I could feel everything go numb in my glove, from the tip of my thumb right up to my forearm.

You've gotta be kidding!

Instantly, I became a one-armed fighter. I went into defensive mode, trying to buy some time and see if the pain subsided. In the corner, between rounds, Mickey berated me.

"What the hell are you doing out there?"

"My hand," I said. "Something's wrong."

Mickey didn't panic, just talked me through it, told me to keep moving and sticking. He didn't realize exactly how much it hurt, or how incapacitated I was. Hell, I didn't know. After the fight I'd discover that I had completely ruptured a tendon in my left thumb—pulled it right off the bone. It's a deal breaker of an injury, the kind that usually results in a fight being stopped. There's nothing you can do to treat it in the heat of battle, no time to take off the glove and wraps, no way to ice it or reduce swelling. You just deal with it.

Or you quit.

I decided to keep fighting, although I didn't look like the guy who was supposedly prepared to fight Julio Cesar Chavez. I had nothing in my left hand, so basically I just danced and clutched for the better part of five rounds, until finally the pain subsided. The hand was still numb, but I could deal with that. I started throwing combinations again, realizing that whatever damage I might have done, it probably wasn't going to get any worse. Finally in the eighth round, I caught him with a left hook, and he went down.

Thank God, I thought. *I can put this guy away.*

But you know what he did? The crazy bastard jumped up off the floor and began clapping his gloves together, like he was applauding my knockdown or something. I'd never seen anything like it.

This guy is nuts!

I ended up winning the last several rounds and came away with a split decision, but it goes to show that taking a fight under those circumstances is always a gamble. I could have lost everything that I'd worked so hard to achieve. And for what? Ten thousand dollars? Mickey was right: It just wasn't worth it.

He knew it, too. We got into a big fight at the airport on the way home. Mickey said something, Sal said something in return, F-bombs fell like rain and I got drenched.

Four months later, in April of 1997, at the Thomas & Mack Center in Las Vegas, I was back in the ring. But a lot had changed. My left thumb had been surgically repaired, but my relationship with Mickey O'Keefe remained damaged. Maybe I shouldn't put it that way. I loved Mickey— always did, always will—but he's one of the toughest, most stubborn men I've ever known, and he wasn't about to take shit from Sal LoNano or anyone else. When Sal decided after the Castillo fight that he wanted Jimmy Connolly to serve as my primary trainer, and Mickey to serve as my second (only the lead trainer is allowed in the ring on fight night), Mickey responded about as you might expect he would. He felt like he'd been demoted, and he blamed me for allowing it to happen. For Mickey, it came down to something fundamental and inflexible: loyalty.

"I want you here," I told Mickey. "But Sal is in charge, and he wants Jimmy, too. Why can't we just make it work?"

There was no reasoning with Mickey on this subject. He wouldn't take a backseat to Jimmy (or any other trainer), and he couldn't stomach being around Sal.

So he left.

I don't know whether Mickey's absence had anything to do with my lackluster performance in Vegas, against an undefeated (16–0) Alfonso Sanchez, or whether Sanchez deserves most of the credit. I do know that I was in big trouble for most of that fight. I felt sluggish and rusty. Sanchez was supposed to be a big hitter, so our strategy was to keep moving, and not trade blows with him in the center of the ring. Unfortunately, for reasons I can't really explain, I couldn't seem to find my rhythm that night. I got knocked down in the fifth round and was trailing by a wide margin late in the fight, so badly that Jimmy Connolly threatened to throw in the towel if I didn't start showing more interest in fighting.

Later I found out that Jimmy wasn't alone. The broadcasting crew from HBO, including Jim Lampley and Larry Merchant, ripped me apart, basically said I was over the hill and had no business getting in the ring anymore. But just as they were calling for a stoppage, as well, in the seventh round, I got off a body punch that clearly hurt Sanchez.

I could see him wince. So I went after him again, tapping the head to free up the body, and then I drove a left into his side.

The crowd was silent at that moment, completely uninterested in what had been, admittedly, a very dull fight. They were waiting for the headliner, a WBC welterweight championship bout between Oscar De La Hoya and Pernell Whitaker. Suddenly, though, the arena came to life, as Sanchez, paralyzed by a perfect shot to the liver, stopped in his tracks and fell to the canvas and began crawling on his hands and knees. Then he rolled over on his side, in obvious agony, as the referee counted him out.

And just like that, with a single punch, I went from has-been to contender. That's the way it goes sometimes in boxing: down one minute, up the next.

Or vice versa.

On August 9, 1997, I met Vince Phillips for the IBF light welterweight title at the Roxy in Boston. This was a serious challenge and a great opportunity. Phillips, who had won the IBF title by beating previously undefeated Kostya Tszyu (who later went on to become a multiple world champion and a member of the Boxing Hall of Fame), was a fighter with a big punch and tons of ability. We were originally supposed to fight in either Atlantic City or at Foxwoods Casino, which would have been fine with me. But to get this fight, for a championship, in my hometown? It was almost too good to be true. Even better was the fact that Mickey and Sal managed to patch things up enough for Mickey to return to the gym. It wouldn't last long, unfortunately, but for the moment Mickey was once again first man in the corner.

Man, the Roxy was jumping that night. It wasn't a big venue, only a couple thousand seats, more like a club than an arena. But it was an intimate and (for Phillips, anyway) intimidating setting, with fans right on top of you, close enough to hear every punch. I wanted to give them one hell of a show, but it wasn't to be. Phillips and I traded punches furiously for the first two rounds, roughly splitting the scoring. It was exactly the sort of hectic fight I expected. What I didn't expect was the trickle of blood that began pouring into my eye roughly one minute into the third round.

I knew it was bad right away. Not because it hurt, but because of how quickly and suddenly it happened. I don't even remember what type of punch it was—a right lead, I think—but as soon as it landed I could feel the skin separate and the blood squirt out. Like when you squeeze an unopened packet of ketchup.

Splat!

It was, for Phillips, a perfectly placed punch. And for me, an incredibly unlucky shot.

I backed up immediately, toward the ropes, to gather my composure, instinctively trying to wipe the blood out of my left eye. I figured if I could just ride out the round, then I'd get to my corner and let the guys work their magic. They'd put me back together and everything would be fine. I wasn't worried about a little blood.

But I never got the chance. The referee, Dick Flaherty, jumped in between us and signaled a temporary halt to the proceedings, never a good sign. Flaherty then walked me to the corner and summoned the ringside physician, Dr. Pat Yoffi.

Pat . . . as in *Patricia.*

At the time, Yoffi was one of the few female fight doctors, and while this will probably sound sexist, I couldn't help but think I would have been better off with a male doc sitting ringside. Women are more sensitive, more likely to err on the side of caution. Sure enough, Dr. Yoffi stopped the fight.

"I'm sorry, Micky," she said, inspecting the cut with a flashlight. "I can see right to the bone."

"Fuck, no!" I yelled. "Let me fight!"

Mickey tried to plead my case, calmly assuring the doc I'd be fine. Of course, this was her business, and though she hadn't worked a lot of big fights, she knew enough to ignore the reassurances of a trainer or fighter. Those are the last people you consult when deciding whether to stop a boxing match.

"Come on, please," Mickey said. "Give us a chance to work on it."

The doc shook her head. "I'm sorry." Then she waved her hands.

The fight was over. Vince Phillips had retained his IBF title by technical knockout. It was the first time in my career that one of my fights had been stopped. I was overwhelmed with frustration and anger. I jumped around the ring, bleeding like the victim in a slasher film. Phillips worked his way toward me and gave me a big hug.

"I'm sorry, man," he said.

"I know."

I was sorry, too, especially for what happened next. As Vince and I stood together, awaiting the formal announcement, the crowd went crazy, throwing cups of beer and other debris into the ring, screaming horrible shit at Phillips, calling him names. I looked out into the arena, and who was leading the onslaught? My friggin' family! My sisters, their husbands and boyfriends. Jesus Christ!

"Stop it!" I screamed while leaning over the ropes. "It's not his fault!"

I'd never been so embarrassed or concerned about another fighter's well-being. Vince didn't deserve this. He was a world champ, coming to my state, giving me a fair shake, and all these drunks from Lowell and Boston were attacking him. I mean, that's what happens when you have a few too many beers at a boxing match. Things don't go the way you want, and you sort of lose your mind.

"HEAD BUTT! HEAD BUTT!" the crowd chanted.

I stared right at a couple of guys sitting ringside and threw my hands in the air.

"What the fuck fight were you guys watching? He hit me with a right hand."

"HEAD BUTT! HEAD BUTT!"

Eventually we all managed to make our way from the ring to the dressing room beneath a steady shower of beer, everyone in my camp (me included) complaining about the stoppage, questioning the wisdom of allowing women to serve as ringside doctors. Then, a little while later, when I got to the emergency room, the tone of the conversation changed.

"You're lucky, Mr. Ward," the doc said as he looked at my cut.

"What do you mean?"

"This thing is really deep," he said. "One more punch and you could have lost the use of that eye."

I felt grateful and ashamed at the same time. Everyone had been blaming Dr. Yoffi, screaming at her, and as it turned out she saved my eyesight. I told her as much the next time I saw her.

"You got a bad rap," I said. "You did what you thought was right, which is exactly what you're supposed to do. And I want to thank you for that. I also want to thank you for saving my eye."

She smiled.

"You're welcome."

Although happy to not be blind in one eye, I was still extremely disappointed with what had happened. I understood the way boxing worked and just naturally figured that Phillips represented my last big shot at a title. But an interesting thing happened: No one else saw it that way. I didn't get beat up or knocked out in the traditional sense. I didn't fight badly. I got stopped on a cut. It happens. Now, the truth is, you don't want a reputation as someone who bleeds, who cuts. That's never good for a fighter (a white fighter, in particular). But no one saw me that way—yet. In reality, I'd begun to accumulate a good deal of scar tissue, and I started cutting more and more after the Phillips fight. On that night, though, what everyone saw was a guy whose nine-fight winning streak was stopped only because of a single, unfortunate cut.

A fluke.

"Relax," Sal told me afterward. "No one is disappointed in you."

He was referring mainly to Bob Arum and Top Rank, whose faith hadn't been shaken, after all. While a victory over Phillips would have given me a belt and likely led immediately to a six-figure payday, a loss wasn't fatal. Eight months later, in April of 1998, I knocked out a journeyman named Mark Fernandez with a body shot in the third round. That fight was supposed to be a tune-up for a bigger fight, and a bigger paycheck. It served its purpose. But I can't say I felt great about it, mainly because once again I'd lost Mickey O'Keefe. It had happened during preparations for the Fernandez fight, when Sal decided to bring in Ruppert "Nell" Brown as a second trainer. Sal did things like that once in a while, for reasons I never quite understood. He liked to shake things up. So he told Mickey, "You'll be in charge in the gym, every day, but during fights I want Nell in the corner."

That was hard, if not impossible, for Mickey to accept.

"Fuck you, Sal!" he screamed one day at the gym. Just like that, the gloves came off. As their argument escalated, I thought the two men might come to blows. Sal tried to remain calm, but his very presence brought out the worst in Mickey. He challenged Sal to a fight.

And then he got angry with me.

"Come on, Mickey," I said. "Take it easy. We're all on the same team here."

Mickey gave me a hard look.

"Fuck you, too, Micky!" he said. Then he walked out the door.

We never worked together again; for a number of years we barely spoke. It wasn't until after I retired that Mickey and I reconciled. Today I'm fortunate to call him one of my closest friends, and one of the most important influences on my life and career. I never meant to hurt him, never meant to allow anyone else to hurt him. I think he knows that. Boxing is a tough business and sometimes you have to make difficult decisions. Inside the ring and outside the ring, people get bruised.

———————

Just two months after the Fernandez fight I got another shot at the big-time: a fight against Zab Judah for the vacant USBA light welterweight title. Judah, a lefty from Brooklyn, was one of the most talented and impressive young athletes in the game, a lightning-quick boxer with some serious pop in his punch. I didn't know him personally, but I knew he was good (15–0 at the time). He had the advantage of youth (only twenty years old), but I had experience on my side. Unfortunately it wasn't enough. Zab was probably the best all-around fighter I ever faced; there's a reason he went on to win five world titles, and continues to contend to this day. He was a lefty, too, which made him naturally more dangerous and confounding. I tried to put pressure on him, but he was just so fast. The main thing I remember about that fight was how tired I felt—it was like I spent the entire night in pursuit of someone who simply couldn't be caught. I think I hit him with one good body shot, but he recovered quickly and got right back on his bicycle. He was so elusive, and I don't mean that in a derogatory way. Zab didn't just run and hide. He would run and stick, run and stick.

I've never felt so confused in a fight, like I was trying to catch a ghost. One second he'd be right in front of me, seemingly a perfect target.

And then he was gone.

Zab had been ringside the night I knocked out Fernandez with a body shot, and he'd obviously learned something in the process, because he never once gave me an opening. Or, if he did, I didn't see it. He was that fast, that slippery. The thing is, I'd never lost a fight by such a wide margin—on all three judges' scorecards, Zab was an overwhelming winner—and yet, I'd never come out of a ten-round fight with less damage. No swelling, no cuts. It was almost like ten rounds of shadow-boxing. That's no knock on Zab. The guy had a brilliant fight plan and he executed it flawlessly.

Someone told me later that the computer stats showed Zab hit me with 270 punches, not one of which hurt. But that's not the point, is it? If you can't knock a guy out, then you have to find another way to beat him. Zab figured that out. I didn't.

Two hundred seventy punches.

You know how many I landed? Ninety. That's pathetic—nine punches per round.

And it felt like even less.

CHAPTER 11

In October of 1998, after spending more than three and a half years behind bars, my brother was released from prison. Hard to believe that anyone who'd screwed up as often as Dicky could be granted early parole, but I guess it just goes to show you: Under the right circumstances, and with the proper motivation, anyone is capable of turning his life around.

I can't tell you exactly what worked for Dicky, and it would be inaccurate to say that he's got life by the balls even today. Things are more complicated than that. But I do know that the man who walked out of jail that fall was a different man than the one who went in. He was clean and sober; healthy and hungry. I was a little surprised by the transformation, to be perfectly honest, partly because I hadn't seen all that much of Dicky in the preceding years. I'd visit him every couple weeks, sometimes more often that that, sometimes less. But I actually found it kind of painful to sit there in the visiting room with Dicky, trying to make small talk, pretending things weren't so bad for him. If you've never been inside a prison, never spent any time meeting with a friend or relative, then you can't understand what it's like. After the initial embrace and the excitement of seeing a loved one, the warmth melts away, replaced mainly by sadness. You very quickly run out of things to say. The inmate just wants to know how everything is going on the outside, and you don't want to know anything about life inside. So the conversation is awkwardly one-directional, almost like an interrogation.

"How's Mom? . . . How's your daughter? . . . How's the training going?"

And so on . . .

Basically he was just trying to get his shit together, which was not an unusual situation for him to be in. I'd heard a lot of talk from Dicky over the years, so I didn't know whether to believe him or not. I was hoping, of course, that he was serious about making changes. But the responsibility was Dicky's; nobody could do it for him. So when he'd start talking that way, making big proclamations, I'd try to steer the conversation in a different direction. Keep it simple. We'd focus mainly on fight talk—what types of workouts I was doing, opponents I might face and what would happen when he was paroled. There was always a carrot that Dicky dangled in front of his own nose.

"When I get out, Mick, we'll show 'em all. You and me. Together again."

I'd usually just nod.

"Sure, Dicky. Of course."

Truth is, I didn't know when he'd get out, or what our relationship would be like, in the gym or out of the gym. I sort of figured in the back of my head that we'd partner up, that Dicky would be my trainer all over again, but I didn't want to talk about it. I had to focus on my own life and career. And each time I visited with Dicky, I left feeling drained and distracted. It hurt too much to see him like that, and to hear the ache in his voice as he talked about how much he missed his son, and how he was going to do things the right way this time around.

Mom was better about handling this sort of thing, which I guess isn't much of a surprise. A mother's love is unconditional, right? Or should be, anyway. Mom used to visit Dicky just about every day, no matter where he was housed, no matter what else was going on in her life. Some people have suggested that my mother's loyalty to Dicky was misguided, and that it might have cost me opportunities along the way. I don't know about that. But I do know that she was Dicky's lifeline when he was in prison, and I don't know what he would have done without her.

Once he got out, though, I became Dicky's lifeline. And I was okay with that. Truth is, I needed him, too.

You'd think a forty-one-year-old man who'd just spent more than three years in prison might have slowed down a step or two, right? Not in Dicky's case. The guy was in ridiculous physical condition. I was only thirty-three years old, and among the top ten light welterweights in the world. But, no bullshit—I couldn't keep up with Dicky. Part of it was because I was laying off a bit when he first got out of jail. I mean, I was still training and running and doing some light work, and obviously there was a residual fitness from all the years of working out. But my right hand had begun giving me serious trouble again after the Judah fight. Apparently the benefits of my lengthy sabbatical had finally worn off, and now I was right back where I'd been years earlier: with a hand so swollen that it required hours of icing after every training session, and pain that never quite subsided. Slowly, over time, I'd lost some of my punching power, and I'd begun to worry about whether it was coming back.

So I took some time off to heal up. From a business standpoint, this might not have been the wisest strategy. Losing to Judah had cost me some momentum and support—more than a few people questioned whether I was capable of making a title run. It's all about timing and contacts in boxing. You can be a hot property one moment, and old news the next. I wanted to keep fighting, try to prove that the Judah fight had been an anomaly. But I couldn't. Until I got healthy, I had to be patient. That meant no hitting, no sparring, no contact of any kind.

Just roadwork and shadowboxing.

Dicky, naturally, became both my trainer and training partner, and I was shocked by his level of fitness. The kid had always been like the Energizer Bunny, but this was ridiculous. I couldn't even stay with him when we went for a run. He'd jog ahead of me, barely even breathing, and I'd lag behind, sucking wind like an old man.

"Yo, Micky! Come on! Who's in training here—you or me?"

"Fuck you, Dicky!"

Then he'd laugh. That same goofy cackle I'd heard since I was a little kid. And then he'd pull away. I know he did a lot of running while he was in prison, laps around the yard at Walpole, but Jesus Christ! This was ridiculous. Maybe Dicky missed his calling; the kid could have been a track star.

A lot of it, I suppose, had to do with the fact that Dicky's system was clean—really clean—for the first time in at least twenty years. He'd purged all the toxins—the drugs and alcohol and whatever other shit he might have been doing—while he was in jail, and that left him feeling and acting like a much younger, healthier man. But some of it was just the way Dicky was built. He's a genetic freak. I was always a worker. Disciplined, devoted, trying to squeeze every ounce of talent out of my body. I knew other guys were faster, stronger, quicker, but no one was going to outwork me. Dicky was just the opposite, getting by on physical tools most fighters could only imagine. Even when he was all banged up, he was a formidable sparring partner. Dicky had that gift, and he still has it to this day, at fifty-four years of age. He still comes down to the gym and gets in the ring. He'll spar with guys three decades younger, and he'll give them all they can handle. I've seen it. He feints and moves, flicks off combinations, and generally frustrates the hell out of kids half his age. It's remarkable.

And maybe a little unfair. But that's the way it goes. Hell, I don't spar at all anymore, because of my concussions. I can't even think about putting on headgear and getting in the ring with another man. How ironic is that? I'm the one with the brain issues, and my brother, who did all the drugs and alcohol, can still get in there and spar.

God must have a sense of humor.

Anyway, Dicky came right back to the gym and we picked up where we left off. We trained at that time primarily at the West End Gym, where Arthur Ramalho was still in charge. I guess some things never change, including Dicky's generally irascible nature when it came to running a camp. You see, a trainer isn't just a trainer. He's the guy who calls the shots on any number of subjects; it's not unusual for a trainer to butt heads with a manager or promoter, and that happened almost right away with Dicky and Sal LoNano. I figured Sal had done all right by me on this go-around, and I knew I wanted Dicky back in my corner, so I tried to play peacemaker between the two of them. It wasn't easy, though. Sal was protective of his turf—his investment (that would be me). He'd put a lot of time and effort into helping me rebuild my career, and I think he was rightfully worried that Dicky would come along and take over everything. And Dicky? Well, it wasn't so much that he didn't like Sal; he was just skeptical of Sal's motives and abilities (particularly when it came to finances). Maybe that had something to do with Sal's relationship with my father, or the fact that Sal had basically run Mickey O'Keefe out of camp. I can't say for sure. But Dicky and Sal didn't see eye to eye on much. They'd bicker and argue, and I'd end up getting in the middle.

"Guys, let's stay on the same page here," I'd say. "We all want the same thing, right?"

From a fighter's standpoint, I couldn't have been happier to have Dicky back in the gym. Don't get me wrong. Mickey O'Keefe had been great. I love the guy. Always will. He was there for me in ways big and small, both in the ring and in my personal life, and I'll always owe him for that. But Dicky and I have a connection that goes beyond what a boxer and trainer typically experience. We're blood. I wasn't sure at first how our relationship would unfold once we got in the gym. A lot of time had passed, and a lot of things had changed. But once we started working out, we fell back into the comfort of an old routine—Dicky holding the mitts, directing sparring sessions, understanding what I needed almost as well as I understood it myself.

We clicked . . . just like in the old days.

Only now, Dicky was clean and clearheaded. I didn't have to worry about whether he'd show up on time, or whether he'd been out drinking all night. I didn't have to worry about anything—other than trying to become the best fighter possible.

In order for that to happen, though, we had to confront the physical limitations presented by my weakened right hand. Rest and rehab was no longer a sufficiently effective formula. Forget about winning a world championship; with my hand the way it felt, I couldn't even rip into a heavy bag. So, with nothing to lose, I went to see a guy who was supposed to be one of the top orthopedic surgeons in New England, Dr. Steven Margles, who was affiliated with the Lahey Clinic in Burlington, Massachusetts. He took a bunch of X-rays, then some more detailed scans, and proceeded to tell me what I already knew—that my hand was a fuckin' mess.

The problems, of course, had started with that incident at the Cosmo, so many years earlier. A normal person probably would have healed up just fine and the hand would have served him well pushing pencils or tapping a keyboard or conducting sales presentations or whatever the hell it is people do when they put on a suit and tie and work in an office. I was a boxer, so the hand never got a chance to properly heal. Repeated trauma—round after round, year after year—had left me with a severely arthritic right hand. Given my chosen profession, there was only one option: surgery.

"Without it," Dr. Margles explained, "I think it's very unlikely that you'll ever be able to fight again. Not without a lot of pain."

"And if I have the surgery?"

He smiled reassuringly.

"Good as new."

I trusted Dr. Margles completely, even though the procedure sounded kind of grisly and complicated, involving lots of cutting and scraping and transplanting. The idea, the doc explained, was to smooth out the rough patches in the damaged section of my hand, and then surgically implant a piece of healthy bone to fill in the resulting gaps. I would donate my own tissue—harvested from my pelvis (which I've since learned is comprised of the strongest bones in the human body), since that yielded the best possible outcome.

Modern orthopedic surgery is an amazing thing, the way these guys take people apart and put them back together again, in better working order. And they do it in a matter of just a few short hours. My procedure involved incisions in my hand and hip. Two separate surgical sites, a lot of hardware, a fair amount of blood and a variety of anesthetic drugs. And yet, the procedure was performed on an outpatient basis—I went into the clinic first thing in the morning, went home that night. The worst part, for me, was not the postsurgical pain, but the nausea associated with general anesthesia. I remember being awake when they first started the surgery, and then they gave me something to knock me out. For whatever reason (my stubborn nature, probably), I fought the drugs, so they had to give me additional medication to keep me under. And that made me sick as a dog. I'd have been home by late afternoon if I hadn't been vomiting so badly. I've never been so sick in my life.

Since then I've had a few procedures. Each time the docs have prescribed a motion sickness patch to combat postsurgical nausea. Works like a charm.

Other than the brutal hangover, my surgery was uneventful. I just wish I'd known it was an option years earlier. Turns out it's a fairly common procedure for boxers. Our hands take a beating; sometimes you have to go in and clean up the mess. Within three or four months I felt better than I had felt since the earliest days of my professional career. Although there was some natural stiffening and pain, and scar tissue that had to be broken down, I knew pretty quickly that I'd made the right decision. The pain that comes with rehab following an injury is very different from the pain of the injury itself. It's "good pain," if there is such a thing.

On St. Patrick's Day, 1999, I returned to the ring with a surgically repaired right hand and with Dicky in my corner for the first time in five years. My opponent was a kid named Jose Luis Mendez, a club fighter from Providence who, let's face it, probably shouldn't have even been in the ring with me. He'd won only three of fourteen fights, and had faced no one of any note. But what the hell? It wasn't like I was ready to fight Oscar De La Hoya. Or even Zab Judah, for that matter. I just wanted, and needed, an opportunity to test my new right hand and regain some confidence in the ring. So, for three rounds, I pushed Mendez around, worked on timing and combination, and then put him down for the count.

A successful comeback, all the way around.

Or so it seemed.

Not long after the Mendez fight, my hand started hurting again. The first time I felt it, I was surprised. Then, as the pain persisted, depression kicked in.

Oh, crap . . . it didn't work!

So I went back to see Dr. Margles. There were more X-rays, more scans. As it turned out, I had experienced a fairly common complication: Some of the hardware that had been used to hold my new hand together was causing irritation and pain. No big deal, the doc explained. They would just remove one of the three screws in my hand. By comparison, it was a quick and uneventful surgical procedure. I was back in the gym within a month, and this time there was no pain whatsoever. Three months after that, on July 16, 1999, I scored a fifth-round technical knockout over Jermal Corbin at the Hampton Beach Casino. Actually, the fight ended between the fourth and fifth rounds, with Corbin on his stool, unable to continue. I'd hit that kid with everything I had for the better part of two rounds. Hit him with a half dozen of my best body punches, blows so solid you could hear the smack of leather against skin deep into the crowd; you could hear the guy grunt. But Corbin wouldn't go down. I knew I'd hit him hard; I knew I'd hurt him.

Sometimes it just takes a while for the will to fade.

––––––––––––––

The first time I saw Charlene Fleming, she was working behind the bar at Captain John's, a local watering hole frequented by many of my friends and relatives. I was between girlfriends at the time. Over the years I'd had a few relationships, some more serious than others. Most of them, believe it or not, had gotten along pretty well with my family, although that's no easy thing. My sisters and my mom could be highly judgmental and argumentative, and so they scared off a lot of women early in the process. I suppose it's somewhat normal for the women in a big family to be protective of the baby boy, but the Ward/Eklund girls sure carried things to an extreme, especially if they felt threatened in any way.

I actually got to know Charlene's brother, Kenny, before I ever met Charlene. He worked at Captain John's as well. But it was my father who first tried to hook me up with Charlene. Dad was a regular at Captain John's, and one day he told me about this young girl who had recently graduated from college and come back to Lowell. She was tending bar to help pay the bills while looking for other work.

"She's really pretty, Micky," Dad said. "Sweet kid, too. You should come on down and meet her."

This went on for a while, my father dropping hints, telling me about how he had been at Captain John's the night before, bragging on his son to the cute new bartender. Eventually I decided to stop by and check her out for myself. Now, you have to understand that I was a sporadic partier in those days. Most of the time, I barely drank at all and spent little time in any of the local bars. Sure, I'd go in after a fight, loosen up for a few days or a couple weeks, but then it was back to the gym. Long periods of time would pass between beers. But there were other times, during layoffs, when I'd hit it pretty hard.

On the night I first saw Charlene, I was in training for the Mendez fight, but I decided to break my self-imposed prohibition for an opportunity to introduce myself. Well, I ain't the smoothest talker in the world, especially when I'm completely sober, so it wasn't like I made the best first impression.

"Hey, I'm Micky," I said, leaning against the bar.

"Yeah? I'm Charlene," she replied, not breaking a smile. "What can I get you?"

"Um . . . just a Diet Pepsi, please."

That, believe it or not, was about the extent of our interaction the first few times I saw her at Captain John's. I'd sit there, practically mute, sipping on a soda, for a couple hours, while Charlene worked the bar with all the charm and energy of a pro. In some ways we were exact opposites. She was outspoken, funny . . . a ballbuster (which is a prerequisite for the job, come to think of it). And I was really laid-back and shy. Also, I was ten years older than Charlene. She was maybe twenty-three at the time, having just come back from the University of Rhode Island, which she attended on a track-and-field scholarship. At 5'9", she was an inch taller than me, with long legs, an incredibly taut, lean body, blond hair and perfect skin; she was also just about the most beautiful girl I'd ever seen.

I fell for her hard.

Unfortunately, Charlene did not fall for me. Not for a while, anyway. I heard from some people that she found me annoying.

"Annoying?!" I'd say. "How can I be annoying when I'm not even talking to her?"

Eventually it dawned on me that "annoying" might not have been the right word. "Creepy" might have been more appropriate. She was just being polite, apparently to avoid hurting the feelings of her new stalker.

The situation improved after the Mendez fight, when, with the aid of a social lubricant (two or three beers), I got up the nerve to carry on a real conversation with Charlene.

"You're a runner, huh?"

"High jumper, actually."

"Yeah, whatever. You did track-and-field, right? You and me should go on a run together sometime."

She shook her head.

"I don't run. I told you—I was a high jumper."

There was a pause as I tried to deal with this little setback.

"Okay, then how about we go for a walk on the boulevard?"

She smiled, ever so slightly.

"We'll see."

That's the way it started. Not nearly as romantic or dramatic, unfortunately, as it was portrayed in *The Fighter*. There was no big chivalrous moment, where I protected her honor by decking some loudmouthed bar patron. I'd long since given up on street fights by that point. Charlene knew nothing about me (other than what she'd heard from my father), and didn't give a rat's ass about boxing. To her, I was just another guy at the bar.

At least a month passed before I got that walk on the boulevard, time devoted to breaking down the pretty bartender by any means necessary. I'd go down to Captain John's all the time—five, six nights a week—and just hang out for hours, nursing a beer or a soda, trying to strike up a conversation. Like a schoolboy with an unbearable crush,

I just wanted to be near Charlene. I chased and chased, asking her the same thing over and over—*"Let's go for a walk . . . Let's go for a run . . . Let's go somewhere else and get a drink"*—until I aggravated the shit out of her and eventually wore her down to the point where for some reason she felt compelled to say . . .

"Yes."

What she didn't say, but probably felt, was *"Anything to get you to shut the hell up and leave me alone!"*

Our first date wasn't exactly a fairy tale, mainly because I screwed up so badly. You know that movie *Taxi Driver*, about a psychotic cabbie trying to clean up the streets of New York (okay, I'm simplifying, but bear with me). Well, in that film Robert De Niro's character has an unhealthy obsession with Cybill Shepherd, who is young and beautiful and smart . . . and way out of his league. Somehow, though, he convinces her to go out on a date. Only De Niro lives in a very small, scum-ridden world, and so he takes Shepherd to see the only kind of movie he knows: a porno flick. She's repulsed, of course, and things go rapidly downhill from there.

Hey, I ain't no Travis Bickle or anything, but I did kind of make a mess of things in the beginning by taking Charlene to a club in Lowell that had a well-deserved nasty reputation. We walked into this place, Charlene looking like a million bucks, as healthy as you'd expect a Division I high jumper to look, and all of a sudden we're surrounded by drunks and lowlifes, an assortment of people who appeared to have more than a passing acquaintance with both drugs and alcohol. Just a bad scene. And right away people started coming up to me, shaking my hand, asking me how I was doing, inquiring about Charlene, who was not impressed.

"So these are your friends?" she asked, a skeptical look on her face.

"Uh . . . Well . . . I know them. I don't know if you'd exactly call them friends."

"Yeah? What would you call them . . . exactly?"

I shrugged, laughed nervously.

"I don't know . . . They're just people."

The truth was a bit more complicated than that. The guy who owned the club was actually a friend of mine, and it had become a place I'd visit when I wanted to have more than just a beer or two; it was a favorite hangout of a lot of sketchy people, and Charlene made it clear right away that she didn't like the place, and didn't really understand why I liked it. What was I going to say? I didn't want her to know that I wasn't hanging out with the best people in the world; that while most of the time I was training and healthy and ambitious, there were other times when I fell back into old habits. And even when I wasn't misbehaving, sometimes I'd stop by the club to see these guys. They didn't always do the right thing, and maybe I should have been more careful about the company I kept, but I didn't hold it against them. That's just the way it was.

That first date very nearly became our last date, as well. I kept going to Captain John's, trying to talk with Charlene, but for the most part she would ignore me. It took a long time for her to get over the idea that I was the kind of guy you'd find at a club like that. Eventually, though, I wore her down again.

"One more chance, Charlene," I said. "Come on. We'll go someplace else. I promise."

We went out for dinner, walked around for a while, then went back to my house and watched TV.

And she never left.

When I think about it now, more than a dozen years later, I can't help but laugh. It's crazy the way I broke her down, how she thought I was so irritating, and yet here we are, still together (married since 2005). Lucky break for me, I can tell you that.

See, right before we met? I was dabbling with cocaine again. Not while training, but during time off. I remember going back to my little one-bedroom apartment one evening, and getting down on my hands and knees. I hadn't prayed in years, but this time I begged God for some guidance and mercy.

"Please put somebody in my life," I said. "Someone who will show me a better way . . . who ain't involved in all this bullshit, and get me away from this stuff that I'm doing to myself."

Yeah, I know, you shouldn't curse when you're talking to God, but he must not have minded. It was the message that mattered. Only a few days later I went to Captain John's for the very first time and met Charlene. Despite being a bartender—or maybe because of it—she was no fan of drunks. And she hated drugs of any kind, had no use for anyone who used, wouldn't tolerate it at all. So, once again, I stopped. Fell off the wagon once more the following year, and Charlene caught me doing it. You know what happened? She walked out on me, right on the spot. No questions, no debate. She was just gone. That was the final wake-up call for me. Our separation lasted about two months, during which I did everything I could to convince Charlene that I would never use cocaine or any other drug again. She came back, vowing angrily, and dead serious, to give me one more chance.

"Never again, Micky," she said. "Or we're done."

And that was it. I got straightened out in short order, and have never used coke again. I can't even think of doing it now, and in fact I can barely remember why I did it in the first place. It's a horrible, insidious drug, and I can certainly understand how it grabbed hold of Dicky and ruined his life. For reasons I'll never completely understand, I got lucky. I'm not much of a Catholic anymore, but I do believe that God put Charlene in my life for a reason, and that if it weren't for her, I might have continued to screw things up. I'm not saying we've had a storybook marriage. You grow up the way I grew up—in a house bursting at the seams, with people screaming at one another all the time, but loving one another, as well—and you abandon certain expectations. Like, for instance, the notion that marriage is one great big honeymoon. It's not. Marriage is mainly hard work and compromise.

Charlene and I have had our ups and downs, especially in the beginning. She drank, I drank . . . We drank together. We'd get in wicked fights. Never physical or anything, but, oh man, would we spar verbally. She'd leave, I'd leave. Whatever. We fought a lot. But now everything is great, and it's been great for a long time. Charlene and I never had any kids of our own, but she became like a second mother (and big sister) to my daughter, Kasie. It's funny—the first time I brought Charlene to meet Kasie, they didn't hit it off. My daughter was maybe eleven years old, and sometimes Charlene would spend the night. Before going to bed Kasie would approach us with a scowl.

"She'd better be sleeping on the couch."

So that was rough for a while, but eventually Charlene won her over, and they became great friends. I wish I could say the same of Charlene's relationship with the rest of my family, but that one followed a different trajectory, one that was very similar to the way it was depicted on film. In other words, it started out bad, got progressively worse and ultimately settled in at just plain awful.

There's no point in sugarcoating it: Charlene has never gotten along with my family, particularly my mother and sisters. They've never actually come to blows, but there have been moments where I thought it was likely to happen. They've had terrible arguments over the years, screaming at one another, calling one another names. To this day there's really no love lost. They're cordial—most of the time, anyway—and that's about it. (A notable exception is my sister Gail, who has always kind of liked Charlene, and who gets along great with her now.) I've never really understood the animosity. From the very beginning, Charlene was put on the defensive. She tried to be friendly, but was met mainly with disapproval and insults. They were always putting her down, trying to make her feel bad.

"Ah, she thinks she's hot shit because she's a college girl."

"Yeah, too good for us, I suppose. Fuck her!"

I'd hear this stuff and I'd be like, "Are you kidding me? Are we talking about the same person?"

It wasn't easy being my girlfriend. My family always felt a need to put down anyone I dated. I didn't get it. Some kind of maternal instinct, I guess, except it wasn't just my mother who did the bashing. My sisters were just as bad, if not worse.

"You know that chick you're seeing? She's a dyke, I hear."

"Nah, she ain't a dyke. She's a whore. Screwin' half of Lowell."

They were like an X-rated peanut gallery. I don't know how anyone could ever measure up. Most girls didn't even want to try. But Charlene was made of stronger stuff. She was smart and resilient, and more than capable of holding her own in an argument. I think she figured out early on that the anger had less to do with her than it did with insecurity on the part of my sisters. They didn't want an "outsider" in their family, and that's what Charlene was. Not just in the genetic sense, but in other ways, as well. Yeah, she was a local girl, as tough as any of my sisters (as foulmouthed, too, when circumstances dictated), but she'd gotten out for a while. The very fact that Charlene went to college made her worthy of distrust in the eyes of my family. I think they presumed she looked down on them, which just wasn't the case at all. Regardless, they tried to bully and frighten her, thinking she'd just run off and want nothing to do with me or my family.

They couldn't have been more wrong.

I got stuck in the middle of all this, naturally, and I was never very good at dealing with it. Years ago I gave up the role of peacemaker. I let them find their own levels of comfort. Quiet coexistence is the best we can hope for, and we've generally achieved that state. But it's not like we spend much time together anymore. There are very few big family gatherings. When your wife doesn't get along with your family, you sort of have to make a choice. I chose Charlene. Simple as that. I used to go over to the house all the time, and Charlene would come once in a while—she really did give it a serious effort. But they always had something to say about her. Dicky was different, of course. He didn't have a problem with Charlene; kind of got a kick out of her, in fact. Dicky admired her spunk, her tenacity, her sense of humor. The feeling, however, was not entirely mutual. Charlene thought Dicky was pretty sketchy—and with good reason, obviously. But they've always gotten along reasonably well.

I'd like to tell you there was a big happy ending, with everyone hanging out together, having dinner on Sunday afternoons. But that's a Hollywood ending, where you put a nice bow on things. Life isn't really like that. Life is a lot more complicated.

CHAPTER 12

Age is the enemy of all athletes. Time erodes skill, speed, strength. I don't care who you are; eventually the years catch up to you and things start to break down. The trick is to delay that process as long as possible, and to take advantage of the things age can offer. Experience, for example. Perspective.

And maturity.

Earlier in my career I couldn't seem to get over the big hurdles placed in my path. When faced with an opponent I simply had to beat— someone who stood between me and a championship opportunity—it seemed like I'd invariably find a way to lose. I had a reputation for toughness; I could take a punch. A lot of them, in fact. But the truth is, I lacked the mental toughness and focus required of a world champion. Not by much, mind you. But enough. I wasn't the strongest fighter; I wasn't the quickest or most talented. So I needed to wring every ounce of ability out of my body, and for some reason I couldn't quite do that when it mattered most.

Now, though, things were different.

On October 1, 1999, three days before my thirty-fourth birthday, I fought the most important match of my career. It was held at the Icenter in Salem, New Hampshire, in front of a relatively small but enthusiastic crowd. ESPN broadcast the fight (my twenty-fourth on the network). My opponent was Reggie Green, one of the top contenders in the light welterweight division. Just six months earlier Reggie had lost by majority decision to WBA titleholder Sharmba Mitchell. Really, though, he hadn't lost at all. One judge awarded the decision to Mitchell; another scored the fight in favor of Green. The third scored it even. So, basically, the two men had fought to a draw, but a champ doesn't lose his belt when that happens. You want his title? Then you have to beat him. But Mitchell had come tantalizingly close—closer than I had ever come, anyway. So I knew I had my work cut out for me. I also understood what went unspoken: This would probably be the last chance to prove myself. I was running out of time to demonstrate that I deserved to be among the best fighters in my division; that I deserved a world title shot and the financial rewards that went with it.

I was promised roughly twenty-five thousand dollars for the Green fight, which was fine. Enough to pay the bills for a while and allow me to keep training more or less full-time. But I knew I had to beat him. There was no margin for error. Earlier in my career I would hear the promises—"Just beat this one guy and the big fight is right around the corner"—and I'd stumble. I don't know why. The pressure, maybe, or the frustration over never getting a taste of the big-time. Or maybe I just wasn't good enough. Who knows? For some reason, I felt calm and confident this time around. I welcomed the challenge, and all that went with it. I knew in my heart that if I couldn't beat Reggie Green, it was probably time to hang up the gloves. Not because he wasn't a worthy opponent, but for precisely the opposite reason. He was a legitimate contender, a guy who had nearly become world champion.

It was time to show I could beat a guy like that.

Reggie was a very dangerous fighter—a counterpuncher like Zab Judah. Unlike Judah, though, he wasn't opposed to mixing it up in close quarters. Dicky and I had done our homework, and we knew that Green wasn't likely to run and hide. The guy didn't have a big, heavy punch, so it probably would have benefited him to stay on his bicycle, force me to try to cut down the ring. But I didn't think he would do that. I figured he'd stick and move, stick and move, and eventually give me a chance to work his body inside. And I was right. From the opening bell, Green appeared almost eager to fight, rather than simply box.

The first two rounds were mostly uneventful as we tried to feel each other out a bit. Then, with less than twenty seconds remaining in the third, Reggie caught me with a nasty left hook. I've watched tape of that fight, and I can't believe how open I was. I tossed off a right coming out of a crouch, and left myself completely exposed. Reggie jumped into the punch with everything he had and caught me flush on the face, splitting my lip wide open in the process. I fell back into the ropes and tried to recover. I was lucky. The punch came in late in the round and caught me on the mouth rather than the chin. While it looked bad—blood streaming down my jaw and onto my chest—it could have been worse. Yeah, the punch did some damage—in fact, I don't know if I've ever been hit harder—but had it landed a couple inches lower, right on the chin, it might have put me down and out. It was nearly a perfect blow.

As it was, I staggered back to my corner, where Dicky and Al Gavin, my cut man, were waiting.

To be honest with you, I don't even recall what they said. I remember Dicky talking calmly, trying to reassure me, and I remember Al sticking his fingers in my mouth and trying to piece together my shredded lower lip. It was a massive cut, big enough for Al to insert two fingers at once; the kind of cut that, when it occurs anywhere else on the face, is enough to stop a fight. And if it had gotten any worse, it might have stopped this one.

At the start of the fourth round I was still practically unconscious. Dicky had to pick me up off the stool, shake my arms out, and give me a little shove toward the center of the ring. If he hadn't supported me for a moment, I might have fallen right down. I wobbled to the middle of the ring, where Green was waiting. Surprisingly, though, he didn't lunge at me. That was a tactical error. For whatever reason—fatigue, uncertainty—Reggie fought conservatively in that round, and in subsequent rounds. He piled up the points, of course, and I fell far behind on the scorecards. But I didn't have much choice; it took that long to regain my composure, to get over the nausea I felt from swallowing so much blood, and to be capable of thinking clearly and executing a fight plan.

Simply put, I was in survival mode.

I lost a lot of blood throughout that fight, and not just from the cut in my lip. In the seventh round Reggie opened a cut on my cheekbone, as well—a cut that would later require seven stitches to repair. I was swollen and sore. I looked and felt like complete shit.

Thank God for Al Gavin. That man was nothing less than a miracle worker. He stopped the bleeding between rounds, reduced the swelling to a manageable degree. You see a cut man in the corner sometimes and you wonder what the hell he's doing, and whether he really serves a vital role. In this case (and in others), Al was indispensable. If not for his steady hand and bag full of tricks, I'm sure I would have lost the Green fight. Al was one of the very best in the business, had been since the 1950s. Not only was he a magician with cuts and bruises, but he was like a ringside psychologist as well. I always felt safe with Al in the corner. He was the only person I knew who could keep Dicky calm. Dicky had a tendency to get all worked up during my fights, which sometimes had exactly the opposite effect than he intended.

"Break him down! For Christ's fuckin' sake! Fight smart, will ya?!"

That would be Dicky in the heat of battle.

But Al was a man of wisdom and patience, quietly going about his business.

"You'll be fine, Micky," he said, poking his fingers into the cut in my mouth. "This is no big deal."

I felt so comfortable with Al in my corner, so at ease. He could handle any emergency.

It wasn't until the seventh or eighth round that I began to feel strong again. Through the last three rounds the fight was a real battle, with the two of us trading shots inside. I felt like I was getting the best of him, but I knew there was no way I was going to win a decision; I'd forfeited too many early rounds. When I came out for the tenth and final round, I realized I needed a knockout. Anything less and I'd lose the fight. And maybe my career.

We touched gloves and engaged. I threw everything I had at Reggie right from the start of the round, and with about a minute remaining I sensed he was exhausted to the point of vulnerability. A left hook sent him wobbling into the ropes. He staggered out to the center of the ring, where we traded blows for a few seconds. Then a strange thing happened. Reggie dropped his guard. He was unprotected, apparently too fatigued to even raise his hands above his waist. So there he was, standing right in front of me, leaning at a 45-degree angle, almost asking me to hit him on the chin. I was equally tired, so the first few punches missed their mark. Then I landed a right to the head. And a left. Three or four consecutive punches found their mark. They weren't sufficient to put Green down, but close enough. Just as referee Norm Bellieux stepped in to stop the fight, I uncorked a left hook that caught Reggie on the chin and drove him into the canvas. He bounced up quickly, but by that point it didn't matter. The fight had been stopped.

Both the ESPN broadcast crew and a few people who wrote about the fight later suggested that the ring official had acted prematurely, and that I'd thrown a punch while he tried to separate us. Bullshit. That's part of boxing. You keep punching until they tell you to stop. I'd already begun throwing that hook before Bellieux stepped between us. It was simply unfortunate timing. He was going to stop the fight anyway. So I make no apologies for that; and if I'd been on the receiving end of the exchange, I'd have expected exactly the same of Reggie Green.

Afterward, Reggie would offer a fighter's compliment, saying he'd never been hit harder or more consistently. I could have said the same thing. I mean, I won that fight, but if you'd seen me in the emergency room afterward, getting stitched up, my mouth so sore that I couldn't even talk, you'd have thought I was the loser. I can still feel the needles going into my face, in and around my lip, one after another, as they prepared to close the cut. Sal LoNano's son, Frankie, drove me to the hospital and sat with me while the docs pieced me together. I'd taken stitches before, of course, but that time . . . oh, man, it was nasty. And it went on and on. More than two dozen in all.

I couldn't eat normally or even give my wife a kiss for a couple weeks, but that seemed a small price to pay. For years I'd heard so many promises, seen so many plans unravel. After a while I had stopped listening.

Now, finally, I'd held up my end of the bargain. I'd beaten a top-five contender on national television. It had been an impressive, entertaining fight.

Better days were ahead.

In January of 2000 I was offered a six-figure payday to fight Shea Neary for the World Boxing Union light welterweight championship. Now, I understood, of course, that the WBU was not one of the three big organizing bodies in professional boxing. It was more like fourth or fifth down the ladder. Still, it was a chance to fight for a world title, and to be paid the kind of money I thought I deserved. It was validation after many years of struggle.

We took the fight with little negotiation. I wanted it, felt like I could beat Neary, and was prepared to go anywhere to meet him. That was a good thing, since the fight would be held in his hometown: London. Neary was a Brit, but, like me, he was of Irish ancestry. I was "Irish" Micky Ward. He was the "Shamrock Express." We were two hard-throwing white guys in a sport dominated by quick, athletic kids of African-American and Hispanic lineage.

An easy sell for HBO, which had agreed to broadcast the fight.

Neary was an undefeated champion, and I appreciated his camp giving me an opportunity to meet him in the ring. To be perfectly blunt, though, I didn't think it was the shrewdest move on their part. Neary was a banger, like me, and historically speaking, I'd done well against that type of fighter. I liked mixing it up inside; I was willing to absorb some damage in order to win a fight. Quicker guys—pure boxers—had always given me trouble. If I were Neary, I might have waited for a bigger paycheck against another world champion. But maybe there was no such fight at that time. Or, perhaps, he simply liked his chances against me.

I knew better. Dicky and I watched a bunch of Neary's fights on videotape, and after only a couple of them, I turned to Dicky.

"I'm going to beat this guy."

He smiled and nodded.

"Fuckin' right, you are. Guy's made for you."

I'm almost reluctant to write these words, because I've never been the type to brag or to take an opponent lightly, or to predict victory. Sure, I always went into the ring confident that I had prepared well and was capable of winning. Never, though, had I predicted victory, not even to myself or the guys in my camp. But I did for this one. I wasn't a tape watcher, either. Just this once, though, I felt like it was prudent to do some homework in addition to training. Neary had never fought outside the United Kingdom; I didn't know a lot about him or the twenty-two people he had beaten. I suspected, looking at his record, that he hadn't seen the kind of competition I'd faced. He didn't know what it was like to have his face cut up by Reggie Green, or to chase Zab Judah for ten rounds. Far as I could tell, the best fighter Neary had seen was Darryl Tyson, and that had been almost four years earlier. I'd made a career out of going nose to nose with world-class fighters like Harold Brazier and Frankie Warren, some of the toughest sons of bitches around. I'd been through so much in my life and career. I knew I had more experience than this kid. I knew I'd felt more pain.

I just knew.

Don't get me wrong—I wasn't cocky. I worked incredibly hard in the months leading up to the Neary fight, mostly at the West End Gym, with Dicky running camp. We brought in a bunch of different sparring partners, including Kippy Diggs, a former NABF champ from the Cape, and Jimmy Lange, who'd recently made a name for himself as one of the stars of Sylvester Stallone's reality television show *The Contender*. Jimmy was tall for a welterweight, nearly six feet, with good, quick hands—perfect for sparring. Dicky got in the ring with me, too, and believe it or not the old guy could still get the job done. By that point I was strong enough to hurt Dicky—if I could catch him, which was no easy task.

Anyway, by the time we left for London, about a week before the fight, I was brimming with confidence. It was the first and only time I ever went into a fight with a bit of an attitude. I didn't even mind the fact that we were going overseas to fight, which always presents a host of potential problems, from culture shock to jet lag to food poisoning. I was excited, and I couldn't wait to get into the ring.

It wasn't like I was a seasoned traveler, either. I'd been to Europe only once in my life, in 1999, when I worked briefly as a sparring partner for Thomas Damgaard in Copenhagen. Nevertheless, I arrived in England with a chip on my shoulder. Neary was a heavy favorite over there, naturally, and it seemed like every time I heard someone mentioning the fight, it was as if the outcome was a foregone conclusion.

"Bloody bastard's gonna get killed."

"Shea's gonna knock that Yank the fuck out!"

I did very little press in advance of the fight, tried to keep to myself. When I'd hear that crap, or read it in the newspaper, I'd just smile.

You'll see . . .

Neary showed up for the weigh-in looking like someone who had been living in the wilderness: scruffy beard, unkempt hair, a snarl on his face. He had a reputation for training in a very Spartan manner: wouldn't sleep on the bed, wouldn't watch television, would eat out of a can. Meanwhile, there I was. I had my wife with me, sleeping in the same bed. I couldn't have been more relaxed.

A word about that whole abstinence thing that is so much a part of boxing mythology. Some people think sex saps your strength, and so they abstain in the days leading up to a fight. I don't believe in that. I think it's important to simply adhere to whatever routine makes you comfortable. If you have sex regularly, during your training, sparring, running, whatever, and then you have sex right before a fight, it's not going to affect you. Now, if you don't have sex for a while, and all of a sudden you have sex the night before a fight . . . well, that's different. That'll drain you. But if it's a daily thing, it won't matter. Other people say you need to be angry and pissed off, and that living like a monk naturally encourages an accumulation of testosterone and, consequently, hostility.

Really?

I don't need to be pissed off before a fight. Not when I've got some guy trying to hit me in the face; that's all the motivation I need.

To each his own, I guess. Neary obviously believed that the more hardship he endured while training, the more rugged he'd be; the more fearsome and intimidating. It's all mental gamesmanship, and I sort of understand it. I just don't think it's necessary. At the weigh-in Neary looked at me like he wanted to kill me. He looked like a mean prick. But you know what? I think it was all an act. From what I heard, he was actually a nice kid. I never really got to know him, didn't even get to shake his hand afterward, but I heard later that he's really a decent guy. He just didn't want me to know it.

There were more than eleven thousand fans in Olympia National Hall on fight night, and I don't think more than a few dozen were rooting for me. It was the most antagonistic, partisan crowd I'd ever faced. I was accustomed to fighting in New England, where everyone rooted for me; or in Atlantic City, where I could count on support from at least half the crowd. Now, though, I was a continent away, on someone else's turf. These were Neary's people, and they let me know it.

In keeping with tradition, I entered the ring first. I tried to stay loose, keep my sweat going as I waited for Neary, who made a long, dramatic entrance, while an Irish Rovers tune played over the sound system and the crowd went nuts. I'm usually pretty calm in the ring; I think about my fight plan, the strategy and science of it all. I don't like getting so agitated that I lose concentration. You need a certain amount of adrenaline flowing through your body, obviously, but you don't want to be so jacked up that you do something stupid. Now, though, I was having trouble staying relaxed. I was nervous, anxious, eager to get it on. The fact that Neary tried to intimidate me only made things worse.

After the introductions, we moved to the center of the ring to hear the traditional prefight instructions from the ring official, Mickey Vann:

"Neutral corner . . . Follow my instructions . . . Protect yourself at all times . . . Good luck . . ." Blah-blah-blah.

The usual stuff. To be honest, it didn't even register. What did get my attention was Neary's insistence on getting right in my face. I've never been that kind of fighter. You treat the other guy with respect and dignity—like a professional. Like a man who has a job to do. I had never—not once—stuck my nose into someone else's face before a fight. But that's what Neary did. He got right into me, tried to break me. The idea, of course, is that if you can make the other guy back down or turn away, then somehow you own him before the fight even starts. I didn't move. Just stood there and let our foreheads come together. Then our noses actually touched.

You motherfucker! After all I've been through . . . all the injuries and disappointments . . . all the cuts and stitches and personal turmoil . . . the years of waiting . . . After all that, you think you're going to scare me or intimidate me by sticking your nose in my face? Fuck you! Let's go, you son of a bitch!

You know, it's interesting: I faced so many great fighters, from Vince Phillips to Zab Judah to Arturo Gatti. They were the most respectful people. Good people. It was the guys I fought in the beginning, who weren't all that talented or accomplished, who tended to run their mouths or play mental games. People used to say Reggie Green was a punk or whatever. Wrong. He was a normal person, and if you treated him with respect, it was reciprocated. A professional understands that; a pretender doesn't. A lot of that nonsense you see in the heavyweight division—the trash talking and the bumping of foreheads—that's about the show more than anything else. It's the glamour division, with a history of theatrical behavior. Really, though, who the hell needs it? Not me, and I resented seeing that shit from Neary. He should have known better. What it actually told me was that the guy was scared, that he needed something extra to boost his confidence.

If his intent was to make me apprehensive, then the strategy backfired.

It helped, too, that Neary was the ideal opponent for someone like me. I knew he was a strong, stubborn fighter—like me—and that he'd almost certainly want to brawl in the middle of the ring. He wasn't quick enough to do anything else, really. My job was to beat him at his own game, and I was pretty sure I could do that.

Neary came out ferociously, throwing big, almost wild combinations, just as I anticipated. I stayed calm, kept my hands up, absorbed most of the blows with my gloves and flicked off a couple jabs just to disturb his rhythm. By the midway point of the round, Neary had repeatedly exposed himself, allowing me to catch him with a hard left hook to the body. As so many opponents had done before, he winced, let out an audible grunt and backed into the ropes. At that moment I knew how the fight would unfold. If I could just be patient, I could hurt him; eventually he would tire, and the accumulation of body shots would take their toll. I just had to be careful, stick to the fight plan. Late in the first round I landed an uppercut. His head snapped back. When the bell rang, I went to my corner, brimming with confidence.

"Great job," Dicky said. "Just keep moving. Don't be a target."

The second round was mine, as well. I dictated the action, stayed busy, tried to land a lot of punches. That was the plan, and there would be no deviation.

"If you can take him out early, take him out," Dicky said. "We want to knock him out. We don't want to go to no decision. All right? Keep your hands up. Let's go!"

A funny thing happened as the fight progressed: The crowd warmed to me. They didn't change allegiance or anything, but they did offer grudging respect. During introductions and early in the first round, I'd heard nothing but boos and whistles. By the third round, though, they seemed to be clapping for both of us, for the fight we were staging. Not all of them, of course, but some. Enough that I felt their energy.

And so did Neary.

He caught me good midway through the third round, rocked me with a right hand to the top of the head. I remember feeling pissed more than anything else. I'd let my guard down briefly, and Neary had seized the opportunity. That's the thing about fighting someone who likes to mix it up: They give you multiple chances to hurt them; they're also dangerous.

That punch stunned me, but it wasn't like the shot I took from Reggie Green. I backed into the ropes and covered up for the better part of thirty seconds, until my head began to clear. In the movie version of my life, that punch put me on the canvas; in reality, I remained on my feet. That was the only time in the entire fight that Neary hurt me. Shea had physical strength, but he was not an accurate puncher. I could see from the opening bell that he was throwing wide, so I could catch his punches with my gloves and counter quickly. He had strong legs and he pushed me around a little bit, because it was to his advantage to do that, but I knew he'd get tired; I knew he'd be susceptible to body shots later in the fight.

I just had to avoid making any more stupid mistakes.

"Hey!" Dicky yelled at me as I took a seat on my stool. "Keep your hands up. Don't take any unnecessary punches; you're not a punching bag. This guy, you can tear his head off with your hands up. Why are you letting him abuse you? You can destroy him with your hands up. All right?!"

Yeah, Dicky. All right.

I felt like the fight was going exactly the way I wanted through the next few rounds, like I was giving more than I was getting. I hurt Neary with body punches on several occasions, while not sustaining any serious damage myself. But enough of his punches were getting through, and the swelling on my face was nearly as bad as the swelling on his. I had to remind myself that I wasn't fighting at the Lowell Auditorium, or the Trump Plaza. I was far from home, facing a defending champion in front of eleven thousand of his countrymen. Nothing could be left to chance.

"Mick, you can't be lazy like that in there," Dicky said after the sixth round. "Putting your hands down."

Al Gavin, always the voice of reason, seconded Dicky's opinion, calmly adding, "You gotta remember, Micky, we're in his country."

"That's right," said Dicky. "We've got to take this with a knockout."

I knew they were right, but I didn't panic. I'd fought with urgency before, and I remained confident that eventually Neary would be susceptible to a thunderous body punch. I just had to keep working and waiting. And looking.

It happened in the eighth round, with about forty seconds remaining. I tapped to the head, and his hands went up. There it was: The ribs were exposed. A left hook took Neary's breath away; a second hurt even more. His hands fell instinctively to his side, leaving his head unprotected. I threw a left uppercut that landed flush on the chin. He tumbled backward to the canvas.

Knockdown.

The first of his career.

You can't question the guy's heart. He got up quickly, but I could see from the look on his face that he was still hurting, probably more from the body punches than the uppercut. There were only twenty seconds left in the round by the time Mickey Vann completed his standing eight count and instructed us to commence fighting. Not much time. I couldn't afford to let him escape the round. With the crowd roaring, I leaned right into him, throwing as many punches as I could, until the lactic acid pooled in my biceps and I felt like my arms were going to fall off.

Left hook to the head . . . right uppercut . . . left to the body . . . three more lefts.

Neary stumbled backward and fell to the floor again. This time Vann jumped in immediately and began waving his arms, before Neary had a chance to get up. That was it. The fight was over.

Dicky met me in the center of the ring and gave me a bear hug as I leapt into the air.

"You did it, Mick," he said. "You're the champ."

Then, for some reason I can't quite explain, I went to my corner, fell to one knee and prayed. Or gave thanks. Maybe both, I guess. As I stood up, I saw my friends and family making their way into the ring. It was a small entourage for this one—England is an expensive trip—just Dicky, Al Gavin, Sal LoNano, my father . . . and, of course, Charlene. In the middle of the postfight madness, she put her arms around me and kissed me on the lips. For a moment I thought I might cry. But I couldn't. I had to maintain my composure for the postfight interview with HBO, during which I was handed the championship belt. I'd won a bunch of trophies over the years, and more than a few belts, but this one meant more than any of the others.

So you can imagine my surprise and disappointment when some guy walked into my dressing room afterward, picked up the belt and began to walk out.

"Whoa, buddy," I shouted. "What the hell are you doing?"

"Sorry, Micky," he said. "Didn't they tell you? This one belongs to Shea. You'll get your belt in a week or so."

I had no idea that was the way things worked. When you win a championship, you're given a custom-made belt, and you get to keep it forever, even when you lose the title. The coronation you sometimes see in the ring moments after a fight is merely ceremonial: The former champion forfeits his title, but the belt he gives up only temporarily, just long enough for the new champion to try it on. Then the belt is returned, and the new champion awaits his model.

In my case the transition did not go smoothly. One week became two months. Eventually, though, I did get my belt. A friend of mine who is also a boxing judge picked it up during a European assignment and brought it back to me. I've still got it; it's the only world champion-ship belt I've ever won.

_____

The day after the fight we all flew home to Lowell, celebrating with a few beers along the way. We flew coach, of course, and somewhere over the Atlantic Ocean the flight crew announced that a new world cham-pion was on board. There was a burst of applause, and a bunch of folks joined in the celebration. I couldn't have planned it better. I'm a working-class Irish guy from Lowell. To me, this was better than sipping cham-pagne in a private jet.

A few days after I got home, right around St. Patrick's Day, a cer-emony was held in my honor at the State House in Boston; another was held in Lowell. People lined up to shake my hand, hundreds of them, some pretty emotional, telling me how much the title meant to them, and how proud of me they were for representing the Commonwealth.

Dicky was there, too, sharing in the victory, along with Charlene and the rest of my family. I'm not sure what was going through Dicky's head, whether he felt any regret or resentment, or merely pride and satisfaction. Some of the people who came down to congratulate me were the same ones who had talked shit about me over the years.

"He'll end up just like his brother: a loser."

I'd let it go then, and I let it go now. I've got big shoulders for a little guy. Dicky seemed pretty happy that day. He's not one to be jealous. I think he felt like he contributed to my accomplishment. Which he did. I suppose it may have bothered him on some level, because he could have done the same thing—and more—had he taken a left instead of a right all those years ago; had he chosen a different path. Maybe it bothered him that way. I don't know. It was hard to tell with Dicky sometimes exactly what was going through his mind.

I do know this: He never wished ill upon me, never wanted to see me fuck up the way he did, or get hurt in any way. Dicky was in my corner, both literally and figuratively. He was my big brother. Even though we were eight years apart, we were close. And he was a good kid. When he wasn't messed up, Dicky was the greatest brother you could hope for.

Hell of a trainer, too.

CHAPTER 13

Nothin' comes easy. The sooner you accept that, and learn to deal with it, the better equipped you are to get on with the business of life.

I'd been around long enough to know that even after beating Shea Neary, the big-money offers weren't going to automatically come rolling in. It was a nice victory, for a decent paycheck, and put me among the top fighters in my division. But that was a crowded and talented group, and for some reason I couldn't quite nudge my way to the front of the pack.

As sometimes happens in those types of situations, the people around me grew frustrated and began pointing fingers. Sal LoNano, as my manager, took heat from my family. They questioned his motives; they suggested he didn't have the juice to take me to the next level; they even questioned his integrity in regard to financial matters. All of which understandably offended Sal. No big deal, as far as I was concerned. It came with the job description. You want to be the manager, you have to accept responsibility for opportunities missed and seized. Even though I got frustrated, too, I had faith in Sal, thought he was doing the best that he could. Boxing is a callous business—fairness isn't part of the equation. Sure, it would have been great if the victory over Neary had led directly to, say, a seven-figure championship fight with someone like Kostya Tszyu, but that didn't happen. No point in blaming Sal or anyone else.

As always, there were only a couple options: retire . . . or keep fighting.

Only one of those made any sense. I was thirty-four years old at the time of the Neary fight. Not exactly a kid, by boxing standards. But I was in the best shape of my life, smarter and more savvy than most fighters, and young and healthy enough to keep plugging away a little bit longer. Besides, what else was I going to do? Go back to construction or working as a corrections officer? Nothing wrong with either of those jobs, but I wanted something more—a chance to provide some stability and financial security for my family. The only place I could do that was in the boxing ring.

So I took what was offered.

First up, in August of 2000, at Foxwoods Casino, was a fight against Antonio Diaz, who was nine years younger than me and had a 34–2 record. Tough fight on paper, even tougher in reality. Win that one, I was told, and maybe Kostya Tszyu would be next. Or Arturo Gatti.

Maybe.

I knew enough not to look ahead. Any fighter is dangerous, and Diaz was not just any fighter. The kid was a serious contender, and I gave him all the respect he deserved, trained like crazy in preparation for the fight. The result? Diaz won a unanimous decision. Less than three months later he fought Shane Mosley for the WBC welterweight championship. Didn't win, but at least he got a shot. Me? I'd taken two steps backward, and now had to prove myself all over again.

I didn't think the next fight would be any easier than the Diaz fight. My opponent, Steve Quinonez, was a skilled kid from California. For the first time in many years, though, I caught a break, hit the kid early with one of the best body shots of my entire career. A perfectly placed left hook to the liver with less than twenty seconds remaining in the first round took all the fight out of Quinonez and resulted in the first short night of work I'd enjoyed in more than four years. Accustomed to brawls that stretched out over eight to ten rounds, and required weeks if not months of recuperation, this one was almost like a gift, and I was happy to accept it. What I didn't know at the time was that it would be the last time in my career that I would fight anything less than an all-out war.

In July of 2001, at the Hampton Beach (New Hampshire) Casino, I went ten rounds with Emanuel Burton. If you had wandered in off the street that night, armed with little knowledge of boxing, you might have expected Burton to roll over. After all, the guy had a 24–17 record. How good a fighter could he possibly have been?

Right?

Wrong.

I knew better. Most of Burton's losses had come early in his career, when he had a reputation for being lackadaisical about training and preparation. Since then he'd adopted a more serious approach and slowly worked his way into the upper echelon of the light welterweight division. He was a strong and busy fighter. And don't forget—he was ten years younger than me. In other words, he was dangerous as hell. Burton was the best 24–17 boxer in the world, a designation that might sound silly . . . unless you saw the fight.

We went at each other for ten rounds. Like me, Burton was the kind of fighter who preferred to stay within inches of his opponent. He didn't run, didn't hide, just challenged you to bang with him. And that was what we did, hitting each other so often and so hard that the fight would later be named Fight of the Year by *Ring Magazine*. The difference, I think, was a body shot that put Burton on one knee in the ninth round. It was the lone knockdown of the fight and just enough to sway the decision in my favor.

Months passed while Sal and Al Valenti tried to make my next fight. Eventually, with the help of Lou DiBella, a promoter who had once been a vice president with HBO Sports, I was offered an opportunity to fight Jesse James Leija, a top contender with a record of 42–5–2. The good news was the size of the purse. Thanks mainly to HBO's broadcasting of the event, I would earn easily the biggest paycheck of my career: roughly a quarter of a million dollars. A victory, I was assured, would lead immediately to even bigger and better things.

The bad news was that the fight would be held in Leija's hometown of San Antonio, Texas.

Not that I was intimidated by going on the road. In some ways, it's harder to fight in your hometown. The noise and excitement of a partisan crowd can make you forget your game plan; you expend too much energy and adrenaline in the early rounds. That's not a concern when you're in the other guy's building, or at a neutral site. The downside, though, is that judges in boxing are not always fair and impartial. It's an imperfect system and you learn to deal with it. I knew when I fought Shea Neary that there was little chance of my winning by decision in London. I had to knock him out. The same was basically true of Jesse James Leija. No way I was going to beat that kid on the scorecards in his hometown. To be on the safe side, I had to put him away. Nothing could be left to chance.

The plan was simple: Get busy from the opening bell. Leija was known to be a bleeder. I figured if I got to him early and did some damage, maybe he'd start to panic and leave himself open. Or, even better, maybe the fight would be stopped. Regardless, I knew I had to be the aggressor. I couldn't afford to fall behind, or to let Leija think he had a chance of winning.

When I landed a hard left hook midway through the first round, and I saw the trickle of blood begin streaming down Leija's face, I couldn't help but feel confident. Here we were, not two minutes into the fight, and already I'd opened a cut over his right eyebrow. Things were looking good.

Or so I thought.

Imagine my shock when the ring official, Laurence Cole, stopped the action and stepped in to examine the cut, then proclaimed to the ringside judges that they were to ignore the impact of that cut, since it hadn't come as a result of a left hook.

"Accidental head butt!" he declared.

I was stunned. I mean, this was ridiculous. Sure, we were fighting in close proximity to each other, leaning on each other a bit between punches, but shit . . . our heads hadn't come close to colliding. I felt the punch that opened the cut above Leija's eye. I knew as soon as I had thrown it that it was a good, clean punch. You hit a bleeder with a hook to the eyebrow, and sometimes the tissue just pops right open. That's what had happened. There was no head butt. Absolutely not.

I was distracted for the remainder of the round, which was a flaw on my part. I allowed Leija to come back strong as the round ended, and when I got to the corner after the bell rang, I was met by both Dicky and Al Gavin. As he had in London, Al was quick to point out the obvious.

"This is Texas, Micky. You can't give him anything."

I'm not implying that Cole deliberately mishandled the fight; I simply think he saw something that hadn't occurred: a head butt. Regardless, I was in trouble. There are strict rules regarding cuts in boxing. An intentional head butt can lead to disqualification; an accidental head butt that results in a fight being stopped because of bleeding has different consequences. If the fight is stopped before the fourth round, the fight is declared a "no contest." If the fight is stopped after the fourth round, then the decision is determined by the judges' scorecards. Either way, this phantom head butt was bad news for me. I was a notoriously slow starter, almost always trailed after the first few rounds. Leija knew this and so did his corner. They knew that if they won the first few rounds, and the fight was stopped, Leija would be declared the winner.

I knew it, too. But I was so pissed at what had happened that I lost some of my focus. I shouldn't have let that happen, and I paid the price. After the fourth round Leija's corner began screaming that the cut above his eye was too severe for him to go on. The ringside physician was summoned, and after a brief consult with Cole, the fight was stopped. I threw my hands in the air in frustration and jumped off my stool.

I'm fucked!

And so I was. Two of the three judges had Leija ahead on points, so he was declared the winner by split decision. I don't blame the judges. The scoring, to that point, was reasonably accurate. But the simple fact of the matter is that it never should have gone to the scorecards in the first place. You can watch the replay of that fight a hundred times, and you won't see a head butt. Because it never happened. Maybe the fight should have been stopped; maybe not. That point is debatable. I've seen worse cuts, that's for sure. But if it was bad enough to cause a stoppage, then I should have won by technical knockout. I'd been screwed. There was no other way to look at it.

The only question that remained was: What next? I had made a promise to myself in the weeks leading up to the Leija fight: *If you lose, you walk away.* I meant it, too. I was thirty-six years old. Time was running out. I figured if I couldn't beat Jesse James Leija, it was time to hang up the gloves. Now, though, I had to rethink that decision. How could I quit after a fight like that? A fight, and decision, that represented everything that's wrong with boxing. I loved the sport too much, and I had too much respect for myself and the game, to retire with that bout as the final entry on my resume. At the same time, I wasn't willing to go back to the starting line at age thirty-six. Maybe, I thought, it wasn't up to me. The game has a way of weeding people out, of pushing them to the margins whether they are ready or not.

Soon enough, I figured, I'd find out whether I had anything left to give.

The fight I wanted—the one that had been held out so seductively in the past—was a matchup with Arturo Gatti. That was the money fight, and everyone knew it. It didn't matter that Arturo wasn't currently a world champion. He'd been one in the past (IBF super featherweight champ), and he remained one of the most marketable names in the sport. Like me, Gatti was a warrior—a fighter with a hard-earned reputation for putting on a good show, and for giving everything he had when he climbed into the ring. Anyone who knew anything about boxing understood that our styles had the potential to produce a memorable fight. It was an obvious and natural matchup, one boxing fans would love. Now, a lot of fights look good on paper but don't pan out in reality. But in this case . . . man, we were made for each other.

Thankfully, despite the debacle in San Antonio, Lou DiBella and HBO agreed. I hadn't even left the dressing room after the Leija fight when I first heard that the Gatti matchup was still a possibility. Within a few weeks, the deal had been made.

I knew Arturo only from the vantage point of a fan and fellow fighter. We'd never met, never spoken. I had seen him fight a number of times, always thought he was an exciting and gifted boxer. More than anything else, though, I admired the guy's strength of will. Arturo had terrific hand speed; he was an effective combination puncher with a surprisingly heavy fist. Mainly, though, he was a little guy with big balls. I could relate to that.

Who knows what shapes a person? How much of it is internal or chemical, and how much is the product of circumstance and surroundings. I grew up in a boxing town, in a big, brawling family, with an older brother who fought, and who introduced me to the sport. Arturo had been born in Italy and raised in Montreal, Canada. He'd started boxing right around the same time I had, at roughly seven years of age. Like me, he also had an older brother who was a fighter. And, like me, he'd turned professional at the age of nineteen, after realizing he'd never be an Olympian. Arturo's rise had been a little quicker than mine. Well, a lot quicker, actually. He won twenty-nine of his first thirty professional fights, picking up the USBA super featherweight title and the IBF super featherweight title along the way. But, like me, Arturo was entertaining in both victory and defeat. His loss to Ivan Robinson in a ten-round decision in 1998, for example, was named Fight of the Year by *Ring Magazine*.

I knew all of this about Arturo, admired his skills and accomplishments and attitude, but until recently had never thought there was much of a chance that we'd ever meet in the ring. He'd fought much of his career at roughly 130 pounds; I was 140. But Arturo was a few years younger than me, and as he matured, he naturally thickened. By 1999 Arturo had gained ten pounds from his earlier days and had begun fighting as a light welterweight. Sometimes a fighter is diminished when he moves up; he's bigger, but no stronger, and suddenly he starts losing to lesser opponents. Not so with Arturo. He won his first four fights as a light welterweight—very nearly killed Joey Gamache, who went into a coma after taking a beating from Gatti. Joey recovered, but never fought again. Arturo and his handlers took some criticism after that one; people said he was too big for Gamache, might have benefited from a questionable weigh-in and that they never should have been in the ring together.

Bullshit.

I mean, we all understand the risks. I honestly never asked Arturo about it, but I'm sure that while he felt bad for Joey, he didn't experience any guilt. This will probably sound kind of cold, but that's just boxing. Anything can happen in the ring, and we all know it. It's in the back of your mind at all times. Any fighter who's being honest will tell you that. It doesn't matter who you are fighting—a local guy with a mediocre record or a world champion. There's always the possibility that you could suffer life-altering damage. So do I think Arturo was saddened by what happened to Joey Gamache? Yeah, probably. But in this sport you can't think like that or you lose the edge.

The truth is, you'd rather it happen to the other guy.

About the only time Arturo slipped was when he agreed to fight Oscar De La Hoya at 147 pounds and got pretty badly beat up (the fight was stopped in the fifth round). That was March of 2001, around the same time I was trying to work my way back into contention. The loss to De La Hoya slowed Arturo's bid for another title shot, but he bounced back by knocking out Terron Millett in January of 2002, around the same time I lost to Jesse James Leija. I think the folks at HBO felt bad for me after what happened against Leija, and that may have contributed to my getting a makeup fight with Gatti. But let's be clear: HBO is a business, and they wouldn't have authorized or supported that fight unless they thought it was good for business.

With Arturo and me, they knew exactly what they were getting—two guys willing to put their bodies on the line.

By February we had a deal: roughly a half million dollars for Arturo, four hundred thousand for me. I didn't care that he was getting more than I was getting. He'd earned it. He'd been a three-time world champion, and I hadn't. He'd been a bigger draw. Anyway, four hundred grand was a pretty good piece of change. There would be more, too, if I could beat Gatti. That much had been made clear. So I was anything but bitter about the split. I was grateful. After so many years and so many fights, I was finally starting to make some decent money.

The fight was to be held on May 18, 2002, at Mohegan Sun, a Native American casino and resort in Uncasville, Connecticut. Close enough to Lowell that I would be assured of crowd support. I trained in Tewksbury, Massachusetts, just a few minutes from my home, with Dicky running the show. I was in great shape for that fight, felt like I was in my twenties again. I did all the usual stuff, with a few little wrinkles designed to improve my fitness, since we all expected a long and grueling fight. For example, when I sparred, I'd rest only thirty seconds between rounds. You get a one-minute break during a real fight, of course, but I figured that if I could get by on less rest during training, a full minute would feel practically like a vacation!

It helped, too, that I had a terrific sparring partner by the name of Peter Manfredo Jr. Peter was a big, strong kid from Providence, only twenty years old at the time, with an unbeaten record. The best thing about Peter, though, was that he was a junior middleweight, roughly 5'10", and weighing 154 pounds. He had good hands, lots of speed and stamina (like Arturo), but he was even bigger, which meant I had to work twice as hard to keep him off me, or to hurt him. Every sparring session with Peter was exhausting; he got me ready like you wouldn't believe.

In the weeks leading up to the Gatti fight I was excited more than anything else. I was never one of those fighters who withdrew completely during training, or tried to transform himself into some sort of psychopath. I'd get a bit quieter, edgy, but nothing crazy. It wasn't like you couldn't talk to me. Yeah, I might be a little snappy at home the last few days, but that's about it. Throughout training camp I'd be playing jokes on people, jumping out from behind walls, trying to scare them, keeping things light and fun. Then, the last few days, I'd get more serious. Don't get me wrong—I always took training seriously. Worked my ass off every time. But I saw no reason to act like an asshole just because I was preparing for a boxing match. It was a business. It was a job. I did it to the best of my ability and always tried to be a complete professional. But it wasn't my nature to suddenly become sullen and uncommunicative while preparing for a fight.

I was a pretty relaxed guy, and that didn't change much, not even when I was getting ready for the most important fight of my life. Just the opposite was true, in fact. I thought we had a solid fight plan, and we were putting in the necessary work. There was no point in being tense. For me, anyway, being loose was always the best strategy. I wanted to have fun. That might sound crazy—the notion of enjoying something as primitive and violent as boxing, but isn't that why you get into any sport in the first place? Because you enjoy it? Sure, there was a lot at stake in this fight. And, yes, at age thirty-six, with more than a hundred amateur and professional fights (and thousands of rounds of sparring) in my system, the odds of sustaining some sort of permanent damage were heightened against a fighter of Gatti's caliber. Nevertheless, I tried to hang on to some of that youthful innocence and playfulness.

Part of it, I think, was a natural defense mechanism, a way of lowering the tension and anxiety among those around me. My wife, for example, never quite grasped the idea that boxing could be anything other than madness and mayhem. She was always nervous during my fights. She'd support me, of course. She'd yell and scream, but she never liked it. Charlene didn't grow up in the sport, and she wasn't a glitzy girl, didn't crave the glamour or the spotlight. She was an accomplished athlete in her own right, so she understood and appreciated the training that went into preparing for a match. She understood competition and preparation. But the violence? The danger?

The paparazzi?

Charlene never really warmed to all that.

By the time the Gatti fight came around, she'd had nearly enough.

"You sure you want to do this?" she asked one day.

"Hon, it's what I've been working toward my whole life. Of course I want it."

She nodded. There was a look of resignation on her face. I wouldn't say she approved, but she understood. She'd been watching me fight for years, usually with her hands over her eyes, sometimes wandering in and out of the building, her anxiety growing with each passing round.

Although it was hard for her to be a boxer's wife (well, technically she wasn't my wife yet—we didn't marry until after I'd retired), she had learned to deal with it. She could do it one more time.

What she didn't know then (hell, I didn't know it myself) was that this wouldn't be the last fight. It would be merely the first part of one of boxing's most memorable trilogies.

Purely from the standpoint of athleticism and skill, Arturo was a better boxer than I was. He was quicker, more agile and capable of throwing combinations with greater speed and accuracy than I was. In short, he was a classic lightweight. By comparison, I was a banger—threw a lot of punches as quickly as possible, but I wasn't a dancer. A lot of people said I was a heavyweight in a light welterweight's body, and I guess that's a fair enough assessment. The thing is—and this is what I really admired about him—Arturo was like some freakish combination of all of these things. He could box and he could brawl. My hope was that he would choose primarily the latter tactic, even if it meant a long and bloody battle, because that was my best chance to win.

I need not have worried. Following a wordless meeting in the center of the ring, Arturo came right at me, bouncing off his stool at the sound of the opening bell. I think he wanted to mark his territory right away, impose his will. As if to say, "Hey, man, I'm here to fight, not mess around."

He caught me quickly, too, using a pair of combinations to open a small cut over my right eye. I actually think it was Arturo's game plan to box a little bit in the beginning, but I ended up getting him into my style of fighting. Arturo didn't seem to mind at all. He was an old-school fighter, never talked or anything. Just tried to take your head off. I was the same way, and we instinctively felt mutual respect—even as we tried to kill each other.

"You're all right," Al Gavin assured me in the corner between rounds, as he went to work on the cut. "It's on the outside."

I wasn't worried. Despite the trickle of blood, I felt strong and confident, and I knew Al was just about the best in the business. You never want to get cut that early in a fight, but I felt like I was in good hands.

As usual, though, my opponent got off to a quicker start. I fell behind in the first few rounds and knew I had to pick up the pace. Arturo was much stronger than I had anticipated—he was deceptively powerful for someone so lean and wiry. His legs were good, too. The guy obviously had put in the work prior to our fight. Like me, he was fit as hell. I knew I had to cut down the ring and make him stay inside—challenge him to a slugfest, with the expectation that he would be too proud and fearsome to back down.

"You gotta get to work," Dicky said. "You trained too hard to let this one get away from you. This guy's a good fighter, but don't show him too much respect."

Dicky was right. There's a fine line between showing an opponent respect and being so cautious that you fail to land enough punches to win the fight. Through the first three rounds Arturo had thrown (and landed) more than twice as many punches as I had; again, though, I wasn't overly concerned. It always took me a while to get warmed up, and a fighter as busy and skilled as Arturo was almost sure to get out to an early lead. By the fourth round we were both beginning to look banged up. My cheeks were swollen; blood continued to leak from above my right eye. Arturo's left eye was badly swollen (this happened to him in virtually every fight). Barring a knockout punch, I figured, this was going to be a long and painful fight.

It nearly ended in the very next round.

A little more than a minute into the fourth, I caught Arturo with a big right hand, snapped his neck right back. He dropped his shoulder and momentarily tried to shield himself with both gloves, a sure sign that he was hurt. He covered up briefly, and I jumped all over him. Most fighters would have needed the remainder of the round to recover from a punch like that—if they recovered at all. Not Arturo. He quickly shook it off and began fighting back.

The pace became almost frantic. I nailed him with a left; he responded with exactly the same punch. And I swear to God, I could hear a little voice in my head, the voice of a fight fan.

Oh, this is gonna be good!

But with just under thirty seconds left in the round, as we jostled near Gatti's corner, he unleashed a big, low left.

Really low.

I went down like I'd been kicked in the nuts, just knelt there for a second as the breath was sucked out of my lungs. Frank Cappuccino, the ring official, immediately signaled "low blow."

Now, here's the thing about boxing: Getting hit below the belt, while illegal, is actually pretty common. Very rarely is a low punch thrown intentionally, and even rarer is the low blow that does any significant damage. Usually you get caught on the hip, or on the protective cup; when that happens, the person who throws the punch often feels more pain than the guy on the receiving end. Sometimes, though, the cup moves around, leaving a very soft and vulnerable target. That's what happened in this case. One of my testicles had been slightly exposed, and when the punch landed it retreated immediately into my abdomen.

"Ohhhhhh. Motherfucker!"

I couldn't breathe, couldn't think, couldn't do much of anything except take a knee and wait for the pain to pass. Not that I would have quit. I had so much adrenaline going that I didn't care if my balls fell off.

"You've got five minutes to recover," Cappuccino said as the round came to an end. Arturo, who had been deducted a point, came over to meet me as I limped back to the corner. He put out a hand and we tapped gloves. Then he rubbed the back of my head.

"Sorry," he said.

But here's the thing: The timekeeper screwed up. The clock should have stopped immediately after the low blow, and not restarted until the end of my five-minute recovery. Instead, the clock continued to run for the final half minute of the round. Once the bell rang, I had only the usual one-minute rest period between rounds. So instead of a five-minute recovery, as stipulated by the rules, I was given only a minute and a half.

Dicky and Al protested loudly, but there was nothing that could be done. And, frankly, I didn't care.

"I'm all set . . . I want to go," I said as the break came to an end. "Okay?"

Dicky nodded and shoved the mouthpiece between my lips.

The next few rounds went by in a blur, as we took turns beating the crap out of each other. It's hard to explain how this felt. Arturo would throw six, seven, eight punches in a row, many of them finding their marks. Then, exhausted, maybe a little frustrated, he let his hands fall slightly.

My turn.

A dozen shots, all direct hits.

Why won't this guy go down?

Finally, in the waning seconds of the eighth round, I hurt him badly with a left hook to the jaw. Arturo stumbled backward into the corner and dropped his arms. I unloaded with everything I had, landing a combination to the head in the final seconds that had Arturo bending over, trying to cover up.

As the bell sounded, though, he was still standing. I took a seat in my corner. As Al cleaned my face and applied an endswell to my swollen right eye, I looked across the ring at Arturo.

I wonder if he's as tired as I am.

Dicky gave me a little tap on the cheek to get my attention, then leaned in and whispered into my ear.

"Time to put him away."

Good advice, but a lot easier in theory than in practice.

I went right after Arturo in the ninth round, chased him into the ropes and unloaded with combinations. Less than twenty seconds into the round, as he stumbled toward the center of the ring, I landed my money combination: tap to the head, big left hook to the body. There was a delayed reaction as Arturo wobbled backward and dropped to one knee. As I retreated to a neutral corner, I could see a look of utter anguish on his face. I'd seen that look before. It was the look of a man whose liver had just been rammed up into his ribs. A look that said, *"I'm all done."*

Watch a tape of HBO's broadcast of that fight.

"He's hurt!" Larry Merchant yells.

"This is it," Emanuel Steward adds. "He's not coming . . . It's not like a head punch."

No, it's not. It's much worse. Anytime I'd hit someone that hard, and that accurately, with a body punch, the fight had ended immediately thereafter. But there was Arturo, trying to fight through the pain. I watched this scene unfold with a mix of admiration and anxiety.

Don't get up . . . Don't get up.

As the count reached six, Arturo struggled to his feet.

Are you shittin' me?!

I knew then that I was not dealing with a normal human being. No one gets up from a punch like that. That's why I started calling Arturo "Jason," from the *Friday the 13th* movies: You couldn't kill the guy. He just kept coming back.

Despite being in excruciating pain, and vulnerable to a barrage of punches, Arturo stayed on his feet. For a while, anyway. I hammered him for the next thirty seconds, must have landed twenty punches, without Arturo even attempting to defend himself. He just staggered around the ring, taking one shot after another, trying unsuccessfully to cover up. But I couldn't knock him out. Midway through the round, with my arms burning from the accumulation of lactic acid, I took a brief break . . . and Arturo started fighting back. He didn't hurt me, but he was active as hell, which was not only astonishing under the circumstances, but made it even more likely that I might lose the fight if we went to the judges' scorecards. I had to get busy again.

With forty-five seconds left in the round I hurt him with a left hook to the head. Arturo stumbled back into the ropes as I peppered him with a series of combinations, throwing everything I could, trying to fight through the exhaustion. The punches landed sharply, and still the son of a bitch would not yield.

What neither one of us could have realized was that we were in the midst of what would come to be regarded as one of the greatest rounds of boxing in the history of the sport.

"Just imagine if you bought a ticket," Lampley yelled this time. Then, moments later, his excitement turned to concern.

"Stop it, Frank. You can stop it anytime."

That's the kind of fight it was. If you were a boxing fan, you had to love it. But you also had to wonder how anyone could take such abuse. And by "anyone," in this case, I mean Arturo. He tried to wrap me in a clinch with twenty seconds left, but Cappuccino pushed us apart.

"Fight on!"

And so we did, right up until the bell.

I look at the tape of that fight now and it's like, *Why didn't they stop the fight?* Years ago they let fights go all the time, well beyond any reasonable limit. By this time, though, caution was more common. I honestly think that if it had been anyone else, Cappuccino would have called it off. But Arturo had such a reputation for being a warrior, for being able to withstand punishment, that he was given more consideration than a typical fighter. I'm not saying it's right or wrong; I'm just saying that's what happened, although obviously I didn't ask the official. Was it a dangerous decision? Maybe. But in Arturo's defense, and in defense of Frank Cappuccino, when the tenth round began, Arturo was a new man. It just goes to show you what kind of recuperative powers he had.

"This guy is done," Al Gavin said between rounds. But he wasn't. Not even close.

Like I said . . . *Jason.*

When I stood for the start of the tenth round, I looked across the ring. Something was happening. Arturo was a mess, with both eyes now practically swollen shut. His corner was busy and crowded. As the bell rang, Buddy McGirt, Arturo's trainer, stood on the ring apron, motioning in some way. I later learned that he had considered stopping the fight after watching his fighter absorb so much punishment in the ninth round.

"That's it!" someone yelled. "Fight's over!"

I couldn't believe it. It seemed almost too good to be true. I threw a fist in the air. Dicky began to celebrate.

"Whoa, whoa!" Frank Cappuccino shouted, as he gestured for both of us to meet in the center of the ring. "Fight ain't over . . . Fight ain't over. No . . . last round!"

I sighed and gave Arturo a little tap on the back of the head as Cappuccino ordered us both to our respective corners. Arturo nodded.

Three more minutes . . .

It was like he wasn't even hurt. The guy started dancing around the ring, bicycling like it was the first round again. I tried chasing him, fired a few more body shots, but I had nothing left. At the end of the round, as the crowd stood and roared, we leaned against each other, supporting each other with our weight. I think if either one of us had simply taken a step back, the other person might have tumbled from sheer exhaustion. As the bell rang, signaling the end of the fight, we stood there for a moment, hands hanging at our sides, heads resting on each other's shoulders. Then we embraced. We didn't speak. Didn't say a word.

Didn't need to.

The decision was every bit as close as I figured it would be. One judge (Frank Lombardi) scored it a draw; the other two (Richard Flaherty and Steve Weisfeld) scored it narrowly in my favor. When the decision was announced—"Irish Micky Ward!"—I closed my eyes and threw both taped fists into the air, more out of relief than anything else.

Thank God. I finally won the big one.

That was my very first thought. Sure, I'd already won a world title, but this fight was bigger, more important, and ultimately more memorable. It had been a test of endurance and willpower. It put me in a different category.

Arturo and I met after the decision was announced. Again, we didn't really speak, just shook hands and nodded respectfully, and went our separate ways. I returned to my hotel room, where Dr. Steven Margles (same guy who had fixed my hand) cleaned me up and stitched me back together. The pain I felt after that fight was different from anything I'd known in the ring. Arturo hadn't landed a single punch that might have threatened consciousness. He didn't knock me down, didn't hurt me with a body punch. But the sheer volume of blows that he had thrown had left me looking bloated and bloody. And his ability to take everything I threw at him had completely sapped my energy. I felt like I'd run a marathon. I was completely spent.

Funny thing about being in a fight like that: You don't realize at the time just how special it is. I mean, I knew it was a war; and I could tell by the crowd response that it was an entertaining fight. But that's about it. You don't think about trying to make history when you're busy fighting for your survival. Pretty quickly, though, word got out.

Ward-Gatti, a lot of people suggested, was the fight of the year (it would later earn that honor from *Ring Magazine*).

Round nine was not just the best three minutes of boxing anyone would see that year, but maybe the round of the century.

To me it seemed almost too much to comprehend: to think that a scrawny little kid from Lowell, who no one expected to go anywhere—a kid who supposedly couldn't win the big one—was involved in something like that.

Fight of the year?

Round of the century?

I guess it just goes to show: Anything is possible, if you believe in yourself.

CHAPTER 14

Charlene paced around the living room, kneading her hands, shaking her head.

"I have to tell you, Micky. I'm not crazy about this one." She paused, gave me a hard look, the kind of look that can melt a man's heart. "I'm worried."

Yeah, no shit. Me, too.

Couldn't say that, of course. Some things you don't tell your wife. Like, when you've been offered a second fight against Arturo Gatti, just a few months after the two of you nearly killed each other in the first fight. Better to focus on the positive, rather than the negative.

"I'm going to make a lot of money, hon. This will change our lives."

Charlene might have been the only person I knew who didn't want to see a Gatti-Ward rematch. The buzz following our first fight was like nothing I'd experienced in the sport, and it had begun within seconds of the final bell, when HBO color commentator Larry Merchant stepped into the ring and brought us together for a postfight interview that had ended with him asking whether we might be interested in staging a sequel. Tough question when you're both battered and bruised and exhausted to the point of barely being able to speak.

For some reason, though, we shook hands and agreed that, yeah, a rematch wouldn't be such a bad idea.

Just like that, the wheels were in motion.

I was in a much better negotiating position this time around, and I didn't mind exercising some of that muscle. Not that I was a jerk about it or anything, but after so many years of struggle, and after fighting so many times without being adequately compensated, there was no way I was going to get back into the ring with Arturo, one of the toughest guys on Earth, for anything less than what I believed to be a fair payday. The number I had in mind: one million dollars.

Without going into details (because there's nothing more boring than a blow-by-blow account of a business deal), let's just say I got what I was asking for. And I have a lot of people to thank for it, primarily Lou DiBella and Sal LoNano. When negotiations got sticky and the deal nearly fell apart, it was suggested to me that I push Lou aside and work directly with Main Events, one of the sport's leading promoters. Everything would go smoothly, I was assured. Well, you know what? I didn't care about smooth. I cared about doing the right thing, which meant remaining loyal to Lou, without whom I would not have gotten the first Gatti fight.

You don't turn your back on someone like that. Not where I come from.

"We can get you the million," Sal had said to me. "If you're sure you want to do it."

He paused.

"Or . . ."

"Or what?"

"We can wait and see what else is out there."

I didn't think about it for long. There was no one else for me to fight. At that point, the notion of winning a world championship—even one of the Big Three world titles—was less important than earning long-term security for my family. A rematch with Gatti would do that. No other fight could.

"What am I gonna do—take three hundred grand for a title fight instead of a million for Arturo?" I said. "Don't make sense."

Sal shook his head. "No, it sure doesn't."

I won't lie. Money was the primary motivating factor. But it wasn't the only factor. Strange as it may sound, I wanted to fight Arturo again. See, I'm a fan, as well as a fighter, and after a little time had passed, and I'd thought about it . . . after I watched the tape of the fight and heard enough people talking about how special it was, I got excited about it, too. Our styles were so perfect for each other; a rematch would be great for the sport!

All I had to do was convince Charlene.

"You honestly think this is a good idea?" she asked.

Smart girl, putting it like that. "A good idea?" No, probably not.

"It's the right thing to do," I said, calmly sidestepping the question.

"Why? We don't need the money. We'll be fine."

She was right about that, too. But there was more at stake.

"I told Arturo that if we could work out a deal, I'd give him a rematch," I explained. "And I'm a man of my word. I don't have any choice."

She rolled her eyes.

Playing the manhood card again!

"Come on, Charlene," I said, taking her hand in mine. "We've come this far."

The rematch was held on November 23, 2002, at Boardwalk Hall in Atlantic City (in association with Bally's hotel and casino). I was thirty-seven years old, and finally hitting the big-time. Fighting on HBO again, this time for seven figures. About the only concession made by my camp was the venue. As the winner of the first fight, I might have been able to hold out for a fight closer to my home, which would have ensured more fan support on my behalf. Ultimately, though, Atlantic City seemed a better gamble (so to speak) for the promoters and for HBO, and I wasn't inclined to argue. The fact that Arturo lived in Jersey City didn't even bother me. I'd developed a pretty good following in Atlantic City as well. Fought there eighteen times in my career. Of course, it had been a while—more than ten years, in fact—but I figured people would remember and support me anyway. Mainly, I just figured Atlantic City was a good fight town and people would show up to watch a Gatti-Ward rematch. And that's pretty much what happened. Oh, don't get me wrong. Arturo was their boy and they rooted for him, but I felt like I had my share of supporters, too.

I trained hard for the second fight—every bit as hard as I had for the first one. I felt the same sense of urgency, the same hunger and desire. I was prepared for everything Arturo might throw at me; the fact that I'd already beaten him once, and had demonstrated that I could take his best punch, gave me confidence. In boxing, though, things don't always pan out the way you want them to, or the way you envision them.

Arturo's game plan was flawless; more important, it was flawlessly executed. As in the first fight, he and his handlers knew the best strategy was to keep some distance between us, to utilize Arturo's superior quickness and hand speed to create space; to fight selectively instead of simply wading in with his chin. I know how hard that must have been for a man like Arturo. I'm sure he wanted to meet me in the center of the ring and prove he was the better, stronger fighter, and not just the superior boxer. But that strategy had backfired the first time around, so he wisely adopted a different approach. He was in better shape than the first time we fought, and he was a more disciplined fighter.

That combination turned out to be more than I could handle.

The real trouble began in the third round. That was when I discovered that Arturo had more punching power than I'd realized. He may not have hurt me in the first fight, but he sure as hell hurt me this time. It happened with 2:20 left in the round, as we were separated from a clinch by referee Earl Morton. Each of us took a step back, and then waded in. As I moved forward and threw a sloppy left to his belly, Arturo wound up and unleashed a thunderous overhand right. My punch barely touched him, and in missing, I lost my balance momentarily and leaned forward, headfirst, just as Arturo's punch came crashing in.

The timing was absolutely perfect. Arturo's fist caught me right behind the left ear; not an illegal punch, but a damn near perfect one. There's a little ball of tissue and bone behind the ear that almost never gets hit. Good thing, too, because it's an incredibly sensitive area.

I'd never felt anything quite like it. Instantly I lost my equilibrium and felt a stinging pain shoot through my skull. After two drunken steps, with arms reaching out for help, I lurched into the corner and fell face-first into the turnbuckle and crumpled to the canvas. The crowd erupted. To that point there had been little action, with Arturo dancing and moving, and me trying vainly to catch him. Now I was in trouble.

"Are you all right?" Morton asked after finishing the mandatory eight count. I didn't respond at first, just focused on trying to clear the cobwebs, shaking my head, bouncing awkwardly from one foot to the other.

"Micky, are you okay?"

"I got punched in the ear," I mumbled, as if that mattered. Morton gave me a strange look, as if to say, *Who gives a shit? You ready to fight or not?*

I have no idea why I said that. Guess it just shows how disoriented I was. The referee would have been well within his rights to stop the fight right then and there. And if it had been anyone other than me and Arturo, he probably would have stopped it. But I think we'd proved something with the first fight.

"Let's box!" Morton instructed, as he motioned us to engage once again.

Arturo was on me in a heartbeat, flailing away, using everything he had to put me down and out.

Keep your hands up . . . Keep your hands up.

This was instinct, the product of dozens of fights and thousands of rounds of sparring. When you get hurt, you try to protect yourself and weather the storm. You hope the other guy gets too excited and wears himself out. If you can hang on for a minute or so, the fog usually lifts and you can resume fighting.

But that's a hell of a minute.

You'll sometimes hear the phrase "out on his feet" in reference to boxing, and wonder exactly what that means. Well, I found out in the third round, because I was as close to unconsciousness as you could possibly be without closing your eyes. Arturo battered me across the arms and shoulders. Punches tried to work their way through my mitts, battering my head and face. At one point Arturo backed me into the ropes, then took a breather. As he stepped back—for some reason that I can't possibly explain—I dropped my hands to my side and patted my own belly, almost antagonistically.

I ain't hurt!

Not true, of course. I think I was just trying to convince myself that everything would be okay, but I must have looked like a clown; it had to have been obvious that I was getting the shit kicked out of me. Arturo stared at me for a moment, with the bemused look of a predator about to devour a feisty prey. Then he fired off another cannon shot, a right hand that knocked me into the ropes and snapped my head back. It looked like a knockout punch, but here's the truth: That punch woke me up! No shit. I got knocked out cold, then got a wake-up call in the same round. I swear to God—that punch kept me upright. If Arturo had stepped back and moved, while I was against the ropes, I might have fallen flat on my face. Instead, he cracked me with a right, and I came back to life. Even landed a sharp left hook to the body in the last minute. Arturo curled up momentarily as my fist burrowed into his rib cage. But it wasn't quite hard enough, not quite low enough. The punch stunned Arturo, but not enough to put him down.

That was basically the story of the fight. Arturo hurt me badly in the third round, and I never got him back. In fact, on two or three separate occasions, he gave me a dose of my own medicine, hurting me with body punches. Each time it happened I kind of groaned a little, covered up and thought to myself, *Oh, you son of a bitch! That's my punch.*

Mainly, though, I think what happened in that fight was that Arturo was in fantastic physical shape, had a perfect fight plan, and he hurt me early. Though I stayed on my feet, I never fully recovered after the third round. Every time I felt like I was gaining some momentum, Arturo would throw a flurry of punches to the head, put me back on my heels, or land a stinging body shot. And all the while, he kept moving, dancing. I kept waiting for him to tire, but he didn't.

"You're going to win this fight," Al Gavin said to me after the eighth round. "You're in better shape than him."

That was Al—always the steady voice of reason. Dicky was less reassuring.

"Throw an uppercut when you come out! Right away!" he shouted. I nodded.

"Bend down . . . then do it! If you can't do it, if you're not up for it, then I'm gonna stop the fight!"

"Come on, Dicky . . ."

I know what he was doing: trying to pump me up and protect me. Desperate times call for desperate measures, right? I was way behind in the scoring, and we all knew it. What I needed was a ninth round like the one I'd put together in the first fight. But it wasn't to be. I kept trying to land something, trying to fight, trying to change the course of the bout. I always keep that mentality: *I'll catch him . . . I'll catch him.* Once you start saying, "Ah, shit, I'm losing," then it's all over. I'd pulled out a lot of fights in the last few rounds, despite falling way behind: Alfonso Sanchez, Reggie Green. I didn't see why this was any different.

Except, of course, that it was different. This time I was fighting Jason.

When the fight ended—after Arturo had earned a unanimous decision—we embraced. I congratulated him on a great effort. There were no excuses. He was the better man that night. I honestly thought in my heart that if I hadn't gotten knocked down in the third round, things might have been different. But I did get knocked down, and that's the way it goes.

In the ring afterward, I stood nearby as Arturo was interviewed. He was asked whether he was surprised I got up after the knockdown. Arturo laughed.

"No, I knew he'd get up. There aren't too many guys like Micky Ward around."

I joined the interview moments later, gave Arturo all the credit he deserved. Then came the question I expected from Larry Merchant.

"Micky, is this the last one . . . or are you going to fight one more fight?"

I shrugged. At that point I knew things were beyond my control.

"If we can get together again, I'll give it one more shot. If not . . . I don't know."

Larry turned to face Arturo.

"Do you think a third fight between you is warranted?"

Arturo smiled.

"Well, I have to thank God we're both healthy. He fought a great fight tonight. It's one-one now, so . . ."

He paused, nodded and smiled again.

"I wouldn't mind."

Boxing is, first and foremost, a business—in some ways it's among the bloodiest and most bloodthirsty of businesses. Sometimes, though, a few honorable men rise above the ugliness and greed and make it something special. Throughout my career I tried to be one of those people, and I was fortunate to encounter a few others along the way.

Arturo Gatti certainly belonged in that group. Within a few weeks it had become apparent that our rivalry would become a trilogy. I wanted a third fight, boxing fans wanted it, HBO wanted it. Most important of all, Arturo wanted it. Let's face it—without his cooperation, there wouldn't have been a third installment. I'm not saying Arturo was being charitable—a lot of money was thrown on the table for Gatti-Ward III—but it wasn't like the guy lacked options. I had given him a rematch, and now he was returning the favor. Years later, after we'd become close friends, Arturo told me that he had received other offers. Big fights for just as much money. Maybe even more money. World championship fights, at a time when Arturo didn't have a belt. But he'd given me his word, and you couldn't put a price on something like that. Not with a man like Arturo.

Did a third fight make sense?

Sure it did. We'd split the first two fights, given fans all they could expect from a boxing match. So why not do a third? I mean, aside from the obvious fact that each of us had absorbed an insane amount of punishment through the first twenty rounds, and figured to be hurt just as badly through the next ten. For me there was no bigger or better option. If I wanted to fight again, Arturo was the only viable candidate. But he had choices, opponents who would have put up less resistance. He made more than a million to fight me, probably could have made at least that much to fight Kostya Tszyu, who held the WBC, WBA and IBF titles at the time. I don't know whether he would have won those fights or not, but I doubt they would have been as grueling as our fights.

Equal or better pay . . . for less effort.

"No, thanks. I want Micky."

You've got to admire a man like that.

I received about seven hundred fifty thousand dollars for the third fight. Maybe I could have held out for more; I think Sal and Lou tried to make the case that Arturo and I should have been considered costars in this event, worthy of equal compensation. I didn't lose any sleep over it. Seven-fifty was pretty good, and would bring my take for the trilogy to more than two million dollars. Where else was I going to make that kind of money? (I earned every penny, though. Let's be clear about that. I mean, think of it this way: Would you go thirty rounds with Arturo Gatti for two million bucks? Didn't think so.)

Charlene was a tougher sell. She didn't want a third fight, didn't see any need for it.

"I don't think you can go through that again," she said. "I don't think I can go through it."

I understood her concern, but there was no way I could turn down the offer. We had unfinished business.

"Honey, I'm doing this," I said. "I know you don't like it, but I'm fighting. When this one is over, I'll retire. But I want to go out giving it my all."

She looked right through me.

"Didn't you give it your all last time?"

Damn good point.

"Really," I said. "One more fight. Then I'm all done. Promise."

I meant it, too, and just to make sure there was no confusion, I went public with the announcement. Win, lose or draw, I'd walk away after the third Gatti fight. I'd taken a lot of punches over the years, suffered numerous concussions and injuries. Recent scans hadn't shown any permanent brain damage, but I'd been around enough to know these things take time. I wanted to get out while I could still think straight.

The main problem with announcing your retirement before the fight is that people have a tendency to question your commitment. It's human nature, I guess. Been a long time since boxing was a winner-take-all proposition. You sign a deal, accept a certain fee and then you fight.

Your paycheck has nothing to do with the outcome of the match. Sure, it has an impact on the next fight, and your value as a commodity, but what if there is no next fight? What then? Where's the motivation to fight . . . to suffer? Some people thought I'd just take the money and run. Or walk. Why get beat up all over again? Why not just move around the ring, protect myself as much as possible and avoid any further damage?

If you thought that, you didn't know me. And you didn't know Arturo (although he had no intention of retiring). We would both fight our asses off. It wasn't just about the money. We were competitors . . . fighters. We were there to win.

I felt great going into the fight: no hand problems, no headaches, no vision or equilibrium issues. This would be my third meeting with Arturo in a span of just fourteen months, so it wasn't like there were any big surprises. With Dicky running camp, I trained with the same intensity I'd brought to the previous two fights. You have to give Dicky a lot of credit for the way he trained me during the last couple years of my career. He worked me hard every day, with a seriousness and intensity that he had sometimes lacked in the past. We ran together, sparred together, spent endless hours discussing strategy together.

Our game plan wasn't a lot different than it had been in the first two fights: Get in great shape and try to cut down the ring. If I let Arturo dictate the pace of the fight, I'd be in trouble. I couldn't let him run. I had to keep him in front of me, try to land as many body shots as possible and avoid getting hurt in the early rounds. When reporters asked what I expected from Arturo, I was cautious and respectful. He was the same way. I think everyone realized we had mutual respect for each other. There was no trash talking whatsoever. That had never been my style, of course, and it wasn't Arturo's, either. He said he felt confident that he would win the fight; I said I thought I'd win. But there was no bragging, no nonsense.

We both knew the third fight was going to be every bit as brutal as the first two had been. I figured I was assured of two things when the evening ended:

I'd get a nice paycheck.

I'd be going to the hospital.

I might win, I might lose, but either way it was going to be a long and difficult night. I wasn't apprehensive or anything about it, though. I'd gotten enough stitches in the past, broken enough bones, sustained enough concussions. A few more wouldn't matter. People would remember this fight. That's what I kept telling myself.

So do it right.

Everything about this fight was special. It felt bigger than either of the first two fights. The promoters expected so much interest they even expanded Boardwalk Hall to accommodate a crowd of fifteen thousand people (there actually was a little more than eleven thousand).

Think about that: more than eleven thousand fans! Arturo and I weren't heavyweights. We weren't even fighting for a championship (the ring announcer, Michael Buffer, introduced us by saying we were fighting for the "unofficial but undisputed blood and guts championship of the world"). We were just two relatively little guys willing to give everything we had. And that seemed to resonate with people.

I drove down to Atlantic City a couple days before the fight, to handle media obligations and get comfortable with my surroundings. At the weigh-in, a curious thing happened. They asked Arturo and me to pose for a photo, and when we looked at each other, trying to put on the tough-guy face boxers usually adopt for these occasions, we both started cracking up. I don't how to explain it, but there was something about Arturo that made me laugh. Through two fights we had developed a connection and a bond that could hardly be put into words. There was no animosity, no anger. I found it impossible to pretend that I hated Arturo—not even for a silly photo opportunity.

So there we were, the two hard-ass fighters, fists upraised, scowls melting away, filling the room with laughter. Where, in boxing, do you see something like that? You don't. It doesn't happen. I remember looking at Arturo as he cackled, and thinking, *Are we really going to fight each other? Because this is kind of weird.*

I'd never been through anything like it. I had never needed anger to prepare for a fight. My personality is such that I can be the nicest guy in the world outside the ring, but will try to take your head off once the bell rings. I'd be that way even in sparring sessions with Dicky, or with guys who were my friends. It wasn't personal. It was just the way I went about my business. I would do the same with Arturo and he would do the same with me. But here, in this moment, laughing like we were brothers, poking fun at the cliché of the prefight weigh-in, it seemed hard to believe that soon we'd be trying to rip each other apart. I mean, I genuinely liked the guy. And I know he liked me.

Maybe that's what made it so special.

I left my hotel room around six o'clock on the night of June 7, a few hours before the fight. Before leaving I gave Charlene a kiss and told her not to worry.

"It's almost over. This is the last time we'll go through it."

She smiled, nervously wished me luck.

"Give it your all," she said. "But be safe."

I nodded.

"I love you, hon. See you soon."

As I sat in my dressing room, getting my hands wrapped and going over the final fight plan one more time, I thought about how far I had come, and what an unlikely journey it had been. I wanted to go out a winner, to put a big fat exclamation mark on my career; mainly, though, I wanted my last fight to be memorable, to be worthy of the excitement it had generated.

There were five of us in the dressing room in the minutes leading up to the fight: me, Dicky, Sal LoNano, Al Gavin and my nephew Sean. Just before leaving we gathered in a small circle and said a brief prayer.

"Please, God, keep an eye on me and Arturo both," I said. "Make sure nobody gets hurt. And give me the strength to go out on my shield."

I did as I promised, going after Arturo from the very beginning, but the guy was even more elusive than he'd been in the previous fight. Maybe it had something to do with age. I was only a few months away from my thirty-eighth birthday now, and even though I'd trained incredibly hard and felt like I was in the best shape of my life (I weighed a solid 142 pounds, same as Arturo), I was giving up seven years to my opponent. Fact is, I was getting older and slower; at barely thirty years of age, Arturo was still getting stronger.

By the third round I'd fallen well behind. Arturo was fighting exactly as he had in our prior meeting, only with even greater confidence, throwing more punches and with better accuracy. I couldn't get close enough to work his body, couldn't get off a single damaging blow. For a few brief moments as I sat on my stool between rounds, I wondered if I'd even be able to keep it close. There is a reason, though, that boxing is among the most fascinating and unpredictable of sports. Everything can change in the blink of an eye.

Or in the time that it takes to throw a single punch.

It happened in the first thirty seconds of the fourth round. Arturo threw a hard left hook, just as I took a step backward and to the side. The punch went low, but instead of hitting me in the groin, it smacked into my hip bone. I barely felt it, but I could tell it had been a disastrous mistake for Arturo. He pulled back instantly and let his right arm hang at his side. A few seconds later, when he tried to throw a right to the body, he winced upon impact.

Holy shit . . . he broke his hand.

It was a freak injury, and I suppose if I'd been merely a fan sitting at home, watching the fight on HBO, I might have felt bad for Arturo. But I was in the ring with him. Accidents happen in boxing. You can get hurt in all kinds of weird ways. It had happened to me against Manny Castillo, when I ruptured a ligament in my thumb. I hadn't quit in that fight, and I knew Arturo wasn't about to quit in this one. His injury was unfortunate, but now it was just part of the game, something to be factored into my fight plan—like a cut above the eye or a broken nose.

"Come on, Mick," Dicky said after the fifth round. "Don't let a one-handed fighter beat you."

The one-handed fighter was still ahead on the scorecards, but I was starting to close the gap, despite having a pretty good slice over my left eye. Knowing that Arturo was unable to get much power behind his right hand gave me confidence, although I knew I had to be careful. By the end of the fifth round he'd started throwing his right hand again, testing his jab to see how much pain he could withstand. That made me believe he was okay, and I knew from experience that the longer the fight went on, the more likely he was to forget about the injury. Same thing had happened with my thumb: If you can hang in there till it goes numb, you can start using it again. The longer I waited, the more dangerous Arturo would become.

So I went after him aggressively, almost recklessly. With five seconds left in the sixth round I caught him with a hard left hook, then followed it up with a big overhand right—practically a haymaker. The punch landed on the top of Arturo's head and sent him instantly to the canvas. He bounced to his feet within seconds as the crowd went nuts and the bell sounded, signaling the end of the round.

It was important to jump on Arturo at the start of the seventh, to take advantage of whatever momentum I'd built. But the strangest thing happened. As I crossed the ring, bouncing from one foot to the other, my body went limp. It wasn't pain, really; it was complete and utter exhaustion. I shook out my arms, tried to coax them back to life; I rolled my shoulders.

Nothing.

I'd never felt anything like it. From one round to the next, I'd grown old. They say boxers age overnight, seemingly advancing a decade between fights. For me, personally? It happened between rounds, in a span of just three minutes.

The seventh round was frantic. Arturo, who had been such a quick and evasive target, suddenly stood in front of me, and we battled like we had in the first fight, throwing punches until we could barely lift our arms. I threw more than eighty punches, Arturo more than one hundred twenty. By this point you'd never have guessed that there was anything wrong with the guy's right hand. He was fighting at full strength.

I was running on fumes. But that wasn't even the biggest problem.

What looked like a fairly innocuous punch to the temple in the seventh round had done serious damage to my brain and eyesight. I didn't go down, but I was disoriented and suffering from double vision. Or triple vision! Between rounds, as Al Gavin worked on the growing cut over my left eye, I kept squinting and blinking hard, trying to chase away the shadows and multiple images.

"What the fuck's wrong?" Dicky asked.

"My eyes," I said. "They're all screwed up."

I tried not to panic, but there's no question that I fought the last three rounds with a growing sense of nervousness. I kept waiting for the condition to clear up. Hell, I'd been hurt before; balance and vision problems aren't unusual when you get hit in the head, but typically they clear up after a minute or two. Not this time. If anything, the problem worsened. I spent three rounds chasing Arturo and his ghosts, never sure which I was trying to hit. But I wouldn't quit. No way. I just kept throwing punches, hoping for the best, trying to survive until the end.

I owed myself that much. I owed Arturo, as well.

At the start of the tenth round it's customary for fighters to tap gloves one last time. As the bell sounded and I looked across the ring, Arturo smiled. I smiled back. We met in the center of the ring, touched gloves . . . and hugged. I gave him a pat on the back of the head as we separated.

And then we went at each other all over again.

That might sound extreme, but it felt somehow appropriate.

I'd lost seven of nine rounds. My only hope was to knock him out. I threw everything I had, tried to find an opening for a left hook to the body, but Arturo was too slippery, too strong. To his credit (or stubbornness!), Arturo did not run or hide in that last round, preferring instead to give the trilogy exactly the conclusion it deserved. We stood there for the better part of the last minute, leaning against each other, throwing everything we had. When the final bell sounded, we fell into a long, tired embrace.

The decision was a formality. I knew Arturo had earned a unanimous victory, and the official announcement was almost anticlimactic.

I begrudged him nothing, felt privileged to have been a part of such a memorable series of fights. And I guess Arturo felt the same way.

"Micky Ward has incredible heart," he said during the post-fight interview. "For someone who's about to retire, he fought a hell of a fight."

I complimented Arturo, thanked him for giving me the opportunity to fight one more time; we shared a single bottle of water right there in the ring. People were amazed by that. It's something you don't often see in boxing, that kind of camaraderie and sportsmanship. After all, how can two men who've just spent the better part of an hour trying to kill each other suddenly behave so warmly toward each other? It's hard to explain, but it's precisely because of what we shared that I felt such affection for Arturo; such respect and admiration.

"Look, I want to beat him more than anything in the world," I explained afterward. "But outside the ring, he's a human, he's a beautiful guy. That's what it's about—respect. It's not about who's tougher."

In the dressing room, as he quietly removed the tape from my hands, Dicky reminded me of the promise I'd made.

"So that's it, then. You're done, kiddo. Hope you realize, if you ever want to fight again, you're doing it without me."

I laughed.

"No need to worry, Dicky."

I walked away with no regrets whatsoever. There was no way I'd fight again, not for all the money in the world. Your body can only take so much, and my body had just about reached its limit.

A short time later, accompanied by Sal and Charlene, I was taken by ambulance to the Atlantic City Medical Center to get more stitches and X-rays, along with a precautionary CAT scan. It was while I was there, sitting in the emergency room, that I ran into Arturo.

"Hey, someone wants to say hello," said Dr. Margles, as he drew back a curtain.

There was Arturo, waiting for the same sort of postfight cleanup. The first thing he said—and this will always stay with me—was "You okay, brother?" Even now, after all these years, it gives me goose bumps just thinking about it. He didn't make any jokes, didn't say anything about the fight or the crowd. Not right away.

He wanted to know if I was all right.

I knew then that I'd made a friend for life.

———————————

Arturo fought several more times over the next few years, and each time I walked with him from the dressing room to the ring. I even trained him for one of his fights, spent two months with him in Pompano Beach, Florida, working with him every day in the gym. That was intense and a little strange, but incredibly rewarding. His handlers offered me the job partly because they thought it would make for great publicity, but also because they knew how well we got along. See, I wasn't going to tell Arturo anything he didn't already know; I was just there to motivate him and help him get in shape. And I got in great shape, too, just by working out with him. Heck, I might have been fitter than Arturo by the time fight night arrived! Not that I was ready for another fight. No more of that for me; by this time the neurologists were routinely telling me that the next head punch could be the last. I wasn't even allowed to spar.

But that's okay. I accepted the diagnosis and its limitations. I was happy just to be a part of Arturo's entourage, and to help him become the best fighter he could possibly be. And even though we were very different people outside the ring, we became friends for life because of boxing, so close that I ended up trying to help him at the oddest of times, and under the strangest of circumstances. Late one night, for example, I was roused from sleep by a phone call from an officer with the Port Authority Police Department in New York.

"Is this Micky?" he asked.

"Yeah, what's up?"

"You gotta get down here and help out your buddy Arturo Gatti," the officer said. "He's been in an accident."

"Is he okay?"

"Yeah, he'll be all right. Just banged up a little. Fell asleep at the wheel while going through the Holland Tunnel. We got your name out of his cell phone. Only one we recognized. Can you help us out?"

"I'd love to, but . . . uh . . . I'm in Boston!"

There was a long pause.

"Oh . . ."

It all worked out okay because I gave them the number of a friend in New York, someone who also knew Arturo. The paramedics took him to the hospital for observation and he was released a few hours later. Arturo had a lot of nights like that: close calls.

Another time he came to Boston to help with a fund-raiser for one of my charities, the Team Micky Foundation (which provides financial assistance to needy children and families). Arturo charmed everyone that night . . . then went out and partied for a while and ended up getting involved in a fight with two huge bouncers at a Boston nightspot. Arturo is a hell of a fighter and more than capable of taking care of himself, but I guess these guys were massive and ended up working him over pretty good. His twelve-thousand-dollar Rolex watch was even missing after the altercation.

That was Arturo. The guy lived life to the absolute fullest, sometimes to the detriment of his own safety. But that's the way he was and I never tried to judge him. He was one of the most generous and thoughtful men I've ever known.

Unfortunately, Arturo's life ended much too soon, under bizarre and tragic circumstances that still raise more questions than answers.

Here's what we know: On July 11, 2009, Arturo was found dead in a hotel room in Brazil, where he was vacationing with his family. His Brazilian wife, Amanda Rodrigues, was initially charged with murder when police discovered bloodstains on the strap of her purse. Somehow, though, the charges were later dropped and Arturo's death was ruled a suicide, a determination I find frankly inconceivable. This was one of the strongest men I've ever known. A man, like me, who would have died in the ring before quitting.

Arturo Gatti killed himself?

No fucking way.

This guy had so much to live for. He had a ten-month-old baby he adored; he had a big real estate venture going well in his home country of Canada. I'd talked to him just a few weeks earlier and I know how excited he was about his life and his new opportunities. Sure, Arturo had demons and addictions; and because of my brother I know better than most people that alcohol and drugs can make a man do things he might not otherwise consider. But to this day I can't see him killing himself. There's no possible way. Do I think his wife did it? No, but I think maybe she might know something about what happened, or who might have had a reason to kill Arturo. The guy supposedly hung himself with a purse strap? Are you kidding me?! Obviously I don't know what happened, and the cops in Canada, where they're trying to reopen the investigation, say it could take years to untangle the mystery. To me, though, it just doesn't add up. And because of where it happened, they'll probably never get to the truth. That's the Wild West down there; if you have enough money, and you know the right people, you can literally get away with murder.

All I know is that my friend is gone, and I miss him terribly.

There were two services for Arturo: a memorial in New Jersey and a funeral in Montreal. I went to both. I was asked to speak at the memorial service, but couldn't bring myself to do it. I was too sad, too overwhelmed. At the funeral, Arturo's casket was open. As I knelt before him, saying a final prayer, it all seemed so senseless and surreal. I kept waiting for him to get up and say something, to let me in on the joke. Finally, after the longest time, I leaned in and gave him a last little chuck on the chin.

"Good-bye, my friend."

And then I walked away.

It still doesn't seem real, that a man with that much heart and passion, who had never quit at anything in his entire life, had made the ultimate submission. I refuse to believe it. I still sometimes expect to hear from Arturo, to get one of those late-night phone calls that we'd share across time zones. I'd be out with friends, and we'd start talking about Arturo and the trilogy.

"What's Gatti really like?" they'd say.

"Great guy," I'd respond. "Here, you can talk to him yourself."

Then I'd dial the number and wait for Arturo to answer. I'd let him talk to some of the other guys, or put him on speaker. And he'd do the same damn thing to me when he was out! The thing is, no one could really understand what he was saying, with that squeaky voice and the

Italian-French accent, all delivered at machine-gun pace. Not that I'm the most eloquent guy in the world. I talk fast, too. When Arturo and I would get together, it was like we were speaking our own language. People would hear us and wonder what the hell we were saying.

But we understood each other. Always had, always would.

EPILOGUE

You might think that a guy who has suffered as much damage as I have would harbor some resentment toward the fight game. But I don't. Not in the least. Whatever I've sacrificed to boxing, I've gotten more in return. If it weren't for boxing, I might never have recovered from the trauma of child abuse. Boxing gave me strength and courage and discipline. It gave me an identity.

Boxing gave me purpose.

And, of course, if not for boxing, there never would have been a movie called *The Fighter*.

The film was in the works for a long time—so long, in fact that at several points along the way I just stopped thinking about it. You hear stories about Hollywood and "development hell," about projects that seem to generate a ton of interest, only to fall apart for any one of a hundred reasons. Well, the stories are true. It takes an enormous amount of hard work and input from a bunch of talented people to bring a movie to life. Based on what I've seen, it's a miracle any movie gets made.

I was lucky.

See, I had Mark Wahlberg in my corner.

The first time I heard about Mark's involvement was sometime in 2005. There had been a documentary in the works about me and Dicky, and the buzz from that project sparked interest in a feature film. There were a number of different writers and producers involved over the years, but until Mark got involved, we were basically spinning our wheels. Mark, of course, is a superstar, a Hollywood A-lister. It turned out that he also was a fan of boxing in general, and a fan of mine in particular. When he heard there was a script about my life and career, he wanted to be a part of it. Fortunately for me, he was the kind of guy who had the clout to get it done.

More important, he had the perseverance. Even as the movie went through different hands—on again, off again—Mark remained committed. He'd always wanted to make a boxing movie, and he trained like crazy to look the part. Even as the project languished for months and even years, Mark stayed in shape, kept training like a fighter, just in case the pieces all came together and the movie was given a green light.

"Micky, I promise we're going to get this movie made," he said to me one day, when I'd all but given up. "I don't care how long it takes."

I'm not sure what drew Mark to the project, or kept him going through all the ups and downs. Maybe, in addition to being a boxing fan, he felt like we had something in common. Like me, Mark had grown up in a big, Irish-Catholic, working-class family, near Boston (in the town of Dorchester). There were nine kids in the Ward-Eklund clan; same exact number in the Wahlberg family. Mark knows the turf; he knows what it's like to try to make something of yourself, to rise above your surroundings. We did the same thing—well, he did it on a much bigger scale, obviously, but you get the point. Mark understood where I'd come from, and that made his involvement really important to me. I felt like I could trust him. Hollywood is a town of lip service and broken promises. Mark must not fit in very well, because he's not like that. He's a real man.

"We're going to do this movie for you, and for Dicky, and we're going to do it right," Mark said.

I had no idea what to expect. Sometimes even after they start shooting, they can still pull the plug. Despite Mark's obvious commitment and dedication, I tried not to get my hopes too high. That's a defense mechanism developed through years of boxing. I'd been disappointed so many times in my career that I found it healthy to hope for the best, but expect the worst. That way it doesn't hurt too much when things turn sour.

But Mark wasn't going to let that happen. He threw himself into every aspect of the production, including adopting a training regimen so rigorous that by the time the movie was complete, I swear he could have been a legitimate professional fighter.

Not a light welterweight, mind you. Mark was roughly 175 pounds of solid muscle for the movie, which made him more of a cruiserweight or light heavyweight. But that had no impact on the realism depicted on-screen. We've all seen sports movies in which the actors look like amateurs. Not so with Mark. He looked every inch the professional fighter. We'd spar together once in a while (just body stuff, below the shoulders—no head shots for me!), and I'll tell you—the guy punches hard; he knows what he's doing. No bullshit—Mark could have been a fighter. A really good fighter. He has that work ethic, that mentality and drive to succeed at whatever he does.

Hey, I'm living proof that ambition and hard work are just as important, if not more important, than talent.

Speaking of talent, it was remarkable to see Christian Bale immerse himself in the role of Dicky. I got to see that process up close and personal, since those guys both came to Lowell, and then invited us to spend time with them at Mark's home in Beverly Hills. We'd talk about boxing all the time, get up early, go to church every morning, and then go to the gym. Every day. We'd run the hills around Mark's house, where you practically need to be a mountain goat. There were morning sessions in the gym, afternoon sessions, evening sessions. That was all we'd do: train, train, train. There was no Hollywood bullshit. No partying or hanging out at clubs. These guys were all business. Total pros. David O. Russell, the director, stopped by frequently. And Christian was there all the time, training and watching Dicky's every move, picking him apart. Sometimes you'd think Christian wasn't looking at Dicky, but he was. You'd see him pull a notebook out of his pocket and start jotting things down. The guy was a genius the way he studied.

And it's all up there on the screen, of course.

The first time I saw *The Fighter* I was completely blown away. When you're involved in the filming process, everything seems to be happening slowly. Then, to see it all come together, on the screen . . . Well, it was amazing. There were only a few people in attendance at that first screening in Los Angeles. Just me and Dicky, along with Mark, Christian, David O'Russell and some of their friends and relatives.

"So, what do you think?" Mark asked me afterward.

I was practically speechless. They'd gotten it right! Sure, it wasn't exactly the way things happened in real life—it's not possible to squeeze everything into two hours—but I thought they did a hell of a job. I couldn't have asked for more. Dicky was a little less enthusiastic, probably because the movie depicted his struggles with glaring (and sometimes ugly) authenticity. If anything, he was even worse. Eventually, though, he came to appreciate the movie and what it would do for his life, and the opportunities it would present.

There were so many great moments surrounding the release of *The Fighter*: premiers in Lowell and Boston, the Academy Awards ceremony in Hollywood. The latter was one of the most remarkable nights of my life, too strange and wonderful to even comprehend. It was like being in a dream. My daughter and wife accompanied me on the trip, and got to be part of all the Hollywood hoopla. I was proud to share it with them. And I was happiest for Mark that night. Yeah, Christian won an Oscar for his brilliant portrayal of Dicky. And Melissa Leo won for her depiction of my mother. Both of them did an awesome job. Mark got stuck with playing me—the boring guy—so he wasn't nominated. But without his commitment to the project, *The Fighter* never would have seen the light of day.

If I have one regret from that whole experience, it's that my mother didn't really get to enjoy it. She made it to the premier in Lowell in 2010, but by the time the Academy Awards rolled around, in the winter of 2011, she was very sick. The last several months of her life were spent in a hospital bed, withering from the effects of heart disease. She died on April 27, after being taken off life support. She was seventy-nine years old.

I'd been with Mom all day, but wasn't there when she passed. I'd gone home for a few hours, leaving Dicky and my sisters to keep an eye on her. The machines had been unplugged for several hours, but Mom, tough and stubborn to the end, wouldn't quit. Eventually a nurse came in and told everyone to take a break, go get something to eat. Then, as soon as the room was empty, our mother passed away.

You know what I think? She didn't want her children there when she drew her last breath. She didn't want us to see her die. That was Mom—always trying to do things her own way.

———————————

Life is good these days. Charlene and I have never been happier together. She and Kasie are my whole life. I'm grateful to have them, and to be able to take care of them. We all live together, in the same house in Lowell that I bought years ago. We also have two English bulldogs, Bubba and GG (as in "Gatti Girl," named after Arturo) and a Pekinese named Ernie.

I have health issues now, for sure, but I'm dealing with them. Life moves on, right? I try to give back to the sport, either through my gym (which is popular with both boxers and mixed martial artists) or through various other means, like taking part in Boston University's Center for the Study of Traumatic Encephalopathy, a long-term behavioral and cognitive study to determine the effect of concussions on degenerative brain disease. There are a number of athletes participating in the project, but I'm the only boxer, and I'm really excited about my involvement. I'll be doing a lot of public speaking, talking to coaches across a wide variety of sports—football, soccer, wrestling—teaching them how to look for the subtle signs of concussions, and how to spot a young athlete who may be trying to hide his condition. The most important thing with concussions is to stay out of competition and training until all symptoms have subsided. You have to give the brain time to heal. This obviously presents a real problem in boxing, where concussions not only come with the territory, but actually represent a tactical objective. How do you guard against concussions in a sport whose ultimate goal is a "knockout?"

Well, you can't. Not completely, anyway. But there are steps that can be taken.

What most people don't realize is that fighters sustain the most brain damage not on fight night, but during the endless months of sparring that precede the actual boxing match. It's the accrued trauma of daily pummeling that takes its toll. Headgear is an illusion, preventing bloody gashes and minimizing the effect of errant elbows or head butts. It does little, though, to prevent the brain from splashing around. To help fighters more, there should be less sparring in the gym. I understand the challenge this presents, since sparring is a crucial thing in boxing. A fighter needs to be desensitized; he needs to get hit, and to grow accustomed to an opponent's style. But if you can minimize the number of sparring rounds and just train more—hit the mitts, the speed bag, do roadwork—I think you can really cut down on the number of concussions.

So, in addition to taking care of my family, that's my purpose in life now.

And Dicky? Well, Dicky trains younger fighters in my gym. Sometimes we work together, and we see each other probably two or three times a week. In a lot of ways I'm still closer to Dicky than I am to anyone else. He is, after all, my brother.

My days are full; I don't have any trouble filling the hours. I work as a driver for Teamsters Local 25. I try to teach other fighters and offer whatever advice I can to help them live longer, more productive lives. I understand that I have some health issues related to past concussions, and that I am a candidate for what is clinically known as pugilistic dementia. So be it. I'll do the most that I can with the time I have left. And when I'm gone the scientists and physicians at Boston University will inherit my brain and spinal column, using whatever is left in the name of research.

That way, even in death, I will remain a fighter.

A warrior.